32 WALKS AROUND LONDON'S

TRACK
THE
PLAQUE

**Derek
Sumeray**

COMMEMORATIVE PLAQUES

32 WALKS AROUND LONDON'S

TRACK THE PLAQUE

Derek Sumeray

COMMEMORATIVE PLAQUES

breedon books
PUBLISHING

First published in Great Britain in 2003 by
The Breedon Books Publishing Company Limited
Breedon House, 3 The Parker Centre,
Derby, DE21 4SZ.

ISBN 1 85983 362 4

Printed and bound by Scotprint, Haddington, Scotland

Cover printing by Scotprint, Haddington, Scotland

Contents

Author's Preface

S IR Walter Besant said 'I've been walking about London for the last thirty years and I find something fresh in it every day'. In the preparation of this book I have enjoyed walking hundreds of miles throughout Greater London. There are so many interesting streets and buildings in England's capital that one need never tire of finding somewhere or something fascinating to see.

My interest in commemorative plaques first began with my love of photography. I happened to be in Hampstead one day when testing a new camera. Wishing to run a film through the camera, I started photographing at random and zoomed in on some blue plaques. When examining the results several days later with a friend, I commented that I had not seen a guide or listing of London plaques. By coincidence, the following weekend my interest was further stimulated when I read a review of the English Heritage *Blue Plaque Guide*, which I promptly bought.

Being newly retired I soon found that the searching out and photographing of London's plaques was an interesting hobby. As I photographed them I ticked them off in the book. The problem was that I kept finding other plaques that were not listed. A search of bookshops proved that there was no other book currently available. Previous publications were more than 15 years old and outdated.

My own listing and photograph collection became so large that it eventually led to the publication of my book *Discovering London Plaques* (Shire Publications), which details over 1,400. Researching the biographies of the people and events commemorated was an interesting activity, although it was a mammoth task that took nearly 10 years of my spare time. My efforts resulted in an accumulation of over 3,000 photographs of plaques and buildings.

Since that publication I have spent three years compiling this book of walks and found a further 150 plaques. I have also attended and filmed many new plaque unveilings and kept my records up to date.

Many amusing incidents have occurred in the course of my researches, and several come to mind. Prominent among them was an occasion when I was photographing a house. The owner appeared, mistook me for an estate agent, and told me not to bother photographing the house as it had now been sold. On another occasion I was accosted by a tramp, who seemed to suddenly appear from nowhere, who asked for the price of a cup of tea. When I presented him with a coin he invited me to join him for a cuppa at the nearby café. This would probably have cost me the price of a breakfast as well.

Another time I was busy photographing a plaque in a deserted street, when a voice suddenly boomed out 'Can I ask what you are doing?' I looked around and found a policeman standing immediately behind me. When I explained, he suddenly became quite interested and asked if I had seen the plaque on a building in a nearby street.

In my travels I have had many experiences, including being offered a free haircut, being accosted by a lady of doubtful morals and being shouted at by tramps and layabouts. This is all part of London life and the experiences have made my researches more pleasurable.

In conclusion I would like to thank some of the people who have assisted me greatly in the preparation of this book. Firstly, my wife Loretta, for her patience and help. Thanks must also go to, among others, Pam Whiffin and Emily Cole of English Heritage and Gillian Dawson of Westminster City Council. Fellow walkers Ralph Temple and Gerald Trevor have spent much time checking my routes and I thank them for their suggestions and comments. Finally, I hope that readers will enjoy many hours of 'plaque hunting' with these walks, as I have done and continue to do.

Derek Sumeray

Foreword

THIS book is invaluable not only to the visitor to London, but also to its residents. Those who enjoy walking and at the same time wish to experience the atmosphere of the city will relive the history of England's vibrant capital. Thirty-two of the most interesting areas are covered, and this volume can be considered a companion book to the author's *Discovering London Plaques* (Shire Publications), which gives a potted history of the events and people commemorated on London's many wall plaques.

London's commemorative plaques are not only blue but can be found in many colours and styles. They have been erected over the last 135 years and have proved an extremely popular way of recording the history and events of the capital, as well as giving the names of eminent people who have lived in or visited the city. Official plaques are nowadays frequently erected by English Heritage. Others are put in place by civic authorities, independent organisations and private individuals. This book is designed so that the reader may see as many of them as possible in the shortest possible time, by the quickest possible route. It can save hours of unnecessary walking for the plaque enthusiast.

The walks detailed in this book have been created to encompass almost all the plaques in each district, so that they are located with ease. They all commence and finish near an underground station and local bus routes are mentioned. Distances and times recorded are approximate, and measured up to the final underground station in each case. As well as the plaques, notable buildings and points of interest are mentioned. There are more than 1,500 commemorative plaques in Greater London and these walks encompass over 1,200 of them, all of which can easily be found. More than 30 new plaques are erected each year in London and it is sometimes possible for the observant hiker to find an unlisted one while engaging in one of the walks. Similarly, due to reconstruction, plaques are sometimes 'lost'.

It is not intended to give full biographies of the people recorded on plaques seen on these tours. Only a brief mention of their vocation or history is given. Possible places for rest and refreshment are mentioned, but no guarantee is given of their current worthiness or suitability. The maps are not drawn to scale and are meant to be a rough guide only of plaque locations. Only main roads and streets mentioned in the text are shown.

Finally, it is recommended that comfortable walking boots should be worn.

Walk 1
Mayfair

Distance:	2 miles (3.2km) short walk, or 4½ miles (7.33km) full walk
Time taken:	1 hour short walk, 2½ hours full walk
Number of plaques:	29 short walk, 66 full walk
Nearest tube stations:	Marble Arch, Bond Street, Green Park, Oxford Circus, Piccadilly
Bus routes:	2, 6, 7, 10, 12, 15, 16, 16a, 23, 30, 36, 73,74, 82, 94, 98, 135, 137, 274

WE begin the walk at Marble Arch tube station. Subway No.2 will bring you across to the beginning of Park Lane and the first plaque on the route. This can be seen on the building to your left, No.140 Park Lane. It is a Westminster green plaque commemorating **Keith Clifford Hall** (1), who was a pioneer of contact lenses and practised here 1945–64. This is directly opposite the Marble Arch and Hyde Park. The arch, which originally stood in front of Buckingham Palace, was designed by John Nash and was moved to this site in 1827. The reliefs on the north side are by Richard Westmacott, whose commemorative plaque we shall shortly see. The corner was for centuries the site of Tyburn gallows, where criminals were hanged in front of applauding crowds.

Take the first turning on the left, which is North Row, and immediately to your right is Dunraven Street. On the left side at No.17 you will find the blue plaque commemorating the writer **P.G. Wodehouse** (2), famous for his stories about Jeeves and Bertie Wooster.

Turn left into Green Street and on the right hand side at No.46 is the plaque of **Sir Thomas Sopwith** (3), who lived here 1934–40. He formed his aircraft company in 1912 and was the designer of the successful World War One Sopwith Camel aeroplane. He later became chairman of the Hawker Siddeley group of companies.

Return along Green Street and turn left at the top into Park Lane. Pass Woods Mews and turn left into Upper Brook Street. At No.22, on the left-hand side, there is a Westminster green plaque commemorating **Leo Bonn** (4), who founded what is now the Royal National Institute for Deaf People here in 1911. The plaque was unveiled by HRH the Duke of Edinburgh. Continue and cross Park Street. On the right at No.51 you will see the Greek flag flying over their embassy entrance. There is also a blue plaque commemorating a former ambassador, **George Seferis** (5), who was a noted poet and Nobel Prize-winner.

Retrace your steps a few yards and turn left into Park Street. Take the first turning on the right, Culross Street, and continue down to the corner of Park Lane. There is a Greater London Council (GLC) plaque on this house commemorating the 19th-century Jewish philanthropist **Sir Moses Montefiore** (6), who lived here for 60 years.

1 Keith C. Hall	18 Lord Raglan	35 Lady D. Nevill	52 G.F. Handel
2 P.G. Wodehouse	19 Benjamin Disraeli	36 George Canning	53 Jimi Hendrix
3 Sir Thomas Sopwith	20 Rufus Isaacs	37 Clive of India	54 Horatio Nelson
4 Leo Bonn	21 Mayfair's Oldest House	38 Queen Elizabeth II	55 Prince Talleyrand
5 George Seferis	22 Sir George Cayley	39 Terence Donovan	56 William Morris
6 Sir Moses Montefiore	23 R.B. Sheridan	40 Sir Alexander Korda	57 Artists Rifles
7 Benjamin Disraeli	24 General Burgoyne	41 Ann Oldfield	58 Horatio Nelson
8 Sir Robert Peel	25 Nancy Mitford	42 C.F. Peczenik	59 Sir Henry Irving
9 James Purdy	26 Nancy Mitford	43 Treaty of Paris	60 Lord Brougham
10 Jack Buchanan	27 Viscount Palmerston	44 Dwight D. Eisenhower	61 George Basevi
11 John C. Winant	28 Charles E. Ives	45 F. Handley Page	62 R.B. Sheridan
12 Anna Neagle/Herbert Wilcox	29 Charles J. Fox	46 John Adams	63 George Grote
13 Florence Nightingale	30 Fanny Burney	47 W. Hines Page	64 Richard Bright
14 Catherine Walters	31 Beau Brummell	48 William Blake	65 Sir Allen Lane
15 Lord Ashfield	32 W. Somerset Maugham	49 Sir J. Wyatville	66 Dr J. Yearsley
16 Charles X	33 Earl of Rosebery	50 William Blake	
17 Sir R. Westmacott	34 Duke of Clarence	51 Ernest Bevin	

Continue along Park Lane to Upper Grosvenor Street. The corner building on your left was the home of the Prime Minister **Benjamin Disraeli** (7) from 1839–73. This is recorded on the rectangular bronze plaque on the side of the house. Continue down Upper Grosvenor Street to No.16 on the left. Here there is an English Heritage blue plaque stating that the father and son reformers and politicians, both named **Sir Robert Peel** (8), lived in this house.

Proceed further along Upper Grosvenor Street, past the side of the US embassy. Cross the pedestrian crossing and turn right into South Audley Street. You will see the first shops and restaurants that we have come across on this walk. The Richoux tearooms and restaurant are excellent for refreshment. For something a little stronger try the Audley public house. On the corner of Mount Street the old established gunmakers' premises are James Purdey & Sons Ltd. The founder, **James Purdey** (9), who had the building specially constructed for his business in 1880, has his own commemorative green plaque here. Turning round you will find the Audley Mansions opposite, on the corner of Mount Street, where a blue plaque can be seen for former resident **Jack Buchanan** (10), the famous stage and screen musical comedy actor and theatrical impresario.

Continuing along South Audley Street, you can see the Grosvenor Chapel, built in 1730, which is typical of the 18th-century style of church building. It was here that American servicemen frequently prayed during World War Two. Opposite is Aldford Street. Walk down to the Flemish-style building on the right, No.7. This building, owned by Sir Winston Churchill, was loaned to the American ambassador **John Charles Winant** (11) during World War Two. The GLC blue plaque records that he lived here 1941–6.

Proceed on to Park Lane and turn left. The next street is South Street and on this corner there is a green plaque which states that the actress **Anna Neagle** (12) and her film producer husband **Herbert Wilcox** lived here 1950–64. On the right at No.10 South Street is the blue plaque commemorating the fact that **Florence Nightingale** (13) died in a house on this site. She was the famous nurse of the Crimean War, known as 'the lady with the lamp'. Across the road at No.15 **Catherine Walters** (14), known to her friends as 'Skittles', lavishly entertained her many society friends. Raised in the Liverpool slums, her good looks attracted the attention of a businessman who brought her to London. She lived here 48 years and is described on the plaque as 'The last Victorian courtesan'.

Continue along South Street, crossing over South Audley Street. The premises of Thomas Goode Ltd were specially built for them 1875–91. An interesting innovation is their entrance step, which, when stood upon, operates a mechanism that opens the front doors. On the left at No.43 South Street is a plaque commemorating **Lord Ashfield** (15), who was the first chairman of London Transport. Return to South Audley Street and, turning to the left, you can see a blue plaque across the road at No.72. This is where the French **King Charles X** (16) lived for nine years, prior to his accession to the throne in 1820.

Almost opposite, at No.14 South Audley Street, there is a blue plaque for the sculptor **Sir Richard Westmacott** (17), who lived and died here. Apart from works that he executed for Westminster Abbey and St Paul's Cathedral, his best known works are probably the 'Achilles' statue in Hyde Park and the reliefs on the Marble Arch.

Continue along South Audley Street, past Audley Square, and turn into Stanhope Gate on your right. Here at No.5 is the London City Council (LCC) plaque for **Lord Raglan** (18), after whom the raglan sleeve was named. This is quite surprising since he lost an arm at the Battle of Waterloo in 1815. Raglan lived in this house when in London between 1835 and 1854. His glory was in winning the battles of Alma and Inkerman, but he was also responsible for the fateful ordering of the Charge of the Light Brigade at Balaclava.

Walking to the end of Stanhope Gate you will see an interesting looking Victorian

Gothic building occupied by a bank, and also the nearby entranceway of the Dorchester Hotel.

Return to Park Lane and turn left into Curzon Street. The first plaque you come to is at No.19, a brown LCC plaque on the house where the then Prime Minister **Benjamin Disraeli** (19) died in 1881. Continue along Curzon Street past the bronze elephant at No.27 and Crockford's gentlemen's club. At No.32 there is a plaque on the house where **Rufus Isaacs** (20), the 1st Marquis of Reading, lived and died. He was Lord Chief Justice in 1913, Ambassador to the US 1918–21 and Viceroy of India 1921–6. After this he had a successful business career. This is an architecturally interesting building to see, because of the two colours in the brickwork and the overhanging first-floor balcony.

Turn back to Derby Street and turn left into Pitts Head Mews. Ahead of you in Hilton Mews above an archway is a green plaque commemorating the site of **Mayfair's Oldest House** (21). This house was actually destroyed by German bombing in the 1940s, but the local residents' association wished it to be remembered and Westminster Council happily obliged.

Continue on and opposite at 20 Hertford Street you can see a blue plaque at the home of the pioneer aviator **Sir George Cayley** (22). He actually piloted an airplane for a short distance 50 years before the Wright brothers' Kitty Hawk flight. Walking further down Hertford Street away from Park Lane, past Wheeler's famous fish restaurant, you will find two blue plaques at No.10 (above). These commemorate the dramatist **Richard Brinsley Sheridan** (23) and the soldier and playwright **General John Burgoyne** (24). Sheridan lived here 1795–1802 and is famous for his plays *The Rivals* (1775), *The School for Scandal*

(1777) and *The Critic* (1779). Burgoyne, who lived and died here, fought in the American War of Independence and later entered Parliament. His comedies included *The Maid of Oaks* (1775) and *The Heiress* (1786).

Walking onwards turn right at Shepherd Street and then left into Trebeck Street. At No.17 (pictured below) a blue plaque records this as being the site of the historic **Mayfair** (25). In 1688 Edward Shepherd began a cattle market here and soon afterwards the two-week May Fair began. After residents' protests in the 18th century the fair was stopped, but the name for the district remained. It has for many years been a haunt of ladies of the night. Shepherd Market, on the right, is today a vibrant area full of restaurants, and is an excellent stop for anything from a snack to a full meal. Ye King's Arms and the Grapes are two popular taverns. The latter is a taxidermist's dream.

Those who have followed the walk so far will have seen 25 plaques. If you wish to leave for the nearest tube station, Green Park, you can easily do so by following the route for the next four plaques.

With the Grapes in Shepherd Market on your right, looking towards the archway you can see the English Heritage blue plaque at No.10 Curzon Street, the former bookshop where the writer **Nancy Mitford** (26) worked from 1943–5.

Turn around and go down White Horse Street to Piccadilly. Turn to your left and at

No.24 on the gatepost is the blue plaque informing you that the 18th-century Prime Minister and statesman **Viscount Palmerston** (27) lived here. Green Park tube station is ahead if you wish to depart. But why not see two more plaques?

To continue take the next turning, Half Moon Street. Near the top at No.17 is the plaque recording the fact that the American composer **Charles Edward Ives** (28) stayed here in 1934. Continue to Curzon Street and turn right.

The next street on the right is Clarges Street. Walk down past the Samuel Pepys pub and at No.46 is the plaque commemorating the famous politician and great orator **Charles James Fox** (29). He was leader of the Opposition at the time of William Pitt and lived here 1803-4. Ahead of you are Piccadilly and Green Park. Turning to the left, the tube station is about 100 yards further along Piccadilly. This is the end of the shorter walk.

To continue the full route turn left into Bolton Street. Half way along at No.11 is the Royal Society of Arts plaque erected in 1885 to commemorate **Fanny Burney (Madame D'Arbley)** (30). This author and diarist wrote several popular novels that could be considered the forerunners of the modern 'soaps'.

Walk on to Curzon Street, turning to the left. Pass the Mirabelle Club, retracing your steps past Shepherd Market, and turn into Chesterfield Street on the right. Standing with your back to No.12 you can now see three plaques. Opposite, at No.4, lived the early 18th-century dandy **Beau Brummell** (31), once a friend of the Prince Regent, later George IV. Next door at No.6 the author **W. Somerset Maugham** (32) lived from 1911-19. At the end of the road at 20 Charles Street is the birthplace of the **Earl of Rosebery** (33). He was a statesman, Prime Minister and keen racehorse owner.

The **Duke of Clarence** (34) lived at No.22 Charles Street in 1826 before taking the throne as William IV four years later. Continue right along Charles Street to No.45, where you can see the plaque on the home of **Lady Dorothy Nevill** (35). She was married to Horatio Walpole, 3rd Duke of Orford, and lived here 1873-1913. A noted horticulturist, she was the author of several publications. The tavern opposite, strangely named the Running Footman, is an excellent place for refreshment. In the 17th and 18th century it was common for a servant to run ahead of a nobleman's coach to carry a flame at night, and to pay tolls and assist passengers.

Continue on and turn left at Berkeley Square. The nightingale can no longer be heard singing but the most outstanding feature is the enormous plane trees, which were planted over 200 years ago. At No.50 on the left is the plaque to **George Canning** (36), the Tory politician who became Prime Minister in the last year of his life. He lived here 1806-7.

No.44 was built 1742-4, and was described by Nikolas Pevsner as 'the finest terrace

house of London'. **Robert Clive of India** (37) lived at No.45 for the last three years of his life. This blue-glazed rectangular-shaped plaque differs from the usual LCC style.

Use the pedestrian crossing and take the footpath across the centre of Berkeley Square Gardens, perhaps first pausing at the gate to read the history of the square. On the other side you will reach Bruton Street. No.17 on the right is the birthplace of **Her Majesty Queen Elizabeth II** (38). The plaque was erected at the time of her Silver Jubilee celebrations in 1977.

Return to Berkeley Square, turning right to the north end where there is a small passage called Jones Street. This takes you into Bourdon Street where you turn to the right. At No.30 a green plaque records the home and studio of the society and fashion photographer **Terence Donovan** (39). Nearby is St George's Buildings, which has five floors with continuous balconies.

Fork back through Bourdon Place and Grosvenor Hill into Broadbent Street, emerging into Grosvenor Street. Cross the road to No.21, where you can see the plaque for **Sir Alexander Korda** (40). This well-known film director had his offices here. His films included *The Third Man, The Scarlet Pimpernel* and *Richard III*. Looking back across the road you can see another blue plaque at No.60, which commemorates the 18th-century actress **Ann Oldfield** (41). She was the first occupant of this house and lived here 1725–30.

Continue along Grosvenor Street to Grosvenor Square. This square is second only in size to Lincoln's Inn Fields, and was built between 1725 and 1731. On the left at No.48, cornering with Carlos Place, is an attractive blue plaque stating that the architect **Charles Edmund Peczenik** (42) lived here. Walking further along you come to the 'Diplomatic Gates' on your right. A circular metal plaque on the ground commemorates the bicentenary of the **Treaty of Paris** (43). Beneath this is a further inscription in large wording on the pavement entrance to the square's centre.

Walk in past the memorial to the airmen of the Eagle Squadrons who died in World War Two. Ahead of you is the statue of Franklin D. Roosevelt. Take the diagonal path towards the north-west corner, approaching the monolithic US embassy. A statue of **President Dwight D. Eisenhower** (44) can be seen at its north corner. His commemorative plaque on the wartime US headquarters can be seen on the red-brick building across the road on the north side. Cross to the plaque and nearby, at No.18, you will find the blue plaque commemorating the aircraft designer and builder **Frederick Handley Page** (45).

At the next corner by Duke Street is the last of the original houses remaining in the square. It was the home in 1785–8 of the American president **John Adams** (46), when he was ambassador to England. The now tarnished rectangular metal plaque is difficult to read. Further round the square, the World War One US ambassador **Walter Hines Page** (47) lived at No.7, just past Brook Street. This rectangular plaque is set rather high on the second floor of the building.

Now walk into Brook Street. **Colen Campbell** (48), the architect who designed the Royal Academy building Burlington House, lived and died at No.76. Continue on past Claridge's Hotel. The cream-painted house, No.39, was the home of **Sir Jeffrey Wyatville** (49) from 1804–40. He was the architect largely responsible for the restoration and improvement of Windsor Castle.

Opposite is the pedestrian precinct of South Molton Street. This is one of the smarter shopping streets of the area and, with several cafés and restaurants, is a good place for rest and refreshment. Walk along to No.17 on the left. A Corporation of the City of London blue-glazed plaque commemorates **William Blake** (50). The artist and poet lived on the second floor with his wife in 1803, before moving to a house near the Strand. Continue to the end, where there is a blue plaque on the apartments at No.34. Socialist politician **Ernest Bevin** (51) lived here 1931–9.

Return to Brook Street, which was developed in the 1720s, and you will see one of the few original houses remaining, No.25. Here **George Frederick Handel** (52) lived from 1723 until his death in 1759. His house is now open to the public as a tribute to the great composer. Unfortunately it is closed on Mondays. Handel's English Heritage blue plaque has a neighbour at No.23, which records that the guitarist and songwriter **Jimi Hendrix** (53) lived here 1968–69.

Turn left again into New Bond Street. One of the two homes in this street where **Viscount Admiral Horatio Nelson** (54) lived is at No.103. An LCC blue plaque records the fact that he was here in 1798. Turn back down New Bond Street and left at the continuation of Brook Street. At the corner, which is No.21 Hanover Square, you can see the plaque of **Prince Talleyrand** (55), the French statesman who lived here 1830–4. A statue of William Pitt can be seen in the centre of the square.

Take the turning to the right of the square, which is St George Street. At No.17 there is a rectangular bronze plaque. This records that a company was established here in 1861, by **William Morris** (56). Continue down St George Street past the church after which it is named. It was built by John James in 1721–4 and has the earliest portico of any London church. Reaching No.8 St George Street on your right you will find a plaque commemorating the **Artists Rifles** (57), a regiment founded here in 1860 at his studio by the artist Henry Wyndham Phillips. A memorial to the 2,003 men of this regiment who lost their lives in World War One can be seen by the entrance to the Royal Academy of Arts in Piccadilly.

Turn right into Conduit Street. This will lead you back to New Bond Street. Turn right to the second of the homes of **Viscount Admiral Horatio Nelson** (58) to be found in this street. It is set rather high at No.147.

Now turn back down New Bond Street, past the junctions of Bruton and Conduit Street and the auctioneers Sotheby's. You will pass the bronze statue of the seated figures of Churchill and Roosevelt, a favourite spot for tourist photographs. The court jewellers Asprey's is on the corner of

Grafton Street. Above their side window at No.15A Grafton Street there is a blue plaque commemorating **Sir Henry Irving** (59), the famous actor, who lived here 1872–99. Continue along Grafton Street to No.5, where an unusual plaque states that **Henry Peter Lord Brougham** (60) lived here. Brougham resided at this address for 30 years until his death. He had a distinguished career in politics and administration but is best remembered by the 'Brougham Horse-drawn Carriage', named after him.

Retrace your steps back to New Bond Street and cross over, turning left and then right, to Clifford Street. This leads into Savile Row. Almost ahead of you across the road at No.17 behind the first-floor balcony can be found the blue plaque at the home of **George Basevi** (61). This architect lived here from 1829 until 1845. He lost his life in a fall while surveying Ely Cathedral. The large white building to the left further up the road on the same side is the head office of English Heritage. They are currently responsible for the erection of the 'official' blue plaques.

Three doors away from Basevi's house, above 'Hardy Amies' at No.14, is the last home of the actor **Richard Brinsley Sheridan** (62). You will recall seeing his other plaque in Hertford Street. This one was erected by the Royal Society of Arts in 1881. Two doors further along at No.12, an LCC plaque records the home of **George Grote** (63). He was a politician and historian of Greece who lived here 1848–71. Next door at No.11 the physician **Richard Bright** (64) lived from 1830–58. 'Brights disease' was named after him.

Continue along Savile Row, past the world famous gentlemen's tailoring houses, to Vigo Street. No.8 opposite was the first business premises of Penguin Books, founded here by **Sir Allen Lane** (65) in 1935.

Turn left and then right into Sackville Street. Halfway down on the right at No.32 is the Westminster green plaque commemorating **Dr James Yearsley** (66), who founded the Metropolitan Ear Institute here in 1838. This is the last plaque on our walk. By now, if you have followed all the directions, you will probably feel exhausted, but can proudly say that you have seen 66 plaques in Mayfair.

Ahead is Piccadilly and turning to the left will bring you to Piccadilly Circus. An interesting pause before departing would be to stop at St James's Church, where there is a daily outdoor craft or antique market. The largest bookshop in Europe, a flagship Waterstone's, is a little further along Piccadilly before you reach the tube station.

Walk 2
West End (1)

Distance:	5½ miles (8.85km)
Time taken:	3 hours
Number of plaques:	66
Nearest tube stations:	Tottenham Court Road, Goodge Street, Warren Street, Regents Park, Baker Street, Bond Street
Bus routes:	10, 24, 29, 68, 73, 91, 134, 168, 188

THE first part of this walk takes you through the garment industry district of London and continues through some very interesting streets of 19th and late 18th-century buildings. Several of these houses are now the practices of physicians and doctors. There are many restaurants and public houses on the route, if refreshment is required.

The walk begins at Tottenham Court Road tube station, where you should leave by exit No.2. Walk along Tottenham Court Road, past the many electronic shops, and turn left into Percy Street. At No.15 we find the blue plaque commemorating the film and stage actor **Charles Laughton** (1), who lived here 1928–31. Next door at No.14 the poet and essayist **Coventry Patmore** (2) lived for a short time. He was a member of the Pre-Raphaelite Brotherhood and many of the plaques in this area have associations with the group (see also Walk 12, Bloomsbury).

Continue along Percy Street to the very end, crossing Charlotte Street, which gives a good view of the Post Office tower. Ahead is Rathbone Street, where you bear right at the Marquis of Granby. A short way along on the left side you will find a small alleyway called Newman Passage. This is the place to go for a London pie and a short cut to Newman Street. Emerging from Newman Passage you will see a bronze plaque a couple of doors to the right at No.28. This was the home of **Thomas Stothard** (3) who was a noted painter and etcher. He also designed monuments, architectural fittings and jewellery.

Turn around and walk along Newman Street to Oxford Street, bearing right to the next corner, where you will find the Plaza shopping centre. On the side of the mall in Berners Street, formerly No.71 Berners Street, there is a plaque marking the site of the home of **Samuel Taylor Coleridge** (4), the poet well-remembered for his poems *The Rime of the Ancient Mariner* and *Kubla Khan*. Walk along Berners Street towards the Middlesex Hospital.

At the end of the road turn right into Mortimer Street, continue into Goodge Street and then turn left into Charlotte Street. Cross over Tottenham Street. On your left at No.81 is the plaque commemorating the architect of the British Museum **Sir Robert Smirke** (5). He also, among other works, designed the General Post Office and the College of Physicians.

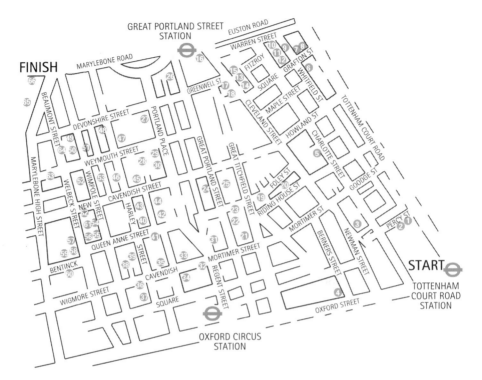

GREAT PORTLAND STREET
STATION

EUSTON ROAD
WARREN STREET

FINISH   MARYLEBONE ROAD

START

TOTTENHAM
COURT ROAD
STATION

OXFORD STREET

OXFORD CIRCUS
STATION

1 Charles Laughton	18 Samuel Morse	35 Sir J. Hutchinson	52 Elizabeth B. Browning
2 Coventry Patmore	19 Henry Fuseli	36 Sir Ronald Ross	53 Sir Evelyn Baring
3 Thomas Stothard	20 Olaudah Equiano	37 Herbert H. Asquith	54 Henry Hallam
4 Samuel T. Coleridge	21 Joseph Noliekens	38 Sir Frederick Treves	55 Samuel Pearce
5 Sir Robert Smirke	22 David E. Hughes	39 Dr G. Dick-Read	56 Hector Berlioz
6 Marie Stopes	23 Edward Malone	40 J.M.W. Turner	57 Thomas Young
7 F. de Miranda	24 Carl M. von Weber	41 Sir George F. Still	58 Sir P. Manson
8 Andres Bello	25 James Boswell	42 Sir Robert Mayer	59 Edward Gibbon
9 Nepali Community	26 Dante G. Rossetti	43 Charles Stanhope	60 Sir J. MacKenzie
10 Mathew Flinders	27 Frances H. Burnett	44 Lutyens/Pearson	61 Thomas Woolner
11 A.W. Hofmann	28 London Amb. Service	4S A. Waterhouse	62 Victor Weisz
12 Charles Eastlake	29 Earl Roberts	46 Lyell/Gladstone	63 Charles Wesley
13 Virginia Woolf	30 Thomas Gage	47 Florence Nightingale	64 J.R. Green
14 George B. Shaw	31 Queens Concert Hall	48 Sir Arthur Pinero	65 Leopold Stokowski
15 Robert G. Cecil	32 Dr Joseph Clover	49 Sir J.M. Rees	66 Charles Dickens
16 Benny Green	33 George E. Street	50 Ethel Gordon Fenwick	
17 John Flaxman	34 Quintin Hogg	51 Sir Arthur Conan Doyle	

The First
BIRTH CONTROL CLINIC
was opened by
Dr. MARIE STOPES
in 1921
at Holloway and
removed here in
1925

Continue along Charlotte Street and Fitzroy Street. Turn right at Maple Street and left at Whitfield Street. On your right at No.108 you will find the first birth-control clinic. This was originally set up in Marlborough Street (1921) and moved here four years later. Its founder, **Dr Marie Stopes** (6), is commemorated with a blue plaque.

Turn right into Grafton Way. At No.58 there are two more

WALK 2: WEST END (1)

blue plaques. These commemorate the Latin American liberators **Francisco de Miranda** (7) and **Andres Bello** (8). A descriptive stone plaque is alongside.

Turn back along Grafton Way and go right again into Whitfield Street. At No.145 on the left you can see a brown plaque marking the first settlement of the **Nepali Community** (9), which began on this site in 1965.

Walk on, turn left at Warren Street, then turn left again into Fitzroy Street. The corner house, No.56, was the home of the naval officer and explorer **Captain Matthew Flinders** (10). His voyages included a survey of the coast of New South Wales and a circumnavigation of Australia (1801–3).

Proceeding to Fitzroy Square you will immediately find two plaques. At No.9 is that of **A.W. Hofmann** (11), and at No.7 that of **Charles Eastlake** (12). Eastlake was a historical painter and first director of the National Gallery. The chemist Hofmann, who was German born, was a director of the Royal College of Chemistry and made many discoveries of organic compounds including formaldehyde. Continue into Fitzroy Square, where on the corner of Fitzroy Street there is a bronze statue of Francisco de Miranda. On the left of the square, a large building has a plaque informing us that it was designed by Robert Adam.

Continuing around Fitzroy Square, the next blue plaque to be seen is at No.29. It commemorates writer **Virginia Woolf** (13). Above this is a brown rectangular plaque which states that the dramatist **George Bernard Shaw** (14) lived here 1887–98. A few doors further along at No.21 another blue plaque commemorates **Robert Gascoyne Cecil** (15), 3rd Marquess of Salisbury, who was three times Prime Minister.

Now continue ahead into Conway Street, turn left again at Warren Street and walk up to Cleveland Street. You will see a privately erected blue plaque on the red-brick building ahead. This is Howard House, No.161, where the musician, writer and broadcaster **Benny Green** (16), is commemorated. He lived here between 1932 and 1962.

Proceeding to your left along Cleveland Street you will reach a public house named the George and Dragon. On the brick building at the rear of this, in Greenwell Street, almost hidden by a fir tree and ivy, is an old RSA plaque commemorating the sculptor **John Flaxman** (17), who lived and died in a house on this site. He was responsible for the monuments to Robert Burns in Westminster Abbey and Lord Nelson in St Paul's Cathedral.

Further along Cleveland Street at No.141 there is a blue plaque which states that **Samuel Morse** (18) lived here 1812–15. Although a recognised painter, he is best remembered for his invention of the telegraph and Morse code.

Four turnings later turn right into Foley Street. Past Candover Street on the left, at No.37, there is an LCC plaque on the house where the artist **Henry Fuseli** (19) lived from 1788 to 1803. His paintings include illustrations of Shakespeare and Milton's works.

Walk into Candover Street and immediately turn left into Riding House Street. You will find the plaque of **Olaudah Equiano** (20) at Nos 67–73. Having been forced into slavery, he obtained his freedom in 1766. He later published his autobiography and campaigned against slavery.

Walk back along Riding House Street, passing Candover Street, then turn left at Great Titchfield Street and right at Mortimer Street. Here on the corner at No.44 the sculptor **Joseph Nollekens** (21) lived and died. He specialised in portrait busts and sculpted many eminent people of his time, including royalty.

Continue and turn right at Great Portland Street. At No.94 on the right **David Edward Hughes** (22) lived and worked. He is credited with the invention of the microphone and a telegraph typewriter. Round the corner to the right at No.40 Langham Street lived the Irish editor of *Shakespeare Magazine*, **Edmond Malone** (23).

Further along Great Portland Street there are two more plaques almost opposite each other. At No.103 the German composer **Carl Maria von Weber** (24) died, two months after his *Oberon* was first performed at Covent Garden. In a house formerly on the site of No.122, the author and biographer of Samuel Johnson, **James Boswell** (25), lived and died.

Proceed along Great Portland Street and turn left into Devonshire Street. Turning right again in Hallam Street will bring you to the plaque commemorating the Pre-Raphaelite artist **Dante Gabriel Rossetti** (26). He was born in a house on this site, near the end of the cul-de-sac.

Returning to Devonshire Street and turning to the right you will reach Portland Place. This majestic wide road has its plaques on the other side. Cross over and bear to the left. The first one reached is at No.63. This was the home of the writer **Frances Hodgson Burnett** (27) from 1893–8. Her most famous books were *The Secret Garden* and *Little Lord Fauntleroy*. The statue in the middle of the road is of the Polish General Wladyslow Sikorski, who has a plaque commemorating him in Buckingham Palace Road. Across the road you can see the Royal Institute of British Architects.

Turn right into Weymouth Street and take the first left into Weymouth Mews. The branch to the right, halfway along, leads round to a small cul-de-sac, where at No.38 you can see a green plaque commemorating the **London Auxiliary Ambulance Service** (28), which had a wartime station here.

Return to Portland Place by the same route and see the small plaque at No.47. Etched into the stonework, it states that **Field Marshall Earl Roberts** (29) lived here 1902–6. The mounted statue of Field Marshall White appears to be looking rather aloof, and he gazes in a different direction. Another soldier, from an earlier period, lived three doors away at No.41. **Thomas Gage** (30) served mainly in North America just before the War of Independence.

Cross the road and walk on past the BBC into Langham Place. Past All Souls' Church is the St George's Hotel. There is a green Westminster plaque here, marking the site of the **Queen's Concert Hall** (31). This was where Sir Henry Wood conducted the first Promenade concerts.

Unveiling of the Queen's Concert Hall commemorative plaque by Sir Andrew Davis, prinicpal conductor of the BBC Symphony Orchestra.

Walk to the traffic lights and cross the road to Cavendish Place. The green Westminster plaque on No.3 states that the pioneer anaesthetist **Dr Joseph Clover** (32) lived in a house formerly on this site. At No.14 across the road lived **George Edmund Street** (33). He was the architect who designed the London Law Courts and many other Gothic style buildings.

Cavendish Place leads into Cavendish Square. To the left at No.5 a plaque states that the founder of the Regent Street Polytechnic, **Quintin Hogg** (34), lived here 1885–98.

Walking back around the square in an anti-clockwise direction, past the telephone boxes, you will find that the surgeon **Sir Jonathan Hutchinson** (35) lived at No.15. Further round at No.18 lived the physician **Sir Ronald Ross** (36). He was the scientist who discovered not only the malaria parasite, but also the fact that it is transmitted by mosquitoes. A few doors away, on the Royal Institute of Nursing, a blue plaque states that the Liberal Prime Minister **Herbert Henry Asquith** (37) once lived in the building.

Turn right and then right again into Wimpole Street. The church of St Peter's Vere Street, which you will have just passed, was built in 1721. Its only remaining decorative features are the windows by Burne-Jones. Cross over Wigmore Street and at No.6 Wimpole Street you will see the blue plaque for **Sir Frederick Treves** (38). He was a founder of the Red Cross Society. Among his patients was the 'Elephant Man', John (Joseph) Merrick, whom he brought to London in 1886.

Return to Wigmore Street and take the second turning left into Harley Street. The first plaque is at No.25 and is a green Westminster type commemorating **Dr Grantly Dick-Read** (39). He was a gynaecologist who promoted natural childbirth and practised here 1935–41.

Now turn left into Queen Anne Street. Above the doorway of No.23 is a relief sculpture of the artist **J.M.W. Turner** (40), who lived in a house formerly on this site. Across the road at No.28 there is a blue plaque stating that the paediatrician **Sir George Frederic Still** (41) lived here. Turn back down Queen Anne Street, crossing over Harley Street, and turn left into Mansfield Street.

The first building on the right has a plaque where **Sir Robert Mayer** (42) lived. He was a great philanthropist and patron of music who founded concerts for children. Further along on opposite sides of the road are the plaques commemorating **Charles Stanhope** (43) at No.20, and **Sir Edwin Landseer Lutyens** (44) and **John Loughborough Pearson** on a shared plaque at No.13. Stanhope was an inventor and politician who married the sister of William Pitt the Younger. Pearson was an architect who specialised in the design of churches. Lutyens, who lived here after Pearson, was also an architect, but more classical in his styling. He was responsible for the designs of the Cenotaph and the Trafalgar Square fountains.

Across the road at No.61 New Cavendish Street lived another architect, **Alfred Waterhouse** (45). His designs include the Natural History Museum in South Kensington, University College Hospital and several University College buildings. Go left to Harley Street and right to No.73. A house on this site belonged to **Sir Charles Lyell** (46), the geologist whose books gave a basis for Darwin's theory of evolution. This plaque is shared with **William Gladstone**, former Prime Minister, who moved into the house the year after Lyell's death.

Cross over Weymouth Street. An inscription commemorating the nurse **Florence Nightingale** (47) is set into the stonework of No.90 on the other side of the road. It was from here that she set out for the Crimea in 1854.

The next plaque on this tour is around the corner in Devonshire Street (below). This is listed as 115A Harley Street and is for **Sir Arthur Pinero** (48). Pinero, who lived here 1909–34, was the author of about 50 dramas and comedies.

Continue along Devonshire Street and turn left into Upper Wimpole Street. The green plaque at No.18 states that the surgeon **Sir John Milsom Rees** (49) lived and practised here from 1914 to 1939. Two doors along there is a blue plaque on the home of the nursing reformer **Ethel Gordon Fenwick** (50), who lived here from 1887 to 1924. Further along, across the road at No.2, the novelist and creator of Sherlock Holmes, **Sir Arthur Conan Doyle** (51) worked in 1891.

Continue into Wimpole Street. At No.50 Wimpole Street, poet **Elizabeth Barrett Browning** (52) lived from 1838–46. Almost opposite at No.36 there is a plaque on the home of the colonial administrator and statesman, **Sir Evelyn Baring** (53). Further along, past New Cavendish Street, the historian **Henry Hallam** (54) lived at No.67. He wrote several detailed works on the history of England.

Now turn right into Queen Anne Street. There are two plaques here. The first is a blue one, privately erected to commemorate **Stephen Pearce** (55). He was a portrait and equestrian painter who lived in this house 1856–84. Close by at No.58 the French composer **Hector Berlioz** (56) stayed in 1851. Proceed on to Welbeck Street where you will see two plaques facing you.

The physicist and linguist **Thomas Young** (57) lived at No.48. He was instrumental in translating the inscription on the Rosetta Stone. Alongside is the GLC plaque on the home of **Sir Patrick Manson** (58). This doctor worked with Sir Ronald Ross on the experiments related to malaria.

Turn left then right into Bentinck Street. Here again we find plaques on opposite sides of the road. **Edward Gibbon** (59), the author of the mammoth work *The Decline And Fall of the Roman Empire*, lived in a house formerly on the site of No.7. Across the road at No.17 lived the physician and cardiologist **Sir James Mackenzie** (60). Walk back and turn left into Welbeck Street, past the end of Queen Anne Street, where an interesting plaque can be found at No.29. A rectangular plaque is placed below a relief portrait of **Thomas Woolner** (61). This sculptor and poet lived here for 32 years until his death.

Welbeck Mansions are at the top of Welbeck Street. Around the corner on the end of the block, in New Cavendish Street, is the plaque of former resident **Victor Weisz** (62). He was a popular newspaper cartoonist who signed his work 'Vicky'. Opposite is Westmoreland Street. Walk down to the King's Head public house. On the wall by the Wheatley Street entrance a blue plaque states that the hymn-writer **Charles Wesley** (63) lived and died in a house on this site. His musician sons Charles and Samuel also lived at the house.

Continue along Westmoreland Street, crossing Weymouth Street, into Beaumont Street. The historian **John Richard Green** (64) lived in a house on the site of No.4. He wrote several books on the subject of English history. Beaumont Street curves near the end and leads into Marylebone High Street. This is an interesting street with a village atmosphere. Take time to enter the garden of rest opposite and read the three plaques on the rear wall.

Next door, No.63 is a school attended by musical conductor **Leopold Stokowski** (65) before he went to the Royal College of Music. The blue plaque is at the side of the building viewed from the peaceful grounds of St Marylebone parish church. As this is near the end of the walk, it is a good place to rest before the final plaque of the tour.

Continue along Marylebone High Street to Marylebone Road. The last and one of the most interesting of the plaques on this walk commemorates **Charles Dickens** (66) and is on the corner building. This is on the site of a house where he lived and wrote six of his novels. The plaque is sculpted in relief and shows a portrait of Dickens with characters from his books.

This is the end of the walk and if followed as written you will have seen 66 plaques. It is now a short walk past Madame Tussaud's and the London Aquarium to Baker Street tube station. Several buses also run along Marylebone Road.

Walk 3
West End (2)

Distance:	4½ miles (7.25km)
Time taken:	2 hours
Number of plaques:	47
Nearest tube stations:	Baker Street, Bond Street, Marble Arch
Bus routes:	2, 6, 7, 13, 15, 16, 23, 30, 36, 74, 82, 98, 113, 135, 139, 189, 274

THIS walk could be taken as a continuation of the previous one or as a separate walk in its own right. It takes in part of the area north of Oxford Street, near some of London's best shopping areas. Restaurants and cafés of all types are abundant.

We begin at Baker Street tube station, where you can leave by the exit for Madame Tussaud's. Close by is the large statue of the fictional detective Sherlock Holmes. Cross Marylebone Road and walk into Baker Street. No.120 was the home during the years 1802–6 of Britain's youngest Prime Minister, **William Pitt** (1). As the plaque is set rather high on the building it is best viewed from the curb edge or from across the road. You will need to cross the road in any case for the next plaque.

Walk back on the other side and cross Marylebone Road. Ahead is Lloyds Bank on the corner, where you can see the green plaque of **Juan Pablo Viscardo Y Guzman** (2), who lived and died at a house formerly at No.185 Baker Street, on this site. He was born in Peru and his essays and writings heralded the Latin American independent states.

Looking across Baker Street towards the station, you can now see two brown plaques

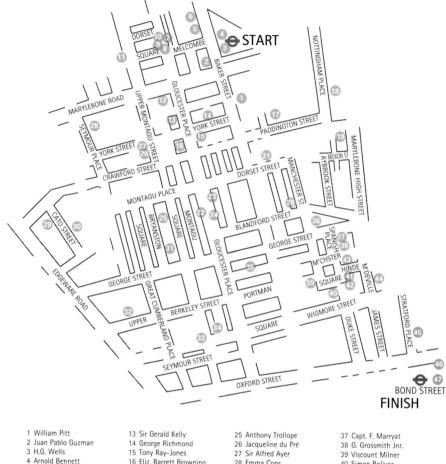

1 William Pitt	13 Sir Gerald Kelly	25 Anthony Trollope	37 Capt. F. Marryat
2 Juan Pablo Guzman	14 George Richmond	26 Jacqueline du Pré	38 G. Grossmith Jnr.
3 H.G. Wells	15 Tony Ray-Jones	27 Sir Alfred Ayer	39 Viscount Milner
4 Arnold Bennett	16 Eliz. Barrett Browning	28 Emma Cons	40 Simon Bolivar
5 Sherlock Holmes	17 Chateaubriand	29 Cato St. Conspiracy	41 Sir Julius Benedict
6 Sherlock Holmes Museum	18 Charles E. Kempe	30 Octavia Hill	42 J.H. Jackson
7 Bentley Motor Car	19 Octavia Hill	31 M. Reschid Pasha	43 Dame Emelie Macauley
8 Free French Forces	20 Michael Faraday	32 Eliz. Garrett Anderson	44 Sir F.P. Tosti
9 Thomas Lord	21 William 'Wilkie' Collins	33 Edward Lear	45 Martin Van Buren
10 MCC	22 William 'Wilkie' Collins	34 Michael W. Balfe	46 HMV
11 G. Grossmith Snr.	23 J.R. Godley	35 Thomas Moore	47 Ernest Bevin
12 VJ Day	24 Benedict Arnold	36 Sir Francis Beaufort	

situated on either side of the entrance to Chiltern Court (left). These are for the novelists **H.G. Wells** (3) and **Arnold Bennett** (4), who both lived here in 1930.

Continue on to the Abbey National building, across the road. A small bronze plaque by the entrance states that this is the site of the home of the fictional detective **Sherlock Holmes** (5), number 221B Baker Street. A few doors away, at No.239, the **Sherlock Holmes museum** (6) has a blue plaque with the same claim. Go back and turn into Melcombe Street.

The third turning on your right is Chagford Street. At No.49 a blue plaque records that the first **Bentley Motor Car** (7) was built here in 1919. Now return to Melcombe Street, turn to your right and cross over Gloucester Place to Dorset Square.

As you turn into Dorset Square you will find a plaque on the corner building, No.1. It was from here that the **Free French Forces** (8) operated during World War Two. Across the road you can see a green wooden hut that supports two plaques. One marks this as the site of the cricket ground laid out by **Thomas Lord** (9) in 1787. This became the home of the **Marylebone Cricket Club (MCC)** (10) and the second plaque was placed alongside to mark their bicentenary in 1987.

Continue to the left, around the square to the far side, to No.28, where you will see a plaque on the home of **George Grossmith Snr** (11). He was a comedy actor who took many leading parts in Gilbert and Sullivan operettas.

Now turn left into Balcombe Street and then left again, crossing Marylebone Road to the majestic council building with the Corinthian columns and seated lions. By the entrance is a black circular plaque, placed by Westminster City Council in 1995 to mark the fiftieth anniversary of **VJ Day** (12).

Turn right into Gloucester Place. The blue plaque at No.117 marks the home of the portrait painter **Sir Gerald Kelly** (13), who lived here from 1916 to 1972. Cross over the road into York Street. At No.20 on the left side there is a blue plaque which commemorates another artist, **George Richmond** (14), who lived here 1843–96. His portraits include the Duke of Wellington, William Gladstone and Cardinal Manning. Return to Gloucester Place and turn left.

The house on the left, No.102, is where the photographer **Tony Ray-Jones** (15) lived and worked. He worked in both London and the US, and taught his art in San Francisco. At No.99, across the road on the corner of Crawford Street, **Elizabeth Barrett Browning** (16) lived for a short time. This rectangular plaque is so tarnished it will need a close examination. To continue turn left into Crawford Street, then cross over Baker Street into Paddington Street.

At the beginning of the railings of Paddington Street Gardens, on the left, past Chiltern Street, there is a Victorian Gothic-style large plinth. Here you will find another tarnished bronze plaque recording the fact that the **Viscount de Chateaubriand** (17) 'lived as an émigré in a garret close to this site where he began his literary career'. He was an author and exile from the French Revolution. Continue and turn left into Nottingham Place. At No.37 the noted stained-glass artist **Charles Eamer Kempe** (18) lived and worked.

Return to Paddington Street, turning to the left. Continue right at Marylebone High Street, then turn right at Moxon Street and right again into Garbutt Place. At No.2, a plaque informs us that the housing reformer **Octavia Hill** (19) began her work here. She was also a co-founder of the National Trust.

Returning to Moxon Street, bear right and then left into Aybrook Street. At the bottom, by the church, turn right into Blandford Street. No.48, just past Manchester Street, was where the scientist **Michael Faraday** (20) served his apprenticeship. This is a Royal Society of Arts plaque erected in 1876.

Turn into Manchester Street, by the Tudor Rose public house. Then turn left at Dorset Street. You will see a green plaque for the computer pioneer **Charles Babbage** (21). Continue forward, crossing Baker Street to Gloucester Place and turning to the left. No.65 is where the novelist **William Wilkie Collins** (22) lived from 1868 to 1876. His novels of mystery and crime are still well read. At No.62 you will see a shield-shaped plaque. This records the fact that **Major General Benedict Arnold** (23) spent the last five years of his life living at this address. Arnold was a traitor to the American cause during the War of Independence. The founder of Canterbury, New Zealand, **John Robert Godley** (24), lived and died at No.48.

Turn right into George Street and take the third entry on your right into the far side of Montagu Square. The prolific writer **Anthony Trollope** (25) lived here at No.39.

Proceed to Montagu Place and into Upper Montagu Street. At No.27 you will see a blue plaque behind the railings commemorating the fact that cellist **Jacqueline du Pré** (26) lived here from 1967-71. This is one of three London plaques commemorating her.

Take the next turning on the left. Around the corner at 51 York Street you will see the plaque commemorating **Sir Alfred Jules Ayer** (27). He was a professor of logic at Oxford University and published many books on philosophy. York Street was built in the early 19th century and numbers 78–84 date from that period. Proceed along York Street and turn right at Seymour Place. **Emma Cons** (28), the philanthropist and founder of the Old Vic theatre, lived and worked at No.136.

Return down Seymour Place and turn right by the traffic lights into Crawford Street. At the junction, cross over into Crawford Place. The Windsor Castle public house is an interesting stop for refreshment. Now take the second left into Cato Street. On the right you will see a blue plaque (left) recording the **Cato Street Conspiracy** (29). This was one of the lesser-known events of parliamentary history. In 1820 a group of conspirators met here in a stable loft and plotted to murder the Cabinet at a meeting in Grosvenor Square. The plan was discovered before any action could be taken, the conspirators were arrested and several were hanged for their involvement in the plot. At Nos 36–38, a little further along Cato Street on the left side, there is a another plaque commemorating **Octavia Hill** (30).

Continue through the archway at the end of Cato Street and turn right to the Edgware Road. Turn left towards Marble Arch and left again at George Street. It is interesting to read the inscription on the old fountain. Take the second entry into Bryanston Square on your left, to see the plaque of **Mustapha Reschid Pasha** (31) at No.1. He was the Turkish ambassador when he lived here in 1839. Cross over George Street into Great Cumberland Place, just behind. Ahead you can see the Marble Arch.

Turn right into Upper Berkeley Street. No.20 bears the plaque of **Elizabeth Garrett Anderson** (32). She was the first woman doctor in Britain and lived here 1860-74. Come back along Upper Berkeley Street, turn right, continue along Great Cumberland Place and turn left into Seymour Street. There are two plaques here. No.30 was the home of the humorist and artist **Edward Lear** (33) and No.12 that of the composer, **Michael William Balfe** (34).

Continue to Portman Square and turn left past the front of the Churchill Hotel, into Gloucester Place. Turn right at George Street. The Irish poet and biographer **Thomas Moore** (35) lived a few doors along at No.85. His best known work was perhaps *The Last Rose of Summer*. Continue and cross Baker Street.

The second turning on the left is Manchester Street. A blue plaque at No.52 records that **Sir Francis Beaufort** (36) lived here. He was the naval officer and hydrographer who developed the wind force measure known as the Beaufort Scale. Return, going left past the rear of the Wallace Collection, and turn right into Spanish Place. In 1890, this magnificent collection of paintings and *objets d'art* was bestowed to the nation, by the widow of Sir Richard Wallace. It was begun in the 18th century by the 1st Marquis of Hertford, an ancestor of Sir Richard.

Two plaques can be found at No.3 Spanish Place. **Captain Frederick Marryat** (37) lived here 1841-3. He was the author of *Children of the New Forest* and *Mr Midshipman Easy*, among other books. The actor/manager **George Grossmith Jnr** (38) also lived here from 1909 to 1935.

SIMON BOLIVAR
EL LIBERTADOR
THE GREAT LATIN AMERICAN
STATESMAN AND PATRIOT
WHO LIBERATED
BOLIVIA COLOMBIA
ECUADOR PANAMA
PERU & VENEZUELA
stayed in this house in
· 1810 ·

Now walk into Manchester Square, bearing to the right. No.14 was the home of the statesman **Viscount Milner** (39). He served in several offices and was a member of Lloyd George's war cabinet. Continue on to Duke Street. At No.4, opposite the Devonshire Arms, the South American revolutionary leader **Simon Bolivar** (40) stayed in 1810. Apart from the original plaque (left) an English Heritage blue plaque has been placed alongside.

Return to Manchester Square and continue to the right corner, where two plaques are located. No.2 was the home of the German musician and composer **Sir Julius Benedict** (41) and No.3 the home of the neurologist and surgeon **John Hughlings Jackson** (42).

Turn right into Hinde Street. There is a plaque at 11-14 Hinde Street, commemorating **Dame (Emilie) Rose Macaulay** (43), whose novels were mainly of a Victorian style.

Turning right again takes you into Mandeville Place. No.12 was the site of the home of the composer **Sir Fransesco Paolo Tosti** (44) from 1886 to 1916. He wrote many popular songs, of which perhaps the best remembered is *Good-bye*. Continue across Wigmore Street, through James Street, to Oxford Street. Turn left and left again into Stratford Place. No.7 was the home of the American ambassador **Martin Van Buren** (45), who progressed to become the eighth president of the US.

Return to Oxford Street. Across the road at No.363, opposite Marylebone Lane, a blue plaque marks the former premises of **HMV** (44). It was here that the Beatles and other popular singers and groups made their first recordings. The final plaque of this walk is opposite Stratford Place, at No.34 South Molton Street, where the Labour foreign secretary **Ernest Bevin** (46) lived from 1931–39.

Bond Street underground station is opposite and this is the end of the walk. If you have followed the route detailed you will have seen 46 plaques on the tour.

Walk 4
Soho and St James's

<table>
<tr><td>Distance:</td><td>4½ miles (7.25km)</td></tr>
<tr><td>Time taken:</td><td>2½ hours</td></tr>
<tr><td>Number of plaques:</td><td>62</td></tr>
<tr><td>Nearest tube station:</td><td>Oxford Circus, Tottenham Court Road, Piccadilly, Green Park</td></tr>
<tr><td>Bus routes:</td><td>3, 6, 7, 8, 10, 12, 13, 14, 15, 19, 22, 23, 24, 25, 29, 38, 53, 55, 73, 88, 94, 98, 139, 176</td></tr>
</table>

THIS walk takes you through the most vibrant area of London. There are so many restaurants, pubs, cafés and snack bars that no particular ones are singled out. The walker can stop almost anywhere and find refreshment within easy reach. The route takes in the younger person's Mecca of fashion, Carnaby Street, the red-light district, the costume jewellery wholesale district, Chinatown, the film district and fashionable Jermyn Street as well as part of the theatre district of London. Two of the oldest official London plaques can also be seen on the route.

We begin the walk at Oxford Circus tube station where the tube traveller will leave by exit No.6. This will lead straight into Argyll Street, where many of the buildings were constructed in the 1730s. The first plaque to be found is at No.10, just before the Palladium Theatre. This commemorates **Major-General William Roy** (1) who lived here 1779–90. He was an antiquarian who founded the Ordnance Survey.

Two doors away, behind the large Palladium wall sign, is a blue plaque recording that the American short story writer **Washington Irving** (2) lived at No.8. He was the originator of the story of *Rip Van Winkle*. If you peer through the left window of the Palladium entrance you will see a blue plaque on the wall commemorating **Lord Grade of Elstree** (3). This theatrical impresario had many associations with the Palladium. Better known as Lew Grade, he was the brother of Bernard Delfont and Leslie Grade. To your right side, on the rear of the Dickens & Jones store, is a blue plaque commemorating **Germaine Necker** (4). She was a French author who lived on this site 1813–14. Ahead of you, you will see Liberty's store, with its impressive façade.

Turn left into Great Marlborough Street. There is a 'Theatreland Plaque' on the side of the **Palladium Theatre** (5). This states that it was opened in 1910 and gives details of its history. Continue to No.18, where an etched plaque informs us that the composer **Franz (Ferenc) Liszt** (6) stayed at a house on this site 1840–1.

Now cross the road to the turning next to Liberty's and walk into Carnaby Street. This street became fashionable with young people in the 'swinging sixties' and is still a popular

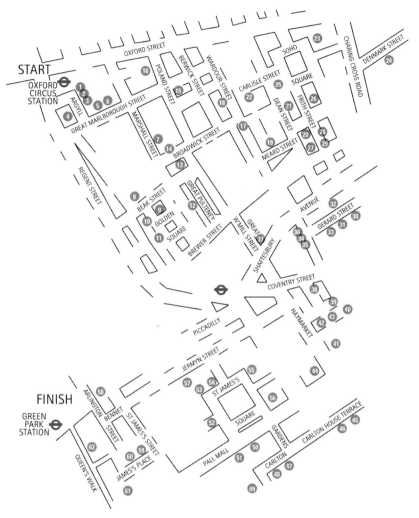

1 William Roy
2 Washington Irving
3 Lord Grade
4 Germaine Necker
5 Palladium Theatre
6 Franz Liszt
7 William Blake
8 Canaletto
9 M. McKenzie
10 John Hunter
11 Marquis of Pompal
12 John Polidori
13 Dr John Snow
14 Charles Bridgeman
15 Percy Shelley
16 Druids

17 Jessie Matthews
18 Thos. Sheraton
19 Thos. Hearne
20 Dr J. Rogers
21 Karl Marx
22 J.C. Smith
23 Arthur Onslow
24 Augustas Siebe
25 Sir Joseph Banks
26 William Hazlitt
27 Dr John Snow
28 Mozart
29 John Logie Baird
30 John Dryden
31 Paul de Lamerie
32 Turk's Head

33 Edmund Burke
34 Willy Clarkson
3S Sarah Bernhard
36 Sir Henry Irving
37 William Hunter
38 Bernard Delfont
39 Sir Isaac Newton
40 Sir M. Wheeler
41 Richard Cobden
42 Oscar Wilde
43 Richard Dadd
44 Ho Chi Minh
45 William Gladstone
46 Nathaniel Curzon
47 Charles de Gaulle
48 Lord Palmerston

49 Earl Kitchener
50 T. Gainsborough
51 Nell Gwynne
52 Napoleon III
53 Ada Lovelace
54 Pitt/Derby/Gladstone
55 Nancy Astor
56 General Eisenhower
57 Sir Isaac Newton
58 Robert & Horace Walpole
59 Frederic Chopin
60 Sir Francis Chichester
61 William Huskisson
62 Sir Henry Pelham

tourist attraction. The Shakespeare's Head, on the corner of Foubert's Place, was originally opened by a relation of the Bard. Details of the pub's history are given in gold letters on a black plaque. Walk down Carnaby Street and turn left into Ganton Street. Turn right into Marshall Street and walk to the wide stone steps on the other side of the road. On the left-hand wall large lettering states that **William Blake** (7) was born on 28 November 1757 in a house that once stood on this site. Continue on to Beak Street, turning to the right.

At No. 41 a plaque records that the artist Antonio Canal, known as **Canaletto** (8), lived here. His views of London were painted 1746–56. Immediately opposite is Upper James Street. This leads into Golden Square. Walking to your right you will find a green plaque at No.33 commemorating the surgeon **Sir Morrell Mackenzie** (9). He founded the first throat hospital here in 1865. The building ahead is No.31 Golden Square. The LCC brown plaque, which formerly stood by the front entrance, is now located at the end of the building in Upper John Street. It has been moved twice due to rebuilding. This plaque was erected to commemorate the surgeon **John Hunter** (10), who lived near here. A weathered stone bust of him can be seen in Leicester Square.

Continue round Golden Square to the red-brick building, Nos 23 and 24. These two houses were used as the **Portuguese embassy** (11) from 1724 to 1747. The Marquis of Pompal, Portuguese ambassador 1739–44, lived here. The statue in the middle of the square is of George II, clad in Roman garb.

Continue on into Lower John Street and turn left into Brewer Street. Three turnings along you reach Great Poultney Street. No.38 was the home of the novelist **Dr John William Polidori** (12). In his short life, he qualified as a medical practitioner and was the first to write a novel about a vampire. He was also a contemporary of Lord Byron and Mary and Percy Shelley. Continue on, turning right and then left into Lexington Street. At the corner with Broadwick Street is the **John Snow** (13) public house. A small plaque around the side records the fact that a coloured kerb-stone marks the site of the 'Broadstreet Pump'. This pump was associated with Dr John Snow's discovery, in 1854, that cholera is conveyed by water. A plaque on the site of Dr Snow's house is in nearby Frith Street on the route. Across the road is a blue plaque at No.54, marking the home of the landscape gardener **Charles Bridgeman** (14).

Looking to the right across the road you can see Poland Street. Walk up to the corner of Poland and Noel Streets. The poet **Percy Bysshe Shelley** (15) lodged at No.15 for a few months in 1811.

Cross over Great Marlborough Street to the King's Arms public house at No.23 Poland Street. Here you will find a blue plaque erected by the **Ancient Order of Druids** (16) to commemorate their re-establishment at this address in 1781. Turn back and go left at Noel Street, then turn right into Berwick Street. The Blue Post public house on the corner of Broadwick Street has a green plaque marking the birthplace of the actress **Jessie Matthews** (17). Continue left through Broadwick Street to Wardour Street and turn to the left again.

Wardour Street has for many years been the centre of offices of the major film companies. No.163 was the home of furniture designer **Thomas Sheraton** (18) from 1793-5. He later had a second home a few doors away (now No.147). Turn back down Wardour Street to Meard Street. A draughtsman and watercolour artist named **Thomas Hearne** (19) lived at No.6.

Walk on to Dean Street and turn left. Opposite, at No.33, on the corner with Bateman

Street, you will see the home of **Dr Joseph Rogers** (20), who was a noted health care reformer. You can see the top of the Post Office tower ahead. Continue along Dean Street to No.28, where a blue plaque, set rather high and easily missed, states that **Karl Marx** (21) lived here 1851-6. Proceed to Carlisle Street, turning to the left. A blue plaque on the offices of *Private Eye* at No.6 records that the composer and friend of Handel, **John Christopher Smith** (22), lived here.

Now cross over Dean Street into Soho Square. This square was originally laid out in the late 17th century and the central gardens are little changed. Go through the gate, where there is a full history of the square detailed, and walk across to the perimeter opposite. You will pass a timbered building in the centre and an original statue of Charles II. No.20 is the site of the home of a former speaker of the House of Commons, **Arthur Onslow** (23). A few yards to the right there is Sutton Row.

Walk through and cross Charing Cross Road. Turn to the right and then left, passing Denmark Place, into Denmark Street. This is the centre of London's music industry. At No.5 you will find a blue plaque on the former home and shop of **Augustus Siebe** (24). This German-born inventor is acclaimed as 'the father of diving'. His diving helmet and rubber suit was first produced in 1840 and versions of his invention remained in use with the Royal Navy until 1989.

Walk back and cross over Charing Cross Road again to Manette Street, which is next to Foyle's famous bookshop. At the end of Manette Street go under the archway of the Pillars of Hercules, where there is an interesting plaque to read. Now turn right to Soho Square and left to the offices of Twentieth Century Fox Film Studios. On the right wall, an etched plaque states that this is the site of the home of **Sir Joseph Banks** (25) and other botanists. He was a founder of Kew Gardens and sailed the world with James Cook, gathering rare plants. The Linnaean Society also met here from 1821 to 1857. Now walk into Frith Street, just behind.

The first plaque we find is at No.6 on the left, where **William Hazlitt** (26) died in 1830. He was an essayist and critic. The next plaque commemorates the previously mentioned **Dr John Snow** (27) and is at No.53. No.20 has a plaque commemorating the fact that **Wolfgang Amadeus Mozart** (28) worked here 1764-5, and two doors away at No.22 **John Logie Baird** (29) first demonstrated his invention of television. Continue along Frith Street and cross over Shaftesbury Avenue into Gerrard Place. Turn right into Gerrard Street.

Gerrard Street is now the centre of London's Chinatown. In the 18th and 19th century it was frequented by writers and artists and was known for its coffee-houses. The first plaque that you will see was erected in 1870. It is one of the oldest of the surviving official plaques and was placed by the Royal Society of Arts. It is at No.43 and commemorates **John Dryden** (30), the poet, who in fact lived on the site of No.44. Three doors away a modern green plaque is on the site of the home of **Paul de Lamerie** (31), the king's silversmith, who lived here 1738–51. Opposite, at No.9, is the site of the **Turk's Head Tavern** (32), where Dr Johnson, with Sir Joshua Reynolds and others, formed 'The Club' in 1764. The inscription on another early plaque, erected in 1876, commemorates **Edmund Burke** (33). This politician lived at No.37 in the 1780s.

At the end of Gerrard Street look across to Nos 41–3 Wardour Street. The theatrical wig-maker **Willy Clarkson** (34) lived and died here. The blue plaque is set very high below the clock. On either side of the entrance are bronze plaques stating that **Sarah Bernhard** (35) laid the foundation stone of this specially designed building in 1904 and **Sir Henry Irving** (36) the coping stone in 1905. Now turn left into Shaftesbury Avenue. Cross over and enter Great Windmill Street. A blue plaque is to be found on the site of the home and museum of the doctor **William Hunter** (37). This is above the telephone boxes at the rear of the Lyric Theatre.

Return along Great Windmill Street, crossing over Shaftesbury Avenue, and turn to the left in Coventry Street. You will see the Prince of Wales Theatre across the road (right). Here a blue plaque commemorates **Sir Bernard Delfont** (38), the theatrical impresario and brother of Lord Grade.

Continue along Coventry Street to the next turning, which is Whitcomb Street. Turn left into Orange Street and you will see the Westminster Reference Library ahead. Engraved into the stonework are the words 'Sir Isaac Newton (39) lived in a house on this site 1710–1727'. A blue plaque for him will be seen later in the walk. Return to Whitcomb Street, bearing left where you will find a blue plaque on No.27, the home of **Sir Mortimer Wheeler** (40). He was an archaeologist and well-known broadcaster. Walk on, turn right and then right again into Suffolk Street. **Richard Cobden** (41), the politician and economist, died at No.23 in 1865.

Further along this cul-de-sac, at the rear of the Theatre Royal, there is a green plaque. It records that **Oscar Wilde** (42) had two of his plays first performed here. Opposite the theatre lived the painter **Richard Dadd** (43) at No.5. During a fit of insanity, Dadd murdered his father in 1843 and consequently spent his remaining years in a mental institution.

Walk back and turn right into Suffolk Place. Looking across Haymarket you can see a blue plaque on the other side of the road. Don't try to cross over, as this is an extremely busy street. This plaque surprisingly records that in 1913, the North Vietnamese leader **Ho Chi Minh** (44) worked at the Carlton Hotel, which formerly stood on this site. He did not wait at table, but worked in the kitchens. Now turn left.

Walk on and turn to the left into Pall Mall East. Cross over at the traffic lights, go

around Canada House and cross over Cockspur Street into Spring Gardens. You will have seen Trafalgar Square and Nelson's Column en route. Go through the iron gates into Cockspur Court. A seated statue of Queen Victoria is on the left and to the right you will see a narrow set of stone steps leading upwards. Mounting these takes you into Carlton House Terrace. This street of terraced houses was designed by John Nash and built betwen 1827 and 1832. You can see another statue of Queen Victoria between Nos 14 and 15. A plaque at No.11 records that Prime Minister **William Gladstone** (45) lived here.

Walking past the Duke of York's lofty column and the statues of Field Marshal Burgoyne and **George Nathaniel Curzon** (46) you reach No.1 Carlton Gardens. This is where Curzon lived and died. He was Viceroy of India 1899–1905 and Foreign Secretary 1919–24. A little further on three plaques can be found at No.4 Carlton Gardens. This was the wartime headquarters of **General Charles de Gaulle** (47) and the Free French Forces. A second inset marble plaque is worded in the French language. The third plaque marks this as a former home of **Lord Palmerston** (48), who was twice Prime Minister in the 19th century. Continue to the large house across the square, No.2 Carlton Gardens, which was the home of **Earl Kitchener** (49) during 1914 and 1915. The rear of a statue of George VI can be seen ahead and behind a statue of General de Gaulle, on the north side.

Retrace your steps to the statue of Lord Curzon and turn left, walking towards Pall Mall. Turn to the left in Pall Mall and proceed to Schomberg House, which is a red-brick

building, numbered 80–82 (above). This is the only original building left in the street. The painter **Thomas Gainsborough** (50) lived here 1774–88. Next door at No.79, the mistress of Charles II, **Nell Gwynne** (51), lived in splendour in a house formerly on this site.

Walk back and cross over the road into St James's Square. The first turning on the left side is King Street. Another old plaque is found at No.1C on the north side. This is on the site of the house where **Napoleon III** (52) lived during his exile in England. The plaque was erected in 1867 and is the oldest surviving official plaque in London.

Continuing around St James's Square a blue plaque commemorating **Ada, Countess of Lovelace** (53) can be seen behind the railings at No.12. She was the daughter of Lord Byron and her friendship with Charles Babbage resulted in her interest in, and involvement with, mathematics and early computing. No.10 was the home of three Prime Ministers; **William Pitt, the Earl of Derby** and **W.E. Gladstone** (54). This blue plaque was erected in 1910.

Ahead you can see a plaque at No.4 on the home of **Nancy Astor** (55), who was the first woman to sit in Parliament. In a verbal duel with Winston Churchill she once said 'Winston, if I were your wife I would put poison in your coffee!' to which he replied 'Nancy, if I were your husband, I would drink it'.

On the centre island opposite is a memorial to the policewoman, Yvonne Fletcher, who was killed here by a single shot from the former Iranian embassy across the road, in 1984. Cut flowers are regularly placed here.

Continue past Charles II Street. At No.31 there are two large bronze plaques on the former wartime headquarters of **General Dwight D. Eisenhower** (56). It was here that 'Operation Torch', for the liberation of North Africa, and 'Operation Overlord', for the liberation of north-west Europe, were planned and directed.

Walk back around the square and leave by Duke of York Street. Turn left into Jermyn Street. The scientist **Sir Isaac Newton** (57) lived from 1700 to 1709 in a house formerly on the site of No.87. Continue along Jermyn Street, then cross over St James's Street into Bennet Street. This leads into Arlington Street, where turning to the right you will find a blue plaque at No.5, recording that this was the home of **Sir Robert Walpole** (58) and his son **Horace**. The father was Prime Minister 1721–42 and the son Horace is best known as a man of letters and builder of the Gothic-style mansion at Strawberry Hill.

Return to St James's Street, turning to the right after Bennet Street. Turn into St James's Place. The first plaque that you can see is at No.4 and commemorates **Frederic Chopin** (59). He lived here in 1848 and left these premises to give his last public performance at the Guildhall. Yachtsman **Sir Francis Chichester** (60) lived at No.9. He won the first transatlantic yacht race in 1957 and later made a solo circumnavigation of the world. At No.28 the politician **William Huskisson** (61), lived 1804–6. His claim to fame is that he was the first person to be killed by a train.

Continuing along St James's Place you will find a narrow passageway next to No.23. Walk through here to Queens Walk, which is at the side of Green Park. Turn right upon exiting. Just past the bollards that straddle the walkway a blue plaque can be seen. This is the rear of 22 Pelham Street, which was the home of **Sir Henry Pelham** (62). He was a statesman who became Prime Minister 1753–4.

This completes the walk. Piccadilly with its buses and Green Park tube station are just ahead.

Walk 5
Westminster

Distance:	4¾ miles (7.64km)
Time taken:	2¼ hours
Number of plaques:	30
Nearest tube stations:	Westminster, Pimlico, Victoria, St James's Park
Bus routes:	3, 11, 12, 24, 53, 88, 109, 211

THIS walk incorporates the areas around the Houses of Parliament, Westminster Abbey, Westminster Cathedral, the Tate Gallery and the London Eye. There are many places for refreshment and relaxation. Unfortunately there are fewer plaques than can be found in some of the other walks, but the area is of such interest that it should not be missed. You will see three plaques commemorating Winston Churchill as well as his statue.

Start the walk at Waterloo underground station. Bear left into York Road upon exiting and then turn right at Chicheley Street. This will bring you to the rear of County Hall, where you will see the first two plaques of the tour. They are commemorating **County Hall** (1), (below) which housed the London governing bodies from 1922–86 and the **Inner London Education Service** (2) from 1922–65. These two plaques were originally placed on the other side of the building, where the London Aquarium is now situated.

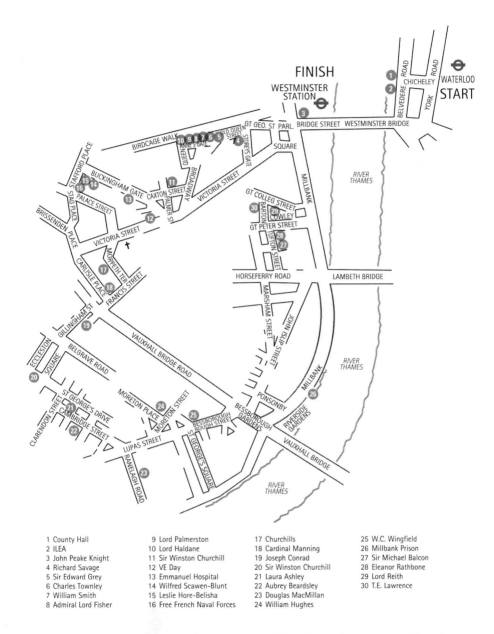

FINISH
WESTMINSTER
STATION

START
WATERLOO

1 County Hall	9 Lord Palmerston
2 ILEA	10 Lord Haldane
3 John Peake Knight	11 Sir Winston Churchill
4 Richard Savage	12 VE Day
5 Sir Edward Grey	13 Emmanuel Hospital
6 Charles Townley	14 Wilfred Scawen-Blunt
7 William Smith	15 Leslie Hore-Belisha
8 Admiral Lord Fisher	16 Free French Naval Forces

17 Churchills	25 W.C. Wingfield
18 Cardinal Manning	26 Millbank Prison
19 Joseph Conrad	27 Sir Michael Balcon
20 Sir Winston Churchill	28 Eleanor Rathbone
21 Laura Ashley	29 Lord Reith
22 Aubrey Beardsley	30 T.E. Lawrence
23 Douglas MacMillan	
24 William Hughes	

Continue along Belvedere Road past County Hall and turn right to cross Westminster Bridge. Crossing the Thames at this point will give you one of the finest views of London. Westminster Bridge leads on to Bridge Street, where you will pass Westminster underground station and St Stephen's Tower, housing Big Ben. The next plaque is found on the corner building with Parliament Street. It is at No.12 Bridge Street, near to which **John Peake Knight** (3) erected the first traffic lights in the world. They were gas-lit and when a fault occurred, the resulting explosion caused the death of a policeman.

Cross over Parliament Street and continue straight ahead along the north side of Parliament Square. You will pass the statue of Sir Winston Churchill on the left and the Cenotaph war memorial can be seen in Whitehall on the right. Continue into Great George Street, past the statue of George Canning. Just after the Institute of Civil Engineers, turn left into Storey's Gate. From Storey's Gate turn right into Old Queen Street.

At No.9 there is a blue plaque, which states that **Richard Savage, 4th Earl Rivers** (4), governor of the Tower of London, lived here 1660–1712. In actual fact he claimed to be the illegitimate son of the 4th Earl, which should have made him the 5th Earl. This street leads you to Queen Anne's Gate.

The plaque at No.3 commemorates **Sir Edward Grey** (5). He was a Liberal statesman who served as foreign secretary (1905–16) and later as ambassador to the US. The next plaque is at No.14, where the antiquary **Charles Townley** (6) lived. After his demise, his collection was purchased by the British Museum.

No.16, next door, has two blue plaques for former residents. These are politician **William Smith** (7) and **Admiral Lord Fisher** (8). Smith was a follower of Fox and an opponent of the war with France. After serving abroad for many years, Fisher became Lord of the Admiralty and later First Sea Lord.

Two doors away, at No.20, a blue plaque marks the birthplace of Prime Minister **Lord Palmerston** (9). Another politician, **Lord Haldane** (10), lived at No.28. He served in several ministries and was the founder of the Territorial Army.

Queen Anne's Gate was originally two separate streets divided by a wall at the point where Queen Anne's statue now stands. You will note the distinctive difference in the styles of architecture. The older part with the decorative door surrounds was built in around 1704. No.28 is the only one still showing the natural wood.

Continue on towards St James's Park station. The Home Office is to your right. Turn left and right into Broadway and walk past New Scotland Yard with its famous revolving sign. Turn right into Caxton Street.

Walking past the Jolly St Ermin's Hotel you come to Caxton Hall. A green plaque informs us that **Sir Winston Churchill** (11) spoke here 1937–42. Proceed to Brewer's Green, where the old Blewcoat School building, erected in 1709, stands. The school was originally founded in 1688 as a charity for 50 poor boys of the parish. It is now a National Trust shop and is interesting to visit.

Continue through Brewer's Green and turn right at the traffic lights into Victoria Street. A short way along you will reach Westminster City Hall. Here a black Westminster Council plaque was placed on the 50th anniversary of **VE Day** (12).

Now return to the traffic lights, by the Army and Navy Stores, and turn left at Buckingham Gate. Walk past the other side of Blewcoat School. At No.51 you will see a stone plaque marking the site of **Emanuel Hospital** (13), which was founded in 1594. Continue past Westminster Chapel and Wilfred Street, almost to the far end. No.15 was the home of **Wilfred Scawen-Blunt** (14). He was a poet, diplomat and traveller and founded the Crabbet Park Arabian Stud.

Ahead of you is Buckingham Gateway, which leads to Buckingham Palace. You may like to have a look, especially if it is time for the changing of the guard at 11.30am.

Turning left from Buckingham Gate, you will find a narrow road leading into Stafford Place. No.16 was the home of Transport Minister **Leslie Hore-Belisha** (15), best remembered for the introduction of 'Belisha beacons' at pedestrian crossings. At the end of Stafford Place there is a stone plaque worded mainly in French. This was the World War Two headquarters of the **Free French Naval Forces** (16).

Turn left and walk around the curving Palace Street. Continue past Westminster City School, with its statue of Sir Sidney Waterlow. Cross over Victoria Street, go under the bridge and bear right. This will bring you to the front of Westminster Catholic Cathedral, which you may like to visit. Walk on and turn left into Morpeth Terrace. At Nos 1–12 Morpeth Mansions you will find a plaque which records that **Winston and Clementine Churchill** (17) lived here 1930–39. Turn right at the end of the road into Francis Street. On the corner of Carlisle Place you will see the bronze plaque commemorating **Cardinal Manning** (18).

From Francis Street, cross over the pedestrian crossing on Vauxhall Bridge Road and bear right. Gillingham Street is the second turning on the left. The blue plaque at No.17 marks the home of novelist **Joseph Conrad** (19).

Cross over Wilton and Belgrave Roads into Eccleston Square. The third plaque on this walk for **Sir Winston Churchill** (20) is at No.34 and records that he lived there 1909–13. Reach this by walking around the right-hand side of the square, where you will find the plaque on the far side.

Continue ahead into St George's Drive. Turn right at Clarendon Street. On the right-hand side corner with Cambridge Street you will see a green plaque on No.83, the house where designer **Laura Ashley** (21) began her business. Turn left into Cambridge Street.

Opposite St Gabriel's Church the illustrator **Aubrey Beardsley** (22) lived at No.114. Walk on, then cross over Gloucester, Charlwood and Lupus Streets into Ranelagh Road. The founder of MacMillan Cancer Relief, **Douglas MacMillan** (23), lived at No.15.

Return to Lupus Street and turn right. At the second junction on the left is Moreton Terrace. Walk into Moreton Street and turn left into Moreton Place. A blue plaque at No.7 marks the birthplace of Australian Prime Minister **William Hughes** (24). Return to Moreton Street, continue and turn right at the next junction, St George's Square. At No.33 on the left corner with Lupus Street is a plaque marking the home of **Major Walter Clopton Wingfield** (25). He was the inventor of the modern game of lawn tennis.

Continue left into Lupus Street, passing Pimlico Station. Proceed through Bessborough Street and Drummond Gate to Vauxhall Bridge Road. Now turn right at the traffic lights into Bessborough Gardens, which is the main road leading to Vauxhall Bridge.

Turn left into Millbank before the bridge and cross the road to Riverside Gardens. Just past the Henry Moore bronze abstract sculptured fountain is a large buttress. A plaque on the front records that it once stood at the top of steps. It was from here that prisoners from nearby **Millbank Prison** (26), sentenced to transportation, embarked on their journey to Australia (below).

It is quite a distance to the next plaque on this tour and there are alternative ways of continuing. If you wish to walk by the riverside, continue along Millbank, turn left at Horseferry Road, opposite Lambeth Bridge, then turn right into Tufton Street. This route takes you past the Tate Gallery, which has free admission and an excellent restaurant. Alternatively, a slightly shorter route is to take the turning opposite, Ponsonby Place, and turn right into John Islip Street, which also leads to Horseferry Road. The former is a more pleasant walk.

Entering Tufton Street, walk on the left-hand side for the best view. A green plaque can be found at No.57 (right). This was the home of the film producer **Sir Michael Balcon** (27). A few doors away at No.59 lived the social reformer **Eleanor Rathbone** (28). She fought for women's rights and was a pioneer of family allowances. Continue and turn right into Great

Peter Street, then left into Cowley Street. At the junction with Barton Street there is a blue plaque commemorating **Lord Reith** (29). He was the Director-General of the BBC and a pioneer of broadcasting, who lived here from 1924 to 1930. The last plaque of this walk is at No.14 Barton Street. This was the home of **T.E. Lawrence** (30), who is better known as 'Lawrence of Arabia'.

Turning right then left at the main road brings you back to Parliament Square. En route to Westminster tube station, you will also pass the Houses of Parliament, St Margaret's Church, and the ancient Jewel Tower. Notice how Oliver Cromwell on his pedestal outside the Houses of Parliament is looking down, as though unable to face the bust of Charles I on the building opposite.

Walk 6
Belgravia

Distance:	4 miles (6.43km)
Time taken:	2 hours
Number of plaques:	45
Nearest tube stations:	Victoria, Sloane Square, Knightsbridge
Bus routes:	C1, C10, 11, 14, 19, 22, 74, 137, 211

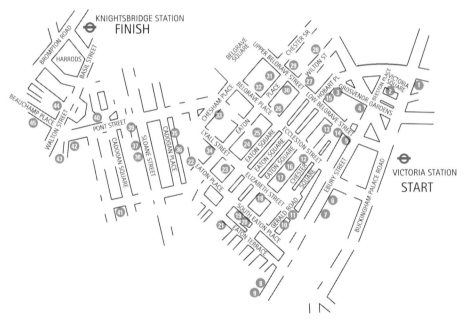

1 General Sikorski	13 Matthew Arnold	25 Stanley Baldwin	37 Sir Charles Dilke
2 Thos. Campbell	14 Queen Wilhelmina	26 Belgian Volunteers	38 Sir H. Beerbohm Tree
3 A. Pitt-Rivers	15 Robert Boothby	27 Walter Bagehot	39 Lillie Langtry
4 F.E. Smith	16 Neville Chamberlain	28 Henry Gray	40 Jane Austen
5 Ian Fleming	17 Prince Metternich	29 Alfred Tennyson	41 Arnold Bennett
6 Edith Evans	18 Vivien Leigh	30 William Ewart	42 George Alexander
7 George Moore	19 Robert Cecil	31 Baron Kelvin	43 Count Raczynski
8 Mozart	20 Philip Noel-Baker	32 John Lubbock	44 P.G. Wodehouse
9 Sackville-West/Nicholson	21 Charles McCall	33 Earl Russell	45 First Test Match
10 Noel Coward	22 Frederic Chopin	34 Thomas Cubitt	
11 Police Station	23 George Peabody	3S Dorothy Jordan	
12 Mary Shelley	24 Lord Halifax	36 William Wilberforce	

THIS district is one of the most exclusive and fashionable areas of central London and was originally part of the Grosvenor estate. The majority of houses in Belgravia were constructed in the early 19th century and were built by the master-builder Thomas Cubitt. Several were designed by George Basevi. The architectural design of the buildings and streets is the main feature of this walk. There are not many shops or restaurants on the route, as it is mainly a residential area, but it terminates by Harrods and Kensington High Street.

The walk begins at Victoria Station, where there are several exits. It is best to take the Victoria Street exit to follow these directions. Turn left and walk towards the trees, then

turn right at the traffic lights into Buckingham Palace Road and continue to the Rubens Hotel. This is past Bressenden Place, and you may find it easier to use the subway to cross under. By the main entrance of the hotel there is a bronze plaque, which records that this was the wartime headquarters of **General Wladyslaw Sikorski** (1). He was commander-in-chief of the Free Polish Forces and premier of the Polish government in exile during World War Two until his deaath in 1943. His excellent bronze statue can be seen in Portland Place during Walk 2.

Return and cross back over Bressenden Place. Cross Buckingham Palace Road at the traffic lights and turn right into Victoria Square. The plaque to the poet **Thomas Campbell** (2) can be seen at No.8 on the left-hand side. His best known works are 'Hohenlinden' and 'Ye Mariners of England'.

Continue through Victoria Square and bear left to Grosvenor Gardens, via Beeston Place. Turn right towards the trees and keep to the left side of the green triangle. Walking on the same side as the green taxi drivers' cabin you will see the sculpture of 'Lioness and Lesser Kudu' in the gardens. The Duke of Westminster commissioned these statues in 2000. Across the road at No.4 you will find the blue plaque of **Augustus Pitt-Rivers** (3). Pitt-Rivers, as well as having a distinguished career in the army, was an eminent archaeologist and anthropologist. He endowed his collection to the museum in Oxford that bears his name.

Walk back down Grosvenor Gardens to the corner of Ebury Street. Here there is a plaque commemorating **F.E. Smith, 1st Earl of Birkenhead** (4). He was a politician, statesman and great orator, who lived here from 1915. Now walk along Ebury Street.

The first plaque found is on the large house with pillars on either side of the entrance (below). This is No.22 Ebury Street, where James Bond originator **Ian Fleming** (5) lived. Having worked as a foreign correspondent in Moscow, a stockbroker, banker and wartime

naval intelligence officer, he was well experienced for writing his exciting novels.

The next two plaques in Ebury Street are on the other side of the road and are for the serious actress **Dame Edith Evans** (6) at No.109 and the Irish-born writer **George Moore** (7) at No.121. While living here he wrote *Conversations in Ebury Street*.

Continue along Ebury Street, crossing over Elizabeth Street, South Eaton Place and Eaton Terrace. The small terrace on the right has two brown plaques. **Wolfgang Amadeus Mozart** (8) composed his first symphony at No.180, when aged only eight, and many years later writer **Vita Sackville-West** lived with her husband **Harold Nicholson** (9) at No.182. If you walk a little further to the road junction you will see a delicate bronze statue of Mozart as a boy.

Walk back and turn left into South Eaton Place. The second turning on the right is Gerald Road. A blue plaque at No.17 informs us that the actor and playwright **Noel Coward** (10) lived here 1930–56. Further along on the same side is a blue plaque on the site of the former **Police Station** (11), which existed from 1846-1993.

Continuing on and crossing over Elizabeth Street again will take you into Chester Square. Walk around St Michael's church towards No.37 on the other side of the square. Behind the railings at No.24 a small rectangular plaque marks the last home of **Mary Shelley** (12). She was the second wife of the poet Percy Bysshe Shelley and was the author of *Frankenstein*.

Towards the end of the square, the poet and critic **Matthew Arnold** (13) lived at No.2. Cross the road to the adjacent corner of the square. At No.77, **Queen Wilhelmina** (14) of the Netherlands had her secretariat here during World War Two.

Walk back to the corner where the post box stands and turn right towards Lower Belgrave Street, then turn left into Eaton Square. Before turning left again, look to the right. Here, at No.1 Eaton Square, **Lord Robert Boothby** (15) lived for 40 years. He was a Member of Parliament and a popular radio and television broadcaster.

Turn left and walk along the southern section of Eaton Square, crossing over Eccleston Street. Prime Minister **Neville Chamberlain** (16) lived at No.37 and the Austrian statesman **Prince Metternich** (17) lived at No.44 in 1848. Continuing over Elizabeth Street you will reach No.54 Eaton Square, where the actress **Vivien Leigh** (18) lived. Continue to the end, turning to the left at South Eaton Place.

There are two blue plaques at No.16. The Tory statesman **Viscount Robert Cecil** (19) lived here from 1923 to 1958 and **Baron Philip Noel-Baker** (20) was also a resident. Apart from being a politician he was captain of the British Olympic team in 1920 and 1924 and won the Nobel Peace Prize in 1959.

Turn right into Chester Row then take the second right into Eaton Terrace. Four turnings along on the left, you will come to Caroline Terrace, where at No.1A you will see a privately erected plaque commemorating the artist **Charles McCall** (21).

Now continue to the very end of Eaton Terrace and bear right. At the corner with Eaton Place you will find a blue plaque with a decorative stone surround. This states that **Frederic Chopin** (22) gave his first London concert in this house on 23 June 1848.

Turn right into Eaton Place and left into the north part of Eaton Square. No.80 was the last London home of American financier and philanthropist **George Peabody** (23). Cross over Lyall Street and walk on to No.86 Eaton Square, where statesman **Lord Halifax** (24) lived. He served as Foreign Secretary and also Viceroy of India. Prime Minister **Stanley Baldwin** (25) lived a few doors away at No.93 in 1920-3.

Continue to the Belgian Embassy, on the corner of Belgrave Place. There is a large gold-coloured plaque here, which was unveiled by the Queen Mother in 1964. It reads 'Many **Belgians** (26) volunteered during World War II to fight with their allies on land, at sea and in the air to liberate their country'.

Proceed to the end of the square, turn left, then turn right into Wilton Street. Immediately on the corner you will find a plaque at the home of **Walter Bagehot** (27). He was a writer and editor of *The Economist* magazine 1860–77. Walk further along Wilton Street to No.9 on the other side of the road. A faded brown plaque records this as being the home of **Henry Gray** (28). Gray's *Anatomy*, published in 1853, has been a standard textbook for medical students since that time.

Return to Upper Belgrave Street and turn to the right. No.9 was the home in 1880–81 of the poet laureate, **Alfred, Lord Tennyson** (29).

Cross over the road into Eaton Place and you will find that the plaques commemorating **William Ewart** (30) at No.16 and **Baron Kelvin** (31) at No.15 are almost opposite each other. It was the MP William Ewart who first proposed the erection of commemorative plaques in London. The first official plaques erected were placed in 1867 by the Royal Society of Arts. The responsibility was then passed to the London City Council (LCC) and the Greater London Council (GLC). Upon the dissolution of the GLC, English Heritage became the custodian of London's commemorative plaques. Baron Kelvin was a physicist responsible for many inventions and scientific works, and the Kelvin temperature scale is named after him.

Continue to No.29. This was the birthplace of **John Lubbock, 1st Baron Avebury** (32), a banker and politician who was also a naturalist. Apart from his scientific work studying ants and bees, he was responsible for the introduction of many bills in Parliament, the most notable being the Bank Holiday Act.

Take the next turning on the right, which is Belgrave Place. On the corner with Belgrave Square you will see the Norwegian embassy. Here there are two interesting relief panels, one on either side of the entrance. A small inscription states 'In 1796 the two coade stone reliefs were affixed to the Danish/Norwegian consulate in Well Close Square, Stepney. In 1968 the reliefs were re-erected on this embassy by courtesy of the Greater London Council'.

Turn left into Chesham Place. No.37 was the home of the **1st Earl Russell** (33). He was a statesman who twice became Prime Minister. Continue and bear left into Lyall Street. Across the road at No.3 the master builder **Thomas Cubitt** (34) lived. He was responsible for the construction of most of Belgravia and died the year Eaton Square was completed.

Walk back to Chesham Place and turn left into Pont Street, which is by the traffic lights. You will pass an interesting statue of two ladies before you reach Cadogan Lane. Walk on and turn left at Cadogan Place.

At No.30 Cadogan Place there is a blue plaque on the home of **Mrs Dorothy Jordan** (35). She was an actress who became mistress to the Duke of Clarence (later William IV). She bore him 10 children and did not retire from the stage until a year before her death. At No.43B Cadogan Place **William Wilberforce** (36) spent his final days at the home of his cousin. This is one of five plaques in London commemorating the slavery abolitionist.

Return to Pont Street and turn left again into Sloane Street. Just past Pavilion Street at No.76 there are two plaques. The statesman and author **Sir Charles Dilke** (37) and the actor and theatre manager **Sir Herbert Beerbohm Tree** (38) both lived here at different times. Tree built and managed Her Majesty's Theatre and was a founder of RADA.

Walk back to the traffic lights, turning to the left into Pont Street. Immediately you come across the plaque of **Lillie Langtry** (39) on the red-brick building on your left. She was an actress and mistress of the Prince of Wales (later Edward VII), who became known as 'Jersey Lily'. This was the title of a painting of her, by the Pre-Raphaelite artist Millais.

Two turnings further along on the left is the beginning of Cadogan Square. From this point looking across the road you can see the entrance to Hans Place. Cross over to see the small plaque which records that **Jane Austen** (40) once stayed in a house on this site (left). Now cross back and walk to the bottom of Cadogan Square. The journalist and editor **Arnold Bennett** (41) lived at No.75 from 1921 to 1930.

Continue round the square, returning to Pont Street, where you turn to the left. No.57 was the home of the actor-manager **Sir George Alexander** (42). Proceed to St Columba's church and turn left into Lennox Gardens, where at No.8 behind the church, you will see the blue plaque for **Count Edward Raczynski** (43).

Now turn right and right again into Walton Street. The novelist **P.G. Wodehouse** (44) lived at No.16 from 1918 to 1920. Walk back to the road junction and turn right into Beauchamp Place. This is one of London's smartest streets for ladies apparel and boutique shops. A short way along on the left you will see the Grove Tavern. A brass plaque on the front states 'The area surrounding the Grove Tavern once included a cricket ground which was the setting for the **first test match** (45) between England and Australia, in 1880. The street in which the pub stands was laid out during that era and was originally named Grove Place to commemorate a nearby grove of trees. The tavern's name is derived from the same source'.

Continue to Brompton Road and turn right. The walk ends at Knightsbridge station, which is just past Harrods.

Walk 7
Chelsea

Distance:	5½ miles (8.46km)
Time taken:	2½ hours
Number of plaques:	56
Nearest tube stations:	Sloane Square
Bus routes:	11, 14, 19, 22, 31, 49, 137, 211, 319, 345

CHELSEA was mentioned in the Domesday Book as a village in Middlesex. It did not become of great importance until Sir Thomas More built a country house there in 1520. Since then artists, authors and actors have lived happily in the area. The King's Road became a centre of youthful fashion in the 1960s and today the atmosphere is both peaceful and bustling.

The starting point for this walk is Sloane Square tube station. Upon exiting the station, walk across towards King's Road. At the traffic lights, cross over to the centre traffic island, by the fountain. Ahead there is an interesting, worn-looking statue. This is a cast replica of the original 1733 statue of Sir Hans Sloane.

Avoiding the traffic, cross over the road and walk to the Peter Jones store, continuing past the front. Towards the end of the store, looking across the road, you will see a blue plaque at No.31 commemorating **Percy Grainger** (1). This Australian-born composer lived here early in the 20th century, before departing to the US in 1915.

Pass Cadogan Gardens and turn right into Blackland Terrace. At the last house on the left there is a plaque where **Earl Jellicoe** (2) lived 1906–8. He was the admiral in charge of the British fleet at the battle of Jutland in 1916. Later he became First Sea Lord and governor of New Zealand.

Turn left and walk along Draycott Place, then turn right into Draycott Avenue. On the left you will see Avenue Court and the blue plaque commemorating **Sir Archibald McIndoe** (3). He was a pioneer in plastic surgery who did much to restore the looks and lives of airmen injured in World War Two.

Return to Draycott Place and turn to the right. Ahead you can see a blue plaque at No.7 Sloane Avenue. The poet **George Seferis** (4) lived here before becoming the Greek ambassador to Britain from 1957 to 1962. Turn to the left and by the Queen's Head public house walk along Tryon Street to King's Road, then turn right. While proceeding along King's Road, apart from the many shops, it is interesting to see the boldly coloured houses in the side turnings.

Continue past Markham Square and you will find, just past Markham Street, an

1 Percy Grainger	15 Miss Rose	29 Sir Thomas More	43 Robert Falcon Scott
2 Earl Jellicoe	16 J.F. Sartorius	30 Elizabeth Gaskell	44 George Gissing
3 Sir A. McIndoe	17 Rosalind Franklin	31 James M. Whistler	45 King Henry VIII
4 George Seferis	18 Robert Fortune	32 Isambard K. Brunel	46 D.G. Rossetti/Swinburne
5 Princess Astafieva	19 Frank Dobson	33 Walter Greaves	47 King Henry VIII
6 Lady Wilde	20 Sir Stafford Cripps	34 Hilaire Belloc	48 George Eliot
7 Sir Carol Reed	21 Sir Alfred Munnings	35 John Tweed	49 Marquess of Ripon
8 Dame Ellen Terry	22 Augustas John	36 Philip Wilson Steer	50 John Singer Sargent
9 Anton Dolin	23 A.A. Milne	37 J.M.W. Turner	51 Lord Haden-Guest
10 Sir Alf Munnings	24 Charles Kingsley	38 Sylvia Pankhurst	52 Oscar Wilde
11 William McMillan	25 Sebastopol	39 Chelsea China/Smollett	53 Peter Warlock
12 Sir Osbert Sitwell	26 Sir C. Wheeler	40 Leigh Hunt	54 Mark Twain
13 Dame Sybil Thorndike	27 Sir Alexander Fleming	41 Thomas Carlyle	55 Brain Stoker
14 De Morgans	28 Crosby Hall	42 Margaret D. Dawson	56 Joseph Losey

impressive entrance way with two classical Greek figures supporting a plinth. Surmounting it is a carriage with four horses. This is all that remains of the original 1769 house. The building behind bears a plaque commemorating the ballet dancer and teacher **Princess Seraphine Astafieva** (5). She trained some of the world's finest ballet dancers here from 1916 until her death in 1934.

Walk on past the Chelsea Antiques Centre and the Town Hall, which is across the road, and come to Dovehouse Green. This was laid out on an old burial site. Various plaques record its history and local heroes. There are several benches here, should you like to pause

The former ballet school in King's Road, run by Princess Seraphine Astafieva.

for a rest. The Farmers' Market behind the square is interesting if you have time for a meander.

Cross King's Road and turn left into Oakley Street. Ahead you can see some of the girders of the Albert suspension bridge. Upon reaching No.87, pause to read the blue plaque on the home of the mother of Oscar Wilde, **Lady Francesca Wilde** (6). She moved here from Dublin after the death of her husband. Apart from being a popular hostess she was a noted poet and essayist. While in Dublin she wrote for a nationalist journal under the pseudonym 'Speranza' and also had several books on Irish folklore published.

Return to King's Road and turn left. The old grey brick houses, built in 1720, were home to **Sir Carol Reed** (7) at No.213 from 1948–76 and **Dame Ellen Terry** (8) at No.215 from 1904–20. Sir Carol was one of Britain's most important film producers and Dame Ellen was

a leading Shakespearean actress of her time. An earlier resident of No.215 was the musician Thomas Arne, who is said to have composed *Rule Brittania* while living here.

Turn left into Glebe Place, where at No.66 you will see a crudely-made private plaque erected to commemorate the ballet dancer and choreographer **Anton Dolin** (9), who lived here 1926–39. Two doors away at No.64 there are two blue plaques. The first of these is for **Sir Alfred Munnings** (10), spelled without the 's', and the second for the sculptor **William McMillan** (11), who lived here

1921–66. You will shortly see another plaque for the former and both of them claim that he lived at their individual addresses from 1920. Did Munnings and McMillan both live at this address 1921–22?

Return to King's Road and walk on as far as Bramerton Street. Now cross King's Road to the narrow entrance, just before the telephone boxes, which leads into Carlyle Square. The author and poet **Sir Osbert Sitwell** (12) lived at No.2 from 1919–63. Nearby, at No.6, the actress **Dame Sybil Thorndike** (13) lived from 1921–32.

Walk on to the end of the square and turn left, then right again into Old Church Street. You can see a blue plaque at first-floor level across the street on the corner of Elm Park Road. This was the home of the artists **William Frend De Morgan** and his wife **Evelyn De Morgan** (14). They were both Pre-Raphaelite ceramic artists and she was also an outstanding painter. They were closely associated with William Morris and Edward Burne-Jones.

A few doors away at No.133 you will see a blue ceramic plaque with the name **Miss Rose** (15) and Latin words. These translate as 'who held sway in this house and holds sway, now and forever, in our hearts'. It is thought that the plaque was erected to commemorate a much-loved cat.

The next plaque to be seen is at No.155 Old Church Street. This is for the artist **John F. Sartorius** (16), who lived here 1807–12. He specialised in hunting scenes and pictures of horses and was a regular exhibitor at the Royal Academy.

Continue to the traffic lights, turn left and cross to the other side of Fulham Road. Four turnings along you will reach Drayton Gardens and Donovan Court, opposite the cinema. The blue plaque here is on the home of the scientist **Rosalind Franklin** (17). As a pioneer in the study of molecular structures, her work was invaluable to later scientific discoveries.

Two more turnings along on Fulham Road turn right into Gilston Road. At No.9 you will find another English Heritage plaque which commemorates the Scottish-born horticulturist **Robert Fortune** (18). Having travelled extensively, he introduced many previously unknown plants to Britain.

Take the next turning right and you will immediately see the next plaque on the corner of Harley Gardens. The sculptor **Frank Dobson** (19) lived at No.14. He was for many years associated with the 'London Group' and was a professor of sculpture at the Royal College of Art until 1953.

Now return to Fulham Road and turn left. Walk along and cross the road to Elm Park Gardens. No.32 was the birthplace of the post-war Chancellor of the Exchequer **Stafford Cripps** (20). During World War Two he had been both ambassador to Moscow and Minister of Aircraft Production.

Now turn right at Elm Park Road and then left into Beaufort Street. The other plaque commemorating **Sir Alfred Munnings** (21) is on the house cornering the second entrance into Chelsea Park Gardens. Sir Alfred, who allegedly lived here 1920–59, was a president of the Royal Academy. He was well known for his paintings of hunting scenes.

Turn left into King's Road and then left again into The Vale. You will have passed the Bluebird food shop and restaurant, which is well worth a visit! The first turning on the right is Mallord Street, where you will see two plaques. The artist **Augustus John** (22) lived and worked at No.28, and further along across the road the children's writer **A.A. Milne** (23) lived at No.13. He was the originator of Winnie-the-Pooh and many other characters beloved by children today.

Turn right at the end of the road and, having crossed King's Road, continue into Old Church Street. No.56 is a large house on the left surrounded by a high brick wall. If the gate is open you will be able to see the blue plaque of the clergyman and writer **Charles Kingsley** (24). Opposite is a small alleyway with a modern development. Curiously you will find a square stone set into the wall with the words 'Established 1798, rebuilt by T. Blanch and Sons 1898. This stone is a portion of the fortifications of **Sebastopol** (25)'. As you walk back you should be able to get a glimpse of the top of the Charles Kingsley plaque on the house opposite, above the main entrance. Kingsley was the author of *The Water Babies* and *Hereward the Wake*.

Fifty yards further along Old Church Street you will reach Hereford Buildings on the right. A yellow convex plaque here commemorates the noted sculptor **Sir Charles Wheeler** (26). He was president of the Royal Academy 1956–66.

Take the next turning right into Paulton Street, which leads into Paulton Square. This square was named after George Stanley, of Paultons in Hampshire. He lived in the 18th

century and married Sir Hans Sloane's daughter. The houses in the square were built in around 1840 and represent a fine example of a uniform square in late Georgian style. Turn left into Danvers Street. The discoverer of penicillin, **Sir Alexander Fleming** (27), lived at No.20.

Continue to the end of the road, where you will reach the much-restored **Crosby Hall** (28). This house was originally built between 1466

Crosby Hall, Cheyne Walk, Chelsea.

and 1475 in Bishopsgate and remnants were moved to this site in more modern times. Former owners and occupants include Sir Thomas More and Sir Walter Raleigh. It is now privately owned. Turn right past Crosby Hall and then right again into Beaufort Street.

By the church at the far end wall of Allen Hall, No.28 Beaufort Street has a plaque recording that **Sir Thomas More** (29), Lord Chancellor of England, canonised in 1935, lived here. Allen Hall stands on the site of Beaufort House, which was built for More in 1521 and demolished in 1766. Return towards the River Thames and turn right into Cheyne Walk.

There are many commemorative plaques in this road, as

you will find. Some are difficult to see because of fencing and trees. As you will be returning along this stretch of the road, it is probably better to walk on the house side and make the return journey on the Thames side. The first plaque is at No.93, where novelist **Mrs Elizabeth Gaskell** (30) was born. She also later lived at a house in Beaufort Street.

At No.96 the artist, famed for the painting of his mother, **James McNeil Whistler** (31), lived in 1866–78. The father and son civil engineers **Marc Brunel** and **Isambard Kingdom Brunel** (32) lived at Lindsey House, now No.98. There is a blue plaque as well as the Lindsey House plaque, which can really only be seen from across the road. Look for it on the way back.

The white-painted house on the corner of Milman's Street, No.104 Cheyne Walk, has two separate blue plaques. They are for the artist **Walter Greaves** (33), who lived here 1855–97 and the writer **Hilaire Belloc** (34), who lived here 1900–5. The latter was a great friend of G.K. Chesterton, who illustrated some of his books.

The plaques of **John Tweed** (35) and **Philip Wilson Steer** (36) are next door to each

other at Nos 108 and 109 respectively (left). Tweed was the sculptor responsible for the statue of Lord Kitchener at Horse Guards' Parade and statues of other notable people of his time. Steer was an artist with skill in varying styles. Having studied in Paris, he worked in an Impressionist manner, but could also paint in the style of Gainsborough.

No.119 was a home and studio of the artist **Joseph Mallord William Turner** (37). His tarnished rectangular bronze plaque is partly covered from view by the garden shrubbery.

The last plaque in this part of Cheyne Walk is at No.120. It was a home of suffragette leader **Sylvia Pankhurst** (38). As a matter of interest, walk into Blantyre Street and look across at the back of 120 Cheyne Walk, from across the road. You will see the comical stone figures straddling the garden wall.

Now return to Cheyne Walk, using the pedestrian crossing to get to the Thames side. Walk back and you will have a different view of some of the houses and plaques. Continue along Cheyne Walk, past Battersea Bridge, Beaufort and Danvers streets, and bear left of the island. The statue of the naked lady in the centre is called 'Awakening' and is by the sculptor Gilbert Ledward. Go past the Chelsea Old Church and the huge painted statue of St Thomas More. The large monument on the corner of the churchyard commemorates Sir Hans Sloane and was erected by his daughters. Turn left into Lawrence Street. Note the attractive relief panels on the corner apartment block. Former residents included Henry James, T.S. Eliot and Ian Fleming.

Right at the end of the road at No.16 (left) there is a blue rectangular plaque recording the site of **Chelsea China** (39). This collectable pottery was manufactured here from 1745 to 1784. The novelist and historian **Tobias Smollett**, who shares the plaque, lived in part of the house in 1750–62. It was Smollett who first translated Cervantes' *Don Quixote* in 1755.

Continue into Upper Cheyne Row. At No.22, opposite the church, is a plaque where the poet and essayist **Leigh Hunt** (40) lived with his large family in 1833–40.

Turn back and then left into Cheyne Row. No.24 was the home in 1834–81 of the historian and essayist **Thomas Carlyle** (41), and a relief bust of Carlyle can be seen on the plaque. This house is now open at limited times to the public, as a museum showing the room settings as they were during Carlyle's occupation. Further down at No.10 a small stone plaque records the home of **Margaret Damer Dawson** (42). She was a founder of the Women's Police Service, an accomplished musician and a holder of awards for animal protection. At the top of the road is the King's Head & Eight Bells, a regular drinking place of Dylan Thomas, which claims to have been a hostelry for great writers and artists. Ahead is the statue of the seated figure of Thomas Carlyle. Turn left.

Walking on, an interesting sculpture confronts you of a naked boy who appears to be flying through the air above a dolphin. To the left is Oakley Street. No.56 on the right side was the home of polar explorer **Robert Falcon Scott** (43). He owned the house from 1905 to 1908, but spent little time there.

Continue along Oakley Street and turn right into Phene Street. The last house on the right is No.33 Oakley Gardens. This was the home of novelist **George Gissing** (44) from 1882–4. Turn right, and going through Cheyne Gardens you will find a blue plaque at Cheyne Studio, which is past No.1 near the end of the road. This refers to **King Henry VIII** (45), who had a manor house on this site.

Proceeding onwards you reach another part of Cheyne Walk. Turning to the right a plaque at No.16 records this as the home of artist and poet **Dante Gabriel Rossetti** (46), who lived here 1862–82. His friend, poet and critic **Algernon Charles Swinburne**, who also spent some time at this address, is named on the same plaque. The house was built in 1717 and is enclosed by railings.

At the corner of Cheyne Mews, the next turning, there is a rectangular blue plaque, which again records this site as being the grounds of **King Henry VIII's** (47) manor house. Walking back to No.4, you will see a plaque that informs you that the writer **George Eliot** (48) spent her final days at this address.

Continue towards the traffic lights and cross over Royal Hospital Road. Walking along the Chelsea Embankment, you will pass the Botanic Gardens of the Society of Apothecaries of London, which has the date 1673 embossed on the gatepost. You can see a large Buddhist shrine across the river and further along the four chimneys of Battersea power station. The **Marquess of Ripon** (49) lived at No.9 Chelsea Embankment from 1890 until his death in 1909. He spent over 50 years in Parliament and colonial service, holding many important offices. Now turn left into Tite Street.

There are four plaques in Tite Street and the first reached is at No.31 on the right. This is an etched stone rectangle, which records that the artist **John Singer Sargent** (50) lived and worked here for 24 years. He was an official war artist in World War One and died in this house in 1925.

The next three plaques are on the other side of the road. No.38 was the home of **Lord Haden-Guest** (51), who was a physician, journalist and Member of Parliament. No.34 was the home of playwright **Oscar Wilde** (52) between 1885 and 1895, and No.30 the home of **Peter Warlock** (53), who was a composer and writer befriended by D.H. Lawrence.

Cross Royal Hospital Road and walk to the top of Tite Street, where you will reach Tedworth Square. The corner house on the right, No.23, was the home of **Mark Twain** (54) 1896-7. This American author is best remembered for his books *The Adventures of Tom Sawyer* and *The Adventures of Huckleberry Finn*. Look down to the basement level to see the murals.

Turn left and walk to the far right corner of the square. This takes you into St Leonard's Terrace, where, at No.18, you can find the plaque of novelist **Bram Stoker** (55). He lived here for 10 years from 1896 and is remembered as the author of *Dracula*.

You are now at the rear of the home of the Chelsea Pensioners. Turn left into Royal Avenue. There is a local borough plaque here which gives you the history of the street and makes interesting reading. Cross the road and walk up to No.29, where you will find the last plaque of this walk. This commemorates the American film director **Joseph Losey** (56), who lived in England after the 1952 McCarthy witch-hunt. His films included *Stranger on the Prowl* (1953), *Modesty Blaise* (1966) *The Go-Between* (1971) and *Steaming* (1984).

Walking up Royal Avenue, turning right into King's Road, will bring you back to Sloane Square and the tube station.

Other nearby plaques not included in the walk:

Sydney Monkton Copeman (1862–1947), physician, 57 Redcliffe Gardens, SW10.
Henry Austin Dobson (1840–1921), poet and essayist, 10 Redcliffe Street, SW10.
William Thomas Du Boulay (1832–1921), vicar, 43 Gilston Road, SW10.
John Ireland, (1879–1962), composer, 14 Gunter Grove, SW10.
George Meredith (1829–1909), novelist and poet, 7 Hobury Street, SW10.

Walk 8
Kensington/Knightsbridge

Distance:	5 miles (8.04km) or 6½ miles (10.45km)
Time taken:	2 hours or 2¾ hours full walk
Number of plaques:	shorter walk 26, full walk 44
Nearest tube stations:	Hyde Park, South Kensington, Gloucester Road
Bus routes:	C1, 9, 10, 11, 14, 19, 22, 49, 52, 74, 137, 211, 319

THIS walk is in an area of London that has some of its most expensive and exclusive property. It incorporates important landmarks such as the Royal Albert Hall, the Albert Memorial, Hyde Park, Harrods and many of London's museums. Several embassies are also located in this area.

Begin at Hyde Park underground station and leave via exit No.3. This will bring you into Grosvenor Place. Walk along Grosvenor Place past the War Memorial of the Royal Regiment of Artillery. On the corner of the second turning, Halkin Street, there is a blue plaque on the home of **Sir Henry Campbell-Bannerman** (1). He was Prime Minister 1905–8 and lived here from 1877 until 1904.

Walk down Halkin Street to the junction and take the pedestrian crossing towards the statue of the 1st Marquis of Westminster. Across the road at 33 Wilton Crescent there is a blue plaque which commemorates the Colombian ambassador **Alfonso Lopez-Pumarejo** (2), who lived and died here. He was twice president of his country.

Continue round Wilton Crescent to No.2. This was the home of **Lord and Lady Louis Mountbatten of Burma** (3).

Now walk back to Wilton Place. No.25 was the home of the botanist **George Bentham** (4). He was a nephew of Jeremy Bentham (see Walk 12), to whom he acted as secretary between 1826 and 1832.

Walk up Wilton Place to Kinnerton Street. The corner house, No.8 Wilton Place, was a home of the music hall actress **Lillie Langtry** (5). One time mistress of Edward VII, she was known as 'Jersey Lily' and had her portrait painted by Millais. The next plaque to be found is over half a mile away.

Continue into Knightsbridge, bear left and walk past the London Park Tower. Proceed across Sloane Street and the top of Brompton Road, keeping to the right of the Scotch House. Opposite the tower block turn left into Rutland Gardens. A synagogue is situated on this corner. A little way down you can walk into Rutland Gardens Mews on the left side of the road. The attractive mews cottage in the corner bears a blue plaque stating that

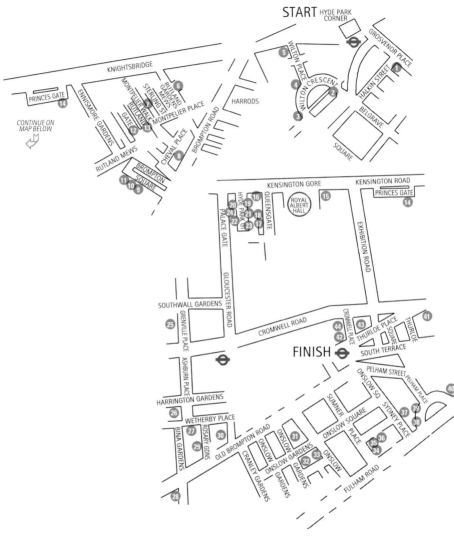

1 Campbell-Bannerman	12 Lord Lugard	23 Sir Leslie Stephen	34 Joseph Hansom
2 Lopez-Pumarejo	13 Sir Francis Galton	24 John E. Millais	35 Admiral Rob. Fitzroy
3 Lord Mountbatten	14 J.F. Kennedy	25 Charles Booth	36 W.M. Thackeray
4 George Bentham	15 Malcolm Sargent	26 Sir W.S. Gilbert	37 Béla Bartók
5 Lillie Langtry	16 Benny Hill	27 Viscount Allenby	38 Sir Nigel Playfair
6 Fonteyn/du Pré	17 Terry Thomas	28 Mervyn Peake	39 François Guizot
7 Bruce Bairnfather	18 Sir Jacob Epstein	29 Sir H. Beerbohm Tree	40 George Godwin
8 Sir Benjamin Thompson	19 Lord Baden-Powell	30 George Borrow	41 Sir Henry Cole
9 Stephane Mallarmé	20 Enid Bagnold	31 William Lecky	42 Hoppe/Millais/Bacon
10 Francis Place	21 Sir Jacob Epstein	32 Andrew Bonar Law	43 Sir John Lavery
11 E.F. Benson	22 Sir Winston Churchill	33 James Froude	44 Sir Charles Freake

Margot Fonteyn and **Jacqueline du Pré** (6) lived here. The famous ballerina cared for the renowned cellist for a period during her fatal illness.

Return to Knightsbridge, retracing your steps and turning right into Trevor Place. Turn right again at the first turning, Montpelier Square. Now take the second left, which is the far side of the square. This will take you into Sterling Street, where the blue plaque of the cartoonist, **Bruce Bairnsfather** (7), can be found at No.1. He was famous for his World War One 'Old Bill' cartoons, and continued working through World War Two.

Turn right, walking towards Montpelier Walk, then left and right at Rutland Street. Follow the road down, going through Cheval Place to the right, and then turn left upon reaching Brompton Road. A short way past the telephone boxes you will reach No.168, where there is a plaque for **Sir Benjamin Thompson (Count Rumford)** (8), who lived here 1799–1802. He was an American-born inventor and traveller. Among other things, he is credited with the invention of the coffee percolator.

Turn back along Brompton Road, walk past Cheval Place and take the second entrance into Brompton Square. The French poet **Stephane Mallarmé** (9) stayed at No.6 in 1863, during one of his many visits to England. He taught the English language while living in Paris. The radical and reformer, **Francis Place** (10), lived at No.21 in 1833–51. More recently the writer **E.F. Benson** (11) lived near the end of the square at No.25. He was the son of an Archbishop of Canterbury and wrote several novels. Return to Brompton Road.

Now retrace your steps back through Cheval Place and into Rutland Street. Around the corner, before you reach the end of this street, you will find a brick wall on the left-hand side with an opening. Go through, up the steps and turn to the left. A few yards along you will see Rutland Gate on the right-hand side. The British colonial administrator **Lord Lugard** (12) lived at No.51 from 1912–19. Across the road, at No. 42 in the corner house, **Sir Francis Galton** (13) lived for 50 years. He was a scientist, traveller and explorer, whose studies led to the science of eugenics and fingerprint identification. The small rectangular plaque was adopted by the LCC in 1959.

Turn back the way you came, past the 'clock house', bear right at Ennismore Street, then turn right again into Ennismore Gardens. Walk past the Russian Orthodox Church to the top of the road by the traffic lights. The main road is Kensington Road, where you should turn left and walk on to Prince's Gate. This is set back from the main road. A blue plaque is immediately visible at No.14, on the Royal College of General Practitioners. This is where **US President J.F. Kennedy** (14) stayed as a young man when studying in London. It is interesting to see that the building was adorned with Native American heads well before his time. Return to the main road and walk on.

Crossing over Exhibition Road you will see a statue of David Livingstone and pass the Royal Geographical Society. Ahead is the Royal Albert Hall, and opposite is the beautifully restored Albert Memorial. On the wall of Albert Hall Mansions, facing the Royal Albert Hall, is a blue plaque that commemorates the famous conductor **Sir Malcolm Sargent** (15), who lived and died here.

Return to the main road, Kensington Gore, and walk on past the Albert Hall and Albert Memorial. Then turn left into Queen's Gate. Walking past the statue of Field Marshall Robert Napier astride his steed, you will reach Nos 1–2 Queen's Gate. A blue plaque marks

this as being the home of the popular comedian **Benny Hill** (16), who lived at this address 1960–86.

Continue along Queen's Gate and take the first turning right, then turn right again into Queen's Gate Mews. Another well-known comedian, **Terry Thomas** (17), lived at No.11 from 1949 to 1981 (left). A few yards further along on the other side (below left) is a plaque marking the studio of sculptor **Sir Jacob Epstein** (18). Retrace your

steps past Benny Hill's house and up to the main road.

Turn left at Kensington Road and left again into Hyde Park Gate, where there are five commemorative plaques. The first you will see is on the left at No.9. This was the home of Boy Scout Association founder **Lord Baden-Powell** (19), who lived here 1861–76. The cream-painted house across the road, No.29, is where novelist and playwright **Enid Bagnold** (20) lived. She was the author of *National Velvet*, which was later made into a film starring the young Elizabeth Taylor.

Crossing back to No.18 another blue plaque is to be found on the home where **Sir Jacob Epstein** (21) lived and died. He did not have far to walk to his studio.

Next door to Enid Bagnold's home is a red-brick house where **Sir Winston Churchill** (22) lived and died. Towards the end of the street at No.22 on the left is a blue plaque honouring **Sir Leslie Stephen** (23). He lived here with his wife and eight children, one of whom was Virginia (Woolf). Sir Leslie's greatest work was editing *The Dictionary of National Biography*.

Return to Kensington Road. Turn to the left, walk past the second section of Hyde Park Gate and turn left into Palace Gate. The painter **Sir John Everett Millais** (24) lived and died at No.2. Walking on you will pass an interesting sculpture called 'Unfurl'.

Proceed along Palace Gate and its continuation, Gloucester Road. This is quite a long walk – nearly half a mile – to the next plaque. Turn right at Southwall Gardens, six turnings down. This will bring you into Grenville Place. Across the road at No.6 the shipping magnate **Charles Booth** (25) lived from 1875 to 1890. He was a pioneer of old-age pensions and did much to assist the poor and needy.

Walk down and cross over Cromwell Road into Ashburn Place. Turn right into Harrington Gardens. The huge Victorian Flemish-style house, No.39 (below), was the home of **Sir William Schwenck Gilbert** (26) from 1893–8. While here, he wrote *The Mikado*, *The Yeomen of the Guard* and *The Gondoliers*.

Those who wish to finish the walk now can return and turn left at Ashburn Place, right at Courtfield Road and then walk on to the underground station at Gloucester Road.

To continue the tour, return to Ashburn Place and turn right. Ahead you can see the blue plaque of **Field Marshall Viscount Allenby** (27) at 24 Wetherby Gardens.

Turn right and then left into Bina Gardens, continuing across Old Brompton Road into Drayton Gardens. On the right you will see the English Heritage blue plaque commemorating **Mervyn Peake** (28), who lived here 1952–62. He was a writer, poet and illustrator, not only of his own books, but also of several well-known classics.

Return to Old Brompton Road and  cross over to Dove Mews. This leads into Rosary Gardens, where you will see the plaque for **Sir Herbert Beerbohm Tree** (29) the actor and theatre manager who lived at No.31. Walk on and turn right at Wetherby Place, then right again into Hereford Square. The writer and traveller **George Borrow** (30) lived at No.22. Continue round the square, turning right at the bottom into Gloucester Road.

Cross over Old Brompton Road. Turn left and walk past the first entrance of Onslow Gardens, going into the second. No.38 was the home of the Irish playwright and historian **William Lecky** (31). Continue to the crossroads. No.24, opposite on the corner, was the home of **Andrew Bonar Law** (32). He was a statesman who, after holding many important posts, became Prime Minister for a few months shortly before his death. Facing his plaque turn left. The next plaque is at No.5 Onslow Gardens, which is on the right opposite Cranley Place. The historian and man of letters **James Froude** (33) lived here 1873-92.

Walk back a few yards and turn right into Onslow Square. Turn right again into Sumner Place. No.27, near the end, was the home of **Joseph Hansom** (34). Apart from being the designer of the hansom cab, he was a distinguished architect.

Retrace your steps and bear right at Onslow Square. No.38 has a blue plaque commemorating **Admiral Robert Fitzroy** (35), who lived here 1854-65. Among his exploits, he circumnavigated the globe with Charles Darwin and later became governor of New Zealand. The novelist **William Makepeace Thackeray** (36) lived next door at No.36 from 1854 to 1862. He is commemorated with a bronze plaque set at a low level and almost hidden by the railings.

Proceed to Sydney Place at the right-hand corner of the square. No.7, where the composer **Béla Bartók** (37) stayed, is actually next door to No.1 Onslow Square. Continue along to Fulham Road, then turn left and left again into Pelham Crescent. The actor-manager **Sir Nigel Playfair** (38) lived at No.26 1910-22. A few doors away, at No. 21, the French politician and historian **François Guizot** (39) lived in exile for a year.

Continue walking round the crescent and turn left at Brompton Road. On the corner of South Terrace and Alexander Square there is a blue plaque on the home of the architect and writer **George Godwin** (40).

Walk up South Terrace and turn right at Thurloe Square. The end house is opposite the main entrance to the Victoria and Albert Museum. The plaque of its first director, **Sir Henry Cole** (41), can be found just around the corner.

Now walk left past the telephone boxes, along Thurloe Place and across the top of Thurloe Square. Cross over Exhibition Road and turn right into Cromwell Place. The large plaque at No.7 across the road bears the names of artists **Emil Otto Hoppe, Sir John Everett Millais** and **Francis Bacon** (42). Across the road at No.5 the painter **Sir John Lavery** (43) lived from 1899-1940. The last plaque of this walk is on the left, at the end of the road, which is No.21 Cromwell Road. This was the home from 1860 of **Sir Charles Freake** (44). He was a builder and patron of the arts.

A short walk back along Cromwell Place will bring you to South Kensington underground station.

Walk 9
Kensington/ Notting Hill

Distance:	5¾ miles (9.25km)
Time taken:	2¼ hours
Number of plaques:	46
Nearest tube stations:	Holland Park, High Street Kensington, Gloucester Road
Bus routes:	9, 10, 12, 27, 28, 31, 49, 52, 74, 94

THIS area contains many architecturally interesting buildings and exclusive squares. Several of them date back to the 18th and early 19th century. There are also several mews cottages and antique shops. Royal parks are nearby. Be prepared for some short steep uphill roads.

Begin at Holland Park tube station, which is in Holland Park Avenue. Turning left will bring you, within a few yards, to Lansdowne Road. Lansdowne House is the high-rise building a short way along on the right-hand side. The blue plaque on its front records the names of six artists, headed by **Charles Ricketts** (1), who had studios here.

Return to Holland Park Avenue, turn left and cross the road. Walking past Holland Park you will see the statue of St Volodymyr, ruler of Ukraine (980–1015). Continue to the third turning, Aubrey Road. This is a very steep uphill road. Follow the road round into Aubrey Walk at the top. There is a blue plaque at No.38, on a home of the singer **Dusty Springfield** (2).

Walk back to Aubrey Road and turn right into Campden Hill Square. This square was built 1827–38 and was originally called Notting Hill Square. There is a plaque in the gardens, which states that the artist J.M.W. Turner 'often painted sunsets near this tree'. Unfortunately access to the central gardens is only available to residents.

Entering the square, turn left and walk down to No.50. It was the home of **Evelyn Underhill** (3), who was a Christian philosopher, writer and lecturer who lived here from 1907 to 1939.

Return to the top of the square, where you can see the plaque of the poet and novelist **Siegfried Sassoon** (4) at No.23 and that of **Charles Morgan** (5) at No.16. Morgan was on the editorial staff of *The Times* 1921–39, but is noted for his novels and plays. Further round

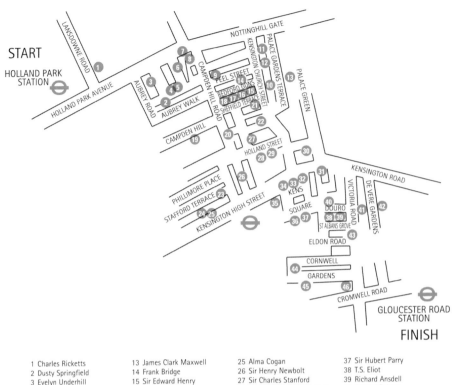

1 Charles Ricketts	13 James Clark Maxwell	25 Alma Cogan	37 Sir Hubert Parry
2 Dusty Springfield	14 Frank Bridge	26 Sir Henry Newbolt	38 T.S. Eliot
3 Evelyn Underhill	15 Sir Edward Henry	27 Sir Charles Stanford	39 Richard Ansdell
4 Seigfried Sassoon	16 G. K. Chesterton	28 Marguerite Radclyffe Hall	40 Samuel Palmer
5 Charles Morgan	17 Wilson Carlile	29 Walter Crane	41 Henry James
6 John McDouall Stuart	18 Agatha Christie	30 W. Makepeace Thackeray	42 Robert Browning
7 James McBey	19 Thomas Macaulay	31 Major R.E.B. Crompton	43 Edward H. Corbould
8 Dame Marie Rambert	20 Ford Madox Ford	32 W. Makepeace Thackeray	44 Ivy Compton-Burnett
9 Sir William Russell Flint	21 Jean Sibelius	33 Edwd. Burne-Jones	45 Joachim Nabuco
10 Muzio Clementi	22 James Joyce	34 Sir John Simon	46 Charles Booth
11 Percy Wyndham Lewis	23 Kenneth Grahame	35 Mrs Patrick Campbell	
12 Sir Max Beerbohm	24 Edwd. Linley Sambourne	36 John Stuart Mill	

the square at No.9 a plaque commemorates **John McDouall Stuart** (6). This explorer, who was the first person to cross Australia from south to north (1860), lived and died here. Continue down and turn to the right upon reaching Holland Park Avenue again.

No.1 Holland Park Avenue was the home of the Scottish etcher and artist **James McBey** (7). You may find the plaque, which is on the outer wall, partly obscured by hanging plants.

Turn right into Campden Hill Road, then right again into Campden Hill Gardens. The Polish-born ballet dancer and teacher **Dame Marie Rambert** (8) lived at No.19. Walk on and turn left, then turn right at Campden Hill Road.

Cross the road and turn left into Peel Street, where you can see a blue plaque a short way down at No.80. This was the studio and home of the watercolour artist **Sir William**

WALK 9: KENSINGTON/NOTTING HILL

Russell Flint (9). Continue along Peel Street, which was named after Sir Robert Peel and built in 1824.

Turning right at the bottom, cross over to the red-brick building No.128, where the Italian pianist and composer **Muzio Clementi** (10) lived 1820-3. Now walk back along Kensington Church Street, past the pedestrian crossing, and turn right into Kensington Mall. Turn right at the end into Palace Gardens Terrace. This attractive street was built in 1860. Opposite the church, at No.61, there is a plaque on the home of **Percy Wyndham Lewis** (11), the artist and writer who lived here 1923-6.

Just past Strathmore Gardens, at No.57, there is a plaque recording the birthplace of **Sir Max Beerbohm** (12). He was a half brother of Sir Herbert Beerbohm Tree and made his name as a caricaturist and writer.

Walking on to No.16 near the end of the road, on the other side you may find that the next plaque is difficult to see. Presumably when the plaque commemorating **James Clark Maxwell** (13) was erected in 1923, the tree obscuring it was very small or had not been planted. Maxwell, who lived here 1860-65, was one of the world's greatest physicists, and made many important discoveries. His most important work was probably developing the theory of electromagnetic radiation.

Now walk through Vicarage Gate into Vicarage Gardens and turn to the right at Kensington Church Street. Cross the road, continue and turn left at Bedford Gardens. The English composer and conductor **Frank Bridge** (14) lived at No.4. He often conducted at Promenade concerts and was a tutor of Benjamin Britten.

Turn back down Kensington Church Street to the previous turning, which is Sheffield Terrace. There are four plaques in this street. **Sir Edward Henry** (15) lived at No.19, on the left. He was a Metropolitan Police commissioner and pioneer of fingerprint identification. Opposite, the novelist **G.K. Chesterton** (16) lived at No.32. This house has a rectangular bronze plaque, which is badly tarnished. Next door at No.34 you can see the plaque for **Wilson Carlile** (17) who lived here 1881-91. He was the clergyman who founded the Church Army. At No.58 there is a blue plaque commemorating the novelist **Agatha Christie** (18).

Walk on and turn to the left, then right into Campden Hill. The Atkins Buildings of Queen Elizabeth College are on the left. Just past 'The Old Coach House', immediately opposite the entrance to Holland Park School, you will see the plaque of **Thomas Babington Macaulay** (19). This is on the building wall at the rear of the car park, set low down. He was a historian, poet and politician who died in the house formerly on this site.

Return to Campden Hill Road and you will see almost opposite at No.80 a blue plaque on the home of **Ford Madox Ford** (20). He is credited with writing about 80 books as well as editing two magazines.

Walk on and turn left into Observatory Gardens. This short road derives its name from the observatory that Sir James South, the astronomer, built here in 1831. It contained for a time, the largest telescope in the world. The existing houses were built in the 1880s.

Bearing left, cross over Hornton Street into Gloucester Walk. The French composer **Jean Sibelius** (21) lived at No.15 in 1909. Continue on, turning right into Kensington Church Street and right again into Campden Grove. The Irish-born novelist **James Joyce** (22) stayed at No.28 in 1931. Walk on, cross over Hornton Street and go back through Observatory Gardens. Turn left at Campden Hill Road.

Now turn right into Upper Phillimore Gardens, left at Argyll Road and right into Phillimore Place. The children's novelist **Kenneth Grahame** (23) lived at No.16 1901–8. He was the author of *The Wind in the Willows* (1908).

Coming back to Argyll Road, bearing right and walking a further two turnings will take you to Stafford Terrace. A small oval plaque below the window of No.18 marks the home of **Edward Linley Sambourne** (24). He was a cartoonist and illustrator, and his house is now open to the public as a museum of his work.

Continue to the end of this road, turn left and then left again at Kensington High Street. This is a good place to stop for a coffee, as you will have walked for an hour or more. Next to the doorway marked 43–52 Stafford Court you will see a Musical Heritage plaque for the popular singer **Alma Cogan** (25), who lived at No.44.

Walking on, turn left into the other end of Campden Hill Road. Passing Kensington Library you will reach the home of naval historian and poet **Sir Henry Newbolt** (26) at No.29.

Continue up the road and turn right at Holland Street. The corner house at the next junction was the home of the composer **Sir Charles Stanford** (27). Although the address is 56 Hornton Street, the blue plaque is in Holland Street. Continuing into Holland Street you will find that **Marguerite Radclyffe Hall** (28), the controversial novelist and poet, lived at No.37 from 1924 to 1929. The blue plaque is set low down behind railings. Further along, at No.13, there is a deeply set blue plaque commemorating another artist and illustrator, **Walter Crane** (29). He was an associate of William Morris and was particularly noted for his book illustrations. The Kandy Tea Room at No.4 is a popular place for refreshment, if you did not stop earlier.

Continue and cross over Kensington Church Street into York House Place. Passing Lancer Square, walk through the narrow walkway to Palace Green. Turn right. The Israeli embassy was the final home of **William Makepeace Thackeray** (30). He had this house specially built for his family, but only survived to live there one year himself. The brown RSA plaque placed in 1887 is set above the central upper window over the flagpole.

Cross over Kensington High Street. The narrow turning opposite is Kensington Court. As the traffic is very heavy on the main road, you may find it safer to cross at the traffic lights.

Entering Kensington Court you will see a lamp post on the left and behind it the words 'Electric Lighting Station'. This was the generating station built by **Colonel R.E.B. Crompton** (31) in 1883. His blue plaque is on the side of the building, further along the passageway. After a distinguished career in the army he formed an electrical company in 1886. This area, which was built during the middle 1880s, was the first private development in London to be lit by electricity.

Go back to Kensington High Street, turn left and then left again into Young Street. The

brick double-fronted house behind Barker's store (No.16) also has a plaque recording it was an earlier home of **William Makepeace Thackeray** (32). He lived here with his family from 1846 to 1855 (above).

Now walk on and turn right into Kensington Square. Halfway along on the right-hand side there is a plaque at No.41 commemorating the Pre-Raphaelite painter **Sir Edward Burne-Jones** (33). Next door at No.40 a plaque is seen on the home of **Sir John Simon** (34). He was a surgeon at St Thomas's who became Medical Officer of Health for London and later Chief Medical Officer to the Privy Council.

Continuing round the square you will see a rectangular plaque recording that **Mrs Patrick Campbell** (35) lived at No.33. She was one of the most highly credited actresses of her day and appeared in plays specially written for her by George Bernard Shaw. Walking round the square past the church, we reach one of the homes of **John Stuart Mill** (36). He was a writer and associate of Carlyle, Coleridge and Tennyson. The composer **Sir Hubert Parry** (37) lived next door at No.17. It is interesting to see that both of these plaques were erected by the LCC, although they differ greatly in style and colour.

Continue straight on through Thackeray Street to Kensington Court Place, where you will see a block of flats called Kensington Gardens. Here there is a blue plaque commemorating **T.S. Eliot** (38). This well-known poet was a member of the Bloomsbury Group and was awarded the Nobel Prize for literature in 1948.

Walk on and turn immediately left into St Alban's Grove. The artist **Richard Ansdell** (39) lived at No.1 near the end of the road. This is now called Atlantic House, Richmond College.

Turn left at Victoria Road and left again into Douro Place. At the end of this cul-de-sac, another artist, **Samuel Palmer** (40), lived at No.16 for 10 years from 1851.

Walk back and cross over Victoria Road. Turn right and left into St Alban's Grove. Turn left into Canning Place then left again into De Vere Gardens. The American novelist **Henry James** (41) lived at No.34 De Vere Gardens from 1886 to 1902. He was a friend of H.G. Wells and in later life took British citizenship. Opposite at No.29 the poet **Robert Browning** (42) spent the last two years of his life. These are both rectangular blue plaques.

Return to Victoria Road, turning to the left, and walk all the way along to the second turning, Eldon Road. The corner house, No.52 Victoria Road, was the home of **Edward Henry Corbould** (43), who was art tutor to Queen Victoria.

Continue along Eldon Road and turn left into Stanford Road. This is a cul-de-sac. In the right-hand corner there is a narrow footpath, which leads into Cornwall Gardens. The block of flats immediately in front is Braemar Mansions. Walk to the right and you will find a plaque on the end wall of the flats. This was the home of novelist **Ivy Compton-Burnett** (44) from 1934 to 1969. Walking round to the other side you will reach the plaque

of **Joachim Nabuco** (45) at No.52 Cornwall Gardens. He was a Brazilian statesman who lived at this address when ambassador for his country.

Proceed along Cornwall Gardens and turn right into Grenville Place, where you come to the last plaque of this route. This is on the home of **Charles Booth** (46) at No.6 Grenville Place (left). He was a shipowner, social reformer and pioneer of old-age pensions. It is only a short walk now down to Cromwell Road and left to Gloucester Road underground station.

Walk 10
West Kensington/ Hammersmith

Distance:	6¾ miles (10.86km)
Time taken:	3 hours
Number of plaques:	44
Nearest tube stations:	Hammersmith, Olympia, Earl's Court, Baron's Court
Bus routes:	9, 10, 27, 28, 391

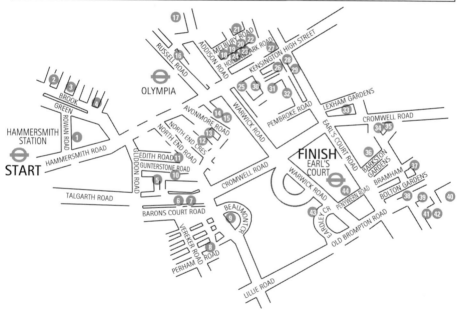

1 Leigh Hunt	12 E. Burne-Jones	23 Lord Frederick Leighton	34 Sir Benjamin Britten
2 Silver Studio	13 Sir Edward Elgar	24 Phil May	35 Alfred Hitchcock
3 Eliz. & Constance Finn	14 Harold Laski	25 G.K. Chesterton	36 Ellen Terry
4 Sir Frank Short	15 Samuel Taylor Coleridge	26 Thomas Daniell	37 Howard Carter
5 John Le Mesurier	16 Mohammed Ali Jinnah	27 Sir David Low	38 Sir Edwin Arnold
6 Sir G. De Havilland	17 Chaim Weizmann	28 G. Lowes Dickinson	39 Beatrix Potter
7 Mahatma Gandhi	18 Sir Hamo Thornycroft	29 Ugo Foscolo	40 Jenny Lind
8 Antonia White	19 Marcus Stone	30 Frankie Howerd	41 Sir Hugh P. Lane
9 Marcus Garvey	20 Michael Powell	31 Cowan Dobson	42 Sir William Orpen
10 Sir Henry Rider Haggard	21 Sir Samuel Luke Fildes	32 Sir W. Rothenstein	43 Hattie Jacques
11 Goossens Family	22 William Holman Hunt	33 Andrew Lang	44 Sir Norman Lockyer

THIS area includes the districts around the exhibition halls of Olympia and Earl's Court. It has many of the older residential buildings of London and some of its fastest moving and busiest roads. Many notable people have lived here and been honoured with plaques. These, however, are not as concentrated in locality as those detailed in some of the previous chapters, and consequently there is a greater distance to be covered. For those who prefer a shorter walk, it will be easy to stop at any time, as there are several tube stations and bus stops along the route.

The tour starts at Hammersmith underground station. Walk along Hammersmith Broadway and Hammersmith Road. This is sign posted A315. Turn left into Rowan Road. No.16 was the last home of the poet **Leigh Hunt** (1). The privately erected plaque may be covered by a vine and be barely visible. Continue up Rowan Road to Brook Green. Turn to the left and take the footpath across to the centre island, opposite the Queen's Head public house.

The three plaques in Brook Green are on this side of the road. Walk to the left, where the first is found at No.84. This is another house where the plaque is hard to find because of plant growth. The blue plaque here records the address being the former premises of the **Silver Studio** (2). This was not a studio making silver goods, but was owned by a family with the surname Silver. They were designers of furnishing fabrics, wallpapers and so on between 1880 and 1963. Turn back and now walk in the other direction. Just past Augustine Road at No.75 there is a blue plaque which reads 'Founded here by **Elizabeth and Constance Finn** (3) the Distressed Gentlefolks Association on the 5th May 1897'. The third plaque in this street commemorates **Sir Frank Short** (4), an engraver and painter who lived at No.56 from 1893 to 1944 – a long time to be in one house!

Continue along Brook Green, passing St Paul's School across the road. Cross the Hammersmith Road at the traffic lights, then walk left and turn right into Edith Road. Take the right fork off Edith Road called Gliddon Road. A short way down you will see the curved balconies of a large block of flats called Baron's Keep. The horseshoe-shaped drive has an arch in the centre. To the left of this is a plaque, which commemorates **John Le Mesurier** (5). This comedy actor lived here 1966–77. His first wife was the actress Hattie Jacques, who herself has a plaque nearby.

Continue along Gliddon Road and cross over the main road, which is Talgarth Road. There are interesting Victorian studio houses to be seen on this corner. Take the turning on the left opposite Baron's Court station. This is Baron's Court Road. Walk along to the plaque of **Geoffrey de Havilland** (6) at No.32. He was the aircraft designer whose company produced the Mosquito aircraft of World War Two and the world's first jet airliner, the Comet. A blue plaque commemorating **Mahatma Gandhi** (7), who lived here when a student, can be seen at No.20.

Turn back to Vereker Road, on the opposite side. Five turnings down you will reach Perham Road, where you turn to the left. The novelist and translator **Antonia White** (8) lived at No.22 from 1899 to 1921.

Proceed and turn left at Challoner Street. Turn right at the second turning, which is Castletown Road. Cross over North End Road at the pedestrian crossing into Beaumont

Crescent. On the right at No.2 is a very worn-looking plaque behind a drainpipe. This records that **Marcus Garvey** (9) lived here. He was one of the first Black Nationalist leaders and lived mainly in the US. He died in 1940 and a park in New York is named after him.

Returning to North End Road, bear right, walk past West Kensington station and cross back over Talgarth Road. The first turning on the left is Gunterstone Road, where the high terraced houses were built in 1882. **Sir Henry Rider Haggard** (10) lived at No.69 1885-8. There is a large tree in the front garden and when this is in leaf the blue plaque, which is above the first-floor balcony, is hardly visible. Rider Haggard was the author of *King Solomon's Mines* and *Allan Quatermain*.

Take the next turning right, Glazbury Road, then turn right again into the other end of Edith Road. No.70 was the home of the **Goossens family** (11) from 1912-27. The father Eugene (1867-1958) was a violinist and conductor. His four children were all musicians in their own right. Continue and cross over North End Road into North End Crescent. Samuel Richardson House is on the site of The Grange, where the Pre-Raphaelite painter **Edward Burne-Jones** (12) lived from 1867 to 1898.

Walk back a few yards and turn left into Stanwick Road and then Matheson Road, which branches off it. Turn left at the end of Matheson Road into Avonmore Road. No.51 was the home of the composer **Sir Edward Elgar** (13) for a year when he was first married. Continuing along Avonmore Road, you can see the Olympia exhibition centre ahead. Upon reaching Hammersmith Road turn right and then right again into Addison Bridge Place. The political theorist **Harold Laski** (14) lived at No.5 1926-50. Two doors away at No.7 the poet **Samuel Taylor Coleridge** (15) lived from 1810 to 1812. He is best remembered for *The Rime of the Ancient Mariner* and 'Kubla Khan'.

Return to the main road, turning right into the start of Kensington High Street. Cross over at the traffic lights to Russell Road. This road runs alongside the rail line next to the Olympia exhibition centre. Walk up past the station entrance. The founder of Pakistan, **Mohammed Ali Jinnah** (16), stayed at No.35 when a young man and law student. Turn right at the next turning, Holland Gardens. Turn left then right at the traffic lights into Addison Crescent, then left at Addison Road. The first President of Israel, **Chaim Weizmann** (17), lived at No.67 between 1915 and 1920.

Now turn back down Addison Road and turn left at Melbury Road. This area is a place where several artists and sculptors made their homes. No.2 Melbury Road was the home of **Sir Hamo Thornycroft** (18). He sculpted the statue of Oliver Cromwell, which stands outside the Houses of Parliament. At No.8 the painter **Marcus Stone** (19) lived from 1877 to 1921. Beneath this is a second plaque commemorating the film producer and director **Michael Powell** (20), who lived here 1951-71. The artist **Sir Samuel Luke Fildes** (21) lived at No.31 from 1878 to 1927. He produced many woodcut illustrations, including those for Dickens's *The Mystery of Edwin Drood*. Architect R. Norman Shaw designed both of these houses. Further round at No.18 the Pre-Raphaelite artist **William Holman Hunt** (22) lived and died. Fildes's plaque is another difficult one to see because of the trees.

Turn right into Holland Park Road. No.12, which is now a museum, was the home of the fine artist and sculptor **Lord Frederic Leighton** (23). At No.20 the caricaturist **Phil May** (24) lived and worked. He drew many cartoons for *Punch* and was one of the earliest practitioners of the modern style of cartoon drawing.

Walk on and turn left upon reaching Addison Road again. Cross over Kensington High Street. Ahead you can see the memorial erected to Queen Victoria in 1904. This is the start of Warwick Gardens. On the left at No.4 the novelist and biographer **G.K. Chesterton** (25) lived with his parents from 1881 until his marriage 20 years later. He was the author of the *Father Brown* stories.

Return to Kensington High Street, turn right and walk into the service road called Earl's Terrace. At No.14 (below) the landscape painter **Thomas Daniell** (26) lived and died. He spent about 10 years living in India and this had a marked impression on his work. Continue along Earl's Terrace and cross the main road at the traffic lights. The large block of flats above the shops is called Melbury Court, where there is a blue plaque on the end wall. This commemorates a former resident, **Sir David Low** (27). He was also a modern cartoonist, well remembered for his character Colonel Blimp. Opposite is the entrance to the Commonwealth Institute and a host of national flags.

Cross back over Kensington High Street and go into Edwardes Square, which you will have previously passed. The first plaque in the square is at No.11, where **Goldworthy Lowes**

Dickinson (28) lived. He was a Cambridge lecturer and author. The Italian-born author and poet **Ugo Foscolo** (29) lived at No.19 in 1817–18.

Retrace the last few steps and go round to the other side of the square. The popular comedian and comic **Frankie Howerd** (30) lived at No.27 from 1966 to 1992. Continue round South Edwardes Square to No.62, where **Cowan Dobson** (31) the portrait painter lived and worked from 1940 to 1980. Pause here to read the council plaque, which details the history of the square. Walk on and turn right into Pembroke Square.

Immediately opposite the Scarsdale Tavern is No.1 Pembroke Cottages. A blue plaque informs you that it was the home of **Sir William Rothenstein** (32). This painter and writer was an official war artist in both world wars and lived here from 1899 to 1902.

Walk on past Pembroke Square to Pembroke Road and turn left. Turn right at the traffic lights then left into Lexham Gardens. Now turn right on reaching Marloes Road.

No.1, which is behind the Cromwell Hospital, has a plaque on the home of **Andrew Lang** (33). This Scottish historian and writer lived here from 1876 until 1912. The plaque, like that of Marcus Garvey's, has a drainpipe in front of it. Coincidentally the only two plaques in London obscured in this way are both on this walk.

Cross Cromwell Road to the blue plaque of the composer **Benjamin Britten** (34). He lived and worked at No.173 in 1931–3 and found it a convenient short walk for him to the Royal College of Music.

Julian Lloyd-Webber at the unveiling ceremony of the plaque commemorating Benjamin Britten.

The house at No.153 was the home of film director **Alfred Hitchcock** (35) from 1926–39. Walk back along Cromwell Road and turn left into Knaresborough Place. Take the third turning on the right, Barkston Gardens. No.22, which is now a hotel, was the home of the actress **Ellen Terry** (36) from 1888 to 1907.

Turn back to Courtfield Gardens, then turn right through Laverton Place to the corner of Collingham Gardens. This was the home of the Egyptologist **Howard Carter** (37), who was famous for his discovery of the tomb of Tutankhamun in 1922.

Walk past Bramham Gardens to Bolton Gardens, turning to the right. **Sir Edwin Arnold** (38) lived and died at No.31. He was an author, journalist and poet who became editor of the *Daily Telegraph* in 1863.

Now turn back past Collingham Gardens and turn right, crossing Old Brompton Road at the traffic lights into Bolton Place. The first house on the left is actually 189 Old Brompton Road. Here you will see a blue plaque set into the pediment above the outer door. The Swedish soprano **Jenny Lind** (39) lived at this house (right) 1876–86.

Return to the traffic lights and turn left into Old Brompton Road. A few yards along on the brick wall of the primary school you will find an attractive rectangular plaque commemorating the children's author **Beatrix Potter** (40). She spent her early years at a house that was formerly on this site.

Take the first turning left and then turn immediately left again into South Bolton Gardens. No.8 (below) has two plaques. These commemorate **Sir Hugh Percy Lane** (41), a director of the Irish National Gallery, and **Sir William Orpen** (42), an Irish artist.

Go back to Old Brompton Road, turn left and continue as far as Eardley Crescent. This is about half a mile and five turnings along on the other side of the road, near the end of the cemetery. Almost at the end of this road at No.67, the comedy actress **Hattie Jacques** (43), lived from 1945 until her death in 1980. She is well remembered for her appearances in the 'Carry On' films and her regular television shows. Continue across Warwick Road into Penywern Road where at No.16 you will see the last plaque of this walk. This commemorates the scientist and astronomer **Sir Norman Lockyer** (44), who is credited with the discovery of helium. Walk to the end of the road and turn left to reach Earl's Court station.

Walk 11
Hammersmith

Distance:	3 miles (4.82km)
Time taken:	1¾ hours
Number of plaques:	16
Nearest tube stations:	Hammersmith, Ravenscourt Park
Bus routes:	9, 10, 27, 33, 72, 190, 209, 211, 266, 267, 283, 391

ALTHOUGH there are not many plaques to see on this tour, it has been included mainly because of the pleasant riverside walk and the attractive 18th century houses. There are many quiet roads and parks, which contrast with the noisy heavy traffic of the Great West Road.

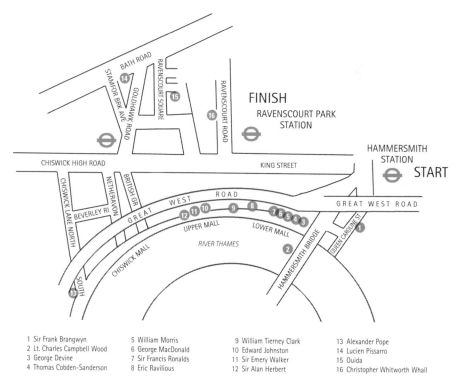

1 Sir Frank Brangwyn	5 William Morris	9 William Tierney Clark	13 Alexander Pope
2 Lt. Charles Campbell Wood	6 George MacDonald	10 Edward Johnston	14 Lucien Pissarro
3 George Devine	7 Sir Francis Ronalds	11 Sir Emery Walker	15 Ouida
4 Thomas Cobden-Sanderson	8 Eric Ravilious	12 Sir Alan Herbert	16 Christopher Whitworth Whall

The walk begins at Hammersmith underground station, which is in the middle of the Broadway shopping centre. There are many exits and you may find it convenient to use a subway to cross the busy road.

The first destination is in Queen Caroline Street, walking away from Hammersmith Broadway. The most obvious landmark to be seen is St Paul's Church. Walk past this and cross the road, going under the flyover. The road passes between a cinema and a block of flats named College Court. You should now be in the older part of Queen Caroline Street. No.51, where the artist **Sir Frank Brangwyn** (1) lived, is set back from the road on the left-hand side. Having been apprenticed to William Morris, his works included furniture, pottery, murals, etchings and interior designs. Continue along Queen Caroline Street and turn right at Worlidge Street. This will take you into Hammersmith Bridge Road, where you turn left and walk towards the bridge. Hammersmith Bridge was designed by Joseph Bazalgette and built in 1883-7.

Take the footpath on the right-hand side of the bridge. Halfway across you will find a brass plaque set on top of the wooden handrail (above). This was placed in memory of **Lieutenant Charles Campbell Wood** (2). He dived from the bridge in 1919 to rescue a woman in distress. Although he saved her life, he lost his own as a result of his injuries. Now walk back to the steps leading off the bridge, before the giant balusters. These steps lead you to the riverside walk named Lower Mall.

Walking with the river on your left proceed to No.9 Lower Mall (facing page, top). The blue plaque records this as the home of the actor and stage director **George Devine** (3). Just past this is the Blue Anchor public house, where Gustav Holst wrote his Hammersmith Suite. A blue plaque is now on his home at The Terrace, Barnes, on the other side of the river.

Continue along Lower Mall, past Furnival Gardens. The large red-brick building that you can see on the other side of the gardens is Hammersmith Town Hall. Bear right opposite Hammersmith Pier and take the opening on the left. The first house is Dove Cottage, where **Thomas Cobden-Sanderson** (4) founded his bookbinding and printing business. He worked with William Morris and Burne-Jones. When he closed down in 1916, he threw all his unwanted typeset into the river. Apart from the blue plaque there is also a small stone one, set in the side wall. The Dove public house is next door.

You are now in the Upper Mall. Walk on to No.26, where a small stone plaque set into the wall informs you that **William Morris** (5) lived here 1878–96. This is also the home of the William Morris Society. A previous tenant was **George MacDonald** (6), a poet and novelist who lived here 1867–77. The adjoining extension of this house has a further plaque (below). This commemorates **Sir Francis Ronalds** (7). He was an inventor who set up

an eight-mile long electric telegraph in 1816. Walk on to No.48, on the corner of Weltje Road. The artist and engraver **Eric Ravilious** (8) lived here 1931–5.

Continue walking on through the covered footpath next to the river, past the Old Ship Inn. Before the Black Lion public house is a wall of arches. On the other side of this wall, facing the pub, is a brown plaque recording that **William Tierney Clark** (9) lived on this waterworks site in around 1839. He was the designer of the first Hammersmith Bridge. The small street to the left, which was built during the middle of the 18th century, is Hammersmith Terrace. The master calligrapher **Edward Johnston** (10) lived at No.3 from 1905 to 1912. He taught at prominent art colleges and wrote on his subject. **Sir Emery Walker** (11), a typographer and antiquary, lived at No.7 from 1903 to 1933. The next plaque is at No.12, which was the home of **Sir Alan**

Herbert (12). He was a writer of comic verse, musical scores and novels, and was also an MP for 15 years.

Continue on past Western Terrace and Eyot Gardens into Chiswick Mall. There are some interesting looking houses along this bankside road. Turn right into Chiswick Lane South and walk up to the Mawson Arms (below). This is where the poet and satirist **Alexander Pope** (13) lived from 1716–19. You will find it is about one mile from here to the next plaque.

Take the underpass to cross the Great West Road. Although the Great West Road is horrendously noisy, the adjoining roads are very peaceful. Turn left on leaving the underpass and continue ahead into Chiswick Road North.

Turn right into Beverley Road, just past the recreation ground. Walk to the end and turn left into Netheravon Road North. Upon reaching Chiswick High Road, turn to the right and then left at the traffic lights into Goldhawk Road. Past the overhead bridge fork left into Stamford Brook Avenue. This will be to the left of the petrol station. Turn right at the top of Stamford Brook Avenue into Stamford Brook Road. The French artist and engraver **Lucien Pissarro** (14) lived at No.27. This house is set back from the road.

Walk ahead over the road junction, to Ravenscourt Square. This is the first turning on the right after the road crossing. No.11 Ravenscourt Square is in the second road entry on the left. The novelist who used the pen name **Ouida** (15) lived here. Her real name was Maria Louisa de la Ramée. Continue walking along Ravenscourt Square, past the Stamford Day Surgery and on to Ravenscourt Gardens, where you turn left. Continue and cross into Ravenscourt Park. Take the right pathway, past the children's playground and paddling pool. Walk straight ahead and do not go under any of the railway bridges. This will bring you into Ravenscourt Road. Turn left and you will find the last plaque of this walk at No.19. It commemorates **Christopher Whitworth Whall** (16). He was a stained-glass artist whose work can be seen in many prominent churches and cathedrals. Ravenscourt Park underground station is just behind, past the bridge.

Walk 12
Bloomsbury

Distance:	4 miles (6.43km) short walk or 6¾ miles (10.85km) full walk
Time taken:	2 hours (short walk), or 3 hours (full walk)
Number of plaques:	50 (short walk), 66 (full walk)
Nearest tube stations:	Tottenham Court Road, Holborn, King's Cross
Bus routes:	7, 8, 10, 18, 24, 25, 29, 30, 55, 68, 73, 91, 98, 134, 168, 176, 188

THIS area includes the British Museum, University College, London, many 18th and early 19th-century buildings and delightful squares. It has been an area frequented by artists and writers, notably the Bloomsbury Group.

Leaving Tottenham Court Road underground station, take exit No.3 leading to the north side of New Oxford Street. Walk along New Oxford Street past the second set of traffic lights into Bloomsbury Way. Turn left into Bury Place, where you will find a blue plaque commemorating the philosopher **Bertrand Russell** (1) on Russell Chambers. Apart from his many philosophical and mathematical publications, he is well remembered as a founder of the Campaign for Nuclear Disarmament (CND) and his anti-religious views.

At the end of the road you can see the British Museum. Turn to the left and within a few yards, at No.46 Great Russell Street, you will find a blue plaque on the home of **Randolph Caldecott** (2). This children's book illustrator lived here 1872–86. The actor-manager **Sir Gerald du Maurier** (3) lived at No.91 across the road, from 1916 until his death in 1934.

Walk on to No.100, where there is a bronze plaque commemorating **Topham Beauclerk** (4) and **Lady Diana Beauclerk**. He was a dandy and descendant of Charles II and Nell Gwynne. Diana was from the Spencer family and a daughter of the second Duke of Marlborough, as well as being a noted artist and engraver. A few doors away at No.106 there is another bronze plaque commemorating the father and son, both named **Augustus Pugin** (5) (page 83, top). They were architects and designers. The son was responsible for much of the design of the Houses of Parliament.

Proceed on to No.14 on the left side. A blue plaque records 'Here lived Charles Kitterbell as related by **Charles Dickens** (6) in sketches by Boz'.

Continue and turn right on reaching Tottenham Court Road. Cross the road to Percy Street, two turnings further along. The stage and film actor **Charles Laughton** (7) lived at No.15 in 1928–31. He is well remembered for his film portrayals of Quasimodo in *The Hunchback of Notre Dame*, Captain Bligh in *Mutiny on the Bounty* and the starring role in

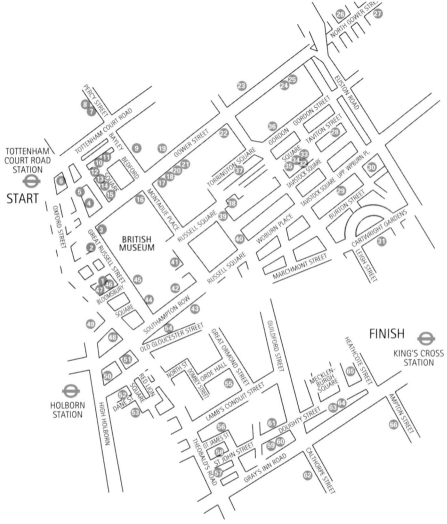

1 Bertrand Russell
2 Randolph Caldecott
3 Gerald du Maurier
4 Topham Beauclerk
5 Augustus Pugin
6 Charles Dickens
7 Charles Laughton
8 Coventry Patmore
9 J. Forbes-Robertson
10 Thomas Wakley
11 Thomas Hodgkin
12 Anthony Hope
13 Thomas Butterfield
14 Bedford College
15 Ram Mohan Roy
16 Earl of Eldon
17 Henry Cavendish

18 M. Garrett Fawcett
19 Pre-Raphaelite Brotherhood
20 Lady Ottoline Morrell
21 James Robinson
22 First Anaesthetic
23 George Dance (Younger)
24 Charles Darwin
25 Richard Trevithick
26 Giuseppe Mazzini
27 Lord David Pitt
28 Hugh Price Hughes
29 Charles Dickens
30 W.B. Yeats
31 Sir Roland Hill
32 Ali Mohammed Abbas
33 John Maynard Keynes
34 Bloomsbury Group

35 Lytton Strachey
36 Robert T. Herford
37 Christina G. Rossetti
38 T.S. Eliot
39 Sir Samuel Romilly
40 Sir George Williams
41 Baron Denman
42 Air Raids
43 Sir John Barbirolli
44 Sir Hans Sloane
45 Dr Robert Willan
46 Dr Robert Willan
47 Isaac D'Israeli
48 Earls of Chesterfield
49 Cardinal Newman
50 Thomas Earnshaw
51 William Lethaby

52 John Harrison
53 Rossetti/Morris
54 Bishop Challoner
55 John Howard
56 Dorothy L. Sayers
57 Benjamin Disraeli
58 Sir John Kirk
59 Brittain/Holtby
60 Charles Dickens
61 Sydney Smith
62 William Lethaby
63 Syed Ahmed Khan
64 R.H. Tawney
65 Hilda Doolittle
66 Thomas Carlyle

Henry VIII. Next door at No.14, the poet and essayist **Coventry Patmore** (8) lived in 1863–4. He worked for 20 years in the British Museum library and was a member of the Pre-Raphaelite Brotherhood.

Turn back and re-cross Tottenham Court Road to Bayley Street, almost opposite. This leads into Bedford Square, which was built 1775–80. Walk straight ahead to No.22. The actor **Sir Johnston Forbes-Robertson** (9) lived here 1888–1937. He was also a manager of the Lyceum Theatre.

Now walk back round the square passing Bayley Street. There are two blue plaques at No.35, both commemorating doctors. **Thomas Wakley** (10) was the founder editor of *The Lancet* and later an MP and coroner. **Thomas Hodgkin** (11) was a physician and pathologist. Hodgkin's Disease, which he identified, was named after him.

Continue past Adeline Place to No.41 Bedford Square. The novelist **Anthony Hope** (12) lived at this address 1903–17. He was the author of *The Prisoner of Zenda* (1894) and *Rupert of Henzau* (1898). Next door at No.42 the architect **Thomas Butterfield** (13) lived 1886–1900. Like Pugin, he was an exponent of the Victorian Gothic style. At No.45 you can see a green plaque commemorating the **Bedford College for Women** (14), which was founded here in 1849. **Ram Mohan Roy** (15) lived nearby at No.49. He was an Indian scholar and reformer, who wrote several books on religion. Roy received the title 'Rajah' three years before his death.

Walk on to No.6 on the next side of the square. The **1st Earl of Eldon** (16) lived here for 20 years. He was a politician and lawyer who became Lord Chancellor (1801–27). Continue up to the corner house of Montague Place. This is actually No.11 Bedford

Square. A bronze plaque on the wall marks this as the home of the **Hon. Henry Cavendish** (17). Cavendish, who lived here 1796–1810, was a physicist who discovered hydrogen.

Walk ahead past the front of the house and you are now in Gower Street. There are four plaques in close proximity to each other here. No.2, which is actually next door, has a blue plaque recording the name of **Dame Millicent Garrett Fawcett** (18). She was a leading suffragette and sister of Elizabeth Garrett Anderson. Across the road at No.7 a blue plaque records that the **Pre-Raphaelite Brotherhood** (19) was founded here in 1848. Opposite, a plaque informs us that **Lady Ottoline Morrell** (20) lived at No.10. She was a literary hostess and patron of the arts. Two doors further along at No.14, the physician and pioneer of anaesthesia, **James Robinson** (21), lived and worked.

Bonham-Carter House stands on the site of No.52 Gower Street. A blue plaque here records that **The First Anaesthetic** (22) given in England was administered on these premises in 1846.

Walk on to No.91, which is on the other side of the road. **George Dance the Younger** (23) lived and died here. He was an architect and painter, and also one of the first members of the Royal Academy.

Walking on you will reach the Biological Science building of University College, across the road. A blue plaque informs us that **Charles Darwin** (24) lived in a house, formerly on this site, 1838–42. This was before he moved to the large house at Downe, in Kent. On another university building, immediately opposite University Street, there is an elaborate bronze plaque commemorating **Richard Trevithick** (25). He was an inventor who ran his first passenger steam locomotive near here in 1808.

An interesting diversion is to see the figure of Jeremy Bentham at University College. Go through the main entrance with the gatekeeper's permission and cross the main quadrangle to the door in the right-hand corner. The dressed padded skeleton and modelled head of Jeremy Bentham sits in a glass fronted box in the foyer.

Continue ahead to North Gower Street, which is the other side of Euston Road. If you enter Euston Square tube station, you will find a subway leading to the other side. At No.183 on the left-hand side you will see the plaque for the Italian nationalist leader **Giuseppe Mazzini** (26). A little further on past Drummond Street, on the other side of the road, there is a plaque at No.200, for **Lord David Pitt** (27). He was a physician and civil rights campaigner.

Now retrace your steps through the subway and turn left into Gower Place. Continue into Endsleigh Gardens and turn right at Taviton Street. The Welsh Methodist preacher **Hugh Price Hughes** (28) lived and died at No.8. He founded *The Methodist Times* in 1885.

Continue and take the next turning left, which is Endsleigh Place. This will bring you into Tavistock Square. Walking forward you can see the British Medical Association building, Tavistock House, across the road. It was at this site that **Charles Dickens** (29) lived, in an earlier building, from 1851–60. He wrote several novels while living here.

Turn left and, walking past the pedestrian crossing, turn right into Woburn Walk. This attractive little street, with its bow-fronted windows, was designed by Thomas Cubitt in

1822. A rectangular plaque records that the poet **W.B. Yeats** (30) lived at No.5 between 1895 and 1919. It is a good place to stop for refreshments.

Walk forward and turn right at Burton Street, then left at Burton Place. Bear right when entering Cartwright Gardens. The next plaque to be seen is on the other side of the centre garden. This is for **Sir Rowland Hill** (31), the postal reformer. The plaque is on Commonwealth Hall, which is another University of London building.

Turn to the right past Leigh Street and into Marchmont Street. Take the first turning right, Tavistock Place, and cross over Woburn Place to the far side of Tavistock Square. Turn to the right and you will find a brown plaque at No.33 Tavistock Square. **Ali Mohammed Abbas** (32), who was one of the founders of Pakistan, lived here 1945–79.

Continue forward, turn left, and then left again. You are now in Gordon Square. The economist **John Maynard Keynes** (33) lived at No.46 for 30 years. Apart from being a member of the Bloomsbury Group, he was an advisor to the British Government in both world wars. A brown plaque at No.50 commemorates **The Bloomsbury Group** (34). Several of its members met here and in neighbouring houses. No.51 was the home of another Bloomsbury Group member, **Lytton Strachey** (35), who was a biographer and critic. You can now walk back a few yards and enter the gate to cross over the Gordon Square garden to Dr Williams's Library. There is a plaque on display to record that **Robert Travers Herford** (36) lived and worked at this address.

Walk to the left across Byng Place and into Torrington Square opposite. The poet **Christina Georgina Rossetti** (37) lived and died at No.30. The bronze plaque above the balcony is easily missed.

Continue along Torrington Square and turn left at Birkbeck College, Clore Management Centre. Ahead you can see a bronze seated figure. Walk on past the School of Oriental Studies into Thornhaugh Street. This leads to the corner of Russell Square. A brown plaque naming the poet and writer **T.S. Eliot** (38) is on the corner building. You need to look back when reaching the corner to see it. He worked for the publishers Faber & Faber from 1925 to 1965.

Turn to the left as you come into Russell Square. The lawyer and MP **Sir Samuel Romilly** (39) lived at No.21. Walking on past Bedford Way you will find another blue plaque on the large building on the left. This is the site of the house where **Sir George Williams** (40) lived 1879–1905. He was a businessman and social reformer, who founded the YMCA.

Cross the road and go through the gardens to the other side of Russell Square. The entrance to the large building on the corner of Bedford Place has a small rectangular plaque, which has been reset after redevelopment of the site. The **1st Baron Denman** (41) lived in a house (No.50) formerly on this site. He was a lawyer and Lord Chief Justice. His son, **Rt Hon. George Denman**, who became a high court judge, was born here. Walk on to the corner of Russell Square and turn right into Southampton Row.

Proceed along to the Bedford Hotel on the right. A small rectangular plaque records that 13 people were killed and 22 injured by a bomb dropped in one of London's first **Air Raids** (42) in 1917. Opposite, at the traffic lights, on another hotel cornering Cosmo Place, there is a blue plaque commemorating the conductor **Sir John Barbirolli** (43) who was born here in 1899.

Take the next turning on the right, which is Bloomsbury Place. The house formerly No.4

was the home of **Sir Hans Sloane** (44) during 1695–1742. He was a physician and naturalist who bequeathed his collection of books and manuscripts to the nation. This became the basis of the British Museum library.

Continue ahead, past the statue of Charles James Fox (by Charles Westmacott, 1816) to No.77 Great Russell Street. The architect **Thomas Henry Wyatt** (45) lived and died here. He was active in the design of country houses, churches and hospitals. Walk back and turn right into Bloomsbury Square.

Bloomsbury Square was laid out in the early 1660s for the Earl of Southampton. The dermatologist **Dr Robert Willan** (46) lived at No.6 from 1800 to 1812. He was the first to classify diseases of the skin in a concise manner. The father of Prime Minister Disraeli, **Isaac D'Israeli** (47), lived at No.6 from 1817 to 1829. He was a noted scholar and writer.

Turn left at the end of the square and cross at the traffic lights to the brick building, No.45, on the corner of Southampton Place. Here there is a dark bronze plaque, which commemorates the **2nd, 3rd** and **4th Earls of Chesterfield** (48).

Continue ahead into Southampton Place to No.17, where you will find a similar plaque on a former home of the eminent **Cardinal Newman** (49). This is one of three plaques in London that commemorate him.

Proceed and turn left, then cross the main road towards Holborn underground station. Immediately opposite the station at No.119 High Holborn there is a blue plaque commemorating **Thomas Earnshaw** (50). He was a watch and chronometer maker and this was the site of his workshops.

You will now have seen 50 plaques on this tour and are probably feeling a little tired. So this is the end of the shorter walk. There are several restaurants and cafes in the area if you would like refreshment before either leaving or proceeding.

To continue, walk up Southampton Row towards the next set of traffic lights. The large building on the right is the Central School of Arts and Crafts. You will find a blue plaque here commemorating the founder and first principal **William Lethaby** (51). Walk back to Fisher Street, which was the last turning you passed. Cross over the main road ahead into Red Lion Square.

The next plaque to be seen is on Summit House in Red Lion Square. The plaque is actually round the corner in Dane Street. Another watch and chronometer maker, **John Harrison** (52), lived and died in a house on this site. He invented the marine chronometer. Further down at No.8 Red Lion Square there is a plaque informing us that **Dante Gabriel Rossetti, William Morris** and **Sir Edward Burne-Jones** (53) all lived in this house. They were founders of the Pre-Raphaelite Brotherhood.

Continue round the square and then turn right into Old North Street. Cross Theobald's

Novelist P.D. James (centre) unveiled the plaque commemorating the author Dorothy L. Sayers.

Road, bearing to the left, and walk along to Old Gloucester Street. **Bishop Richard Challoner** (54), who was Vicar Apostolic of the London district, lived and died at No.44.

Continue ahead into Queen Square, named after Queen Anne. None of the original early 18th century houses are now remaining, but a relic is the water pump. This provided water from a reservoir to the Greyfriars of Newgate Street.

Turn right into Great Ormond Street, where you will find the world-renowned children's hospital. Opposite the hospital there is a plaque at No.23, where the great prison reformer **John Howard** (55) lived 1777–89.

Continue right into Lamb's Conduit Street. Walk all the way down and turn left at Theobald's Road. Take the second left, which is Great James Street. Near the end at No.22 you will find a blue plaque on the home of the novelist **Dorothy L. Sayers** (56). She is remembered as the author of the Lord Peter Wimsey stories and lived here 1921-9.

Walk through Northington Street, opposite, and turn right at King's Mews. This will take you to Theobalds Road, where you turn right again. No.22 Theobald's Road was where the Prime Minister **Benjamin Disraeli** (57) was born and spent his childhood.

Continue and turn right into John Street. There is an interesting plaque at No.32 on the left. This has a relief bust of **Sir John Kirk** (58) on the house where he lived. This philanthropist is remembered for his assistance to crippled and needy children.

Proceed past Northington and Roger Streets to No.58 Doughty Street. The blue plaque here commemorates **Vera Brittain** and the novelist **Winifred Holtby** (59). Vera Brittain was a socialist writer who came to fame with her novel *Testament of*

Youth. This described her experiences as a nurse during World War One. She was also the mother of the MP Shirley Williams.

The novelist **Charles Dickens** (60) lived at No.48 Doughty Street from 1837 to 1839 (below). Although there are 10 commemorative plaques in London for Dickens, this is the only original surviving London house where he lived. It is now a museum dedicated to him. Across the road at No.14 **Sydney Smith** (61) lived between 1803 and 1806. This clergyman was a canon at St Paul's and a noted author and wit.

Take the next turning right, which is Guilford Street. Cross over Gray's Inn Road into

Calthorpe Street. The second plaque on this tour naming **William Lethaby** (62) is on his home at No.20, where he lived 1880–91.

Walk back to Guilford Street and turn right into the continuation of Doughty Street. This brings you into Mecklenburgh Square, named in honour of Queen Charlotte, who was formerly Princess of Mecklenberg-Strelitz. No.20 on the right has two blue plaques. The Muslim reformer and scholar **Sir Syed Ahmed Khan** (63) lived here 1869–70 and the historian and writer **Richard Henry Tawney** (64) 1952–62. The latter was a professor of economic history at the University of London.

Continue round the square to No.44. The American-born poet and novelist **Hilda Doolittle** (65) who used the pen name 'H.D.' lived here 1917–18. From 1937 she made her home in Switzerland.

Walk back and turn left into Mecklenburgh Street. Then turn right at Heathcote Street and left into Gray's Inn Road. Continue along Gray's Inn Road and turn right at Ampton Street. No.33 was a home, from 1831 to 1832, of **Thomas Carlyle** (66), who was one of the most renowned of historians and essayists. His Chelsea home, where he died, is open to the public as a museum.

This is the last plaque of the tour. Continuing along Gray's Inn Road will bring you to King's Cross main line and underground stations, a distance of almost half a mile.

Walk 13
Bayswater/Notting Hill/Paddington

Distance:	5½ miles (8.85km) short walk or 7¾ miles (12.47km) full walk
Time taken:	2¼hours or 3¼ hours extended walk
Number of plaques:	33 (short walk) or 39 (full walk)
Nearest tube stations:	Marble Arch, Bayswater, Notting Hill Gate, Westbourne Park, Royal Oak, Paddington
Bus routes:	6, 7, 12, 15, 16, 18, 23, 27, 36, 94, 98

THE varied remnants of the history of this area make it a delight to walk. From the grisly relics of the Tyburn gallows, to the cosmopolitan district of Queensway and the antiques of Portobello Road, there is much to see and enjoy.

The walk begins at Marble Arch underground station, where it is best to exit at the north side of Oxford Street. Turn to the right and cross over Great Cumberland Place to the corner of the Edgware Road. The first plaque is difficult to see as it is at pavement level on the traffic island at the top of the Edgware Road. Railing barriers prevent you from crossing to this traffic island. Although it had been a place of execution since the 14th century, the plaque marks the spot where the **Tyburn Tree Gallows** (1) stood from 1571 to 1783. Now take the underpass to the other side of the Edgware Road and turn to the right.

The first turning on the left in Edgware Road is Connaught Place, where the corner house has a blue plaque. This was the home of **Lord Randolph Churchill** (2), the father of Sir Winston and a noted statesman himself.

Continue along the Edgware Road and turn left when you reach Kendal Street. The large block of flats Park West, opposite, has a plaque recording that the singer **Richard Tauber** (3) lived here 1947–8. Turn left into Portsea Place. No.16 was the home of **Olive Schreiner** (4) for just six months, during 1885–6. She was a South African novelist and ardent supporter of women's rights.

Walk on and cross over Connaught Street into Connaught Square, which dates from the 1820s. The Italian ballerina **Marie Taglioni** (5) lived at No.14 on the left side during 1875–6.

Continue straight down to Bayswater Road and turn to the right. A short way along is the Tyburn Shrine, where a green plaque was erected in memory of the 105 **Tyburn Martyrs** (6) who lost their lives on the nearby gallows between 1535 and 1681 purely because of their Catholic faith. The nuns who look after the shrine will be pleased to show visitors around and let them see the relics on display.

The unveiling of the plaque commemorating the Tyburn Martyrs.

Walk on to No.23 Hyde Park Place (Bayswater Road). Here there is a ceramic plaque with the heading **ORANJEHAVEN** (7). 'This building served as a club endowed in 1942 by Her Majesty Queen Wilhelmina of the Netherlands for Dutchmen having escaped from their occupied country to join the Allied forces'. Take the next turning on the right, Albion Street. The last Rajah of Sarawak, **Sir Charles Vyner Brooke** (8), lived at No.14, and a few doors away at No.18, a private blue plaque records that the novelist **William Makepeace Thackeray** (9) lived here. He seems to have moved frequently as there are three other plaques in London with the same claim.

Turn left at the top of the road and then left again at Hyde Park Street. The

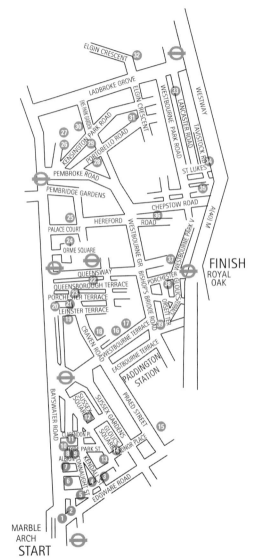

FINISH
ROYAL
OAK

MARBLE
ARCH
START

1 Tyburn Tree Gallows	11 Sir Giles Gilbert Scott	21 John & Jane Loudon	30 Sir William Crookes
2 Lord Randolph Churchill	12 Sir Winston Churchill	22 Constantine Cavafy	31 Susan Garth
3 Richard Tauber	13 Lady Violet Bonham-Carter	23 Sir William Sterndale	32 Jawaharlal Nehru
4 Olive Schreiner	14 Robert Stephenson	Bennett	33 Miodrag Purkovic
5 Marie Taglioni	15 Sir Alexander Fleming	24 Sir Rowland Hill	34 W.H. Hudson
6 Tyburn Martyrs	16 Susan Lawrence	25 Alice Meynell	35 Sadar Patel
7 Oranjehaven	17 Charles Manby	26 Dame Marie Rambert	36 Guglielmo Marconi
8 Sir Charles Vyner Brooke	18 Tommy Handley	27 Ashley Dukes	37 Thomas Hardy
9 William M. Thackeray	19 Francis Brett Harte	28 George Orwell	38 Szmul 'Artur' Zygielbojm
10 W.H. Smith	20 J.M. Barrie	29 Louis Kossuth	39 Alexander Herzen

founder of the newsagents and booksellers **W.H. Smith** (10) lived at No.12. Turn right upon reaching Bayswater Road and then right again into Clarendon Place.

The architect **Sir Giles Gilbert Scott** (11) designed his home Chester House, which is on the corner of Clarendon Close. He was also the architect of Waterloo Bridge, as well as many public buildings and is also credited with the design of the famous London red telephone box.

Take the next turning to the left, Hyde Park Gardens. Turning right at the end will bring you into Sussex Square. On the right-hand side, just past the post box, **Sir Winston Churchill** (12) lived in a house on the site of No.3 from 1921 to 1924.

Walk back a few yards to Stanhope Terrace, then turn left, proceeding over Sussex Place into Gloucester Square. Walk the length of Gloucester Square to No.43. This is at the beginning of Southwick Place. You will see a blue plaque on the corner of Hyde Park Square, which commemorates **Lady Violet Bonham-Carter** (13). She was the daughter of H.H. Asquith and governor of the BBC from 1941 to 1946, as well as being president of the Liberal Party 1944-5.

Cross the road and walk into Radnor Place. On the left at No.35 Gloucester Square there is a brown LCC plaque, which was originally on a house where **Robert Stephenson** (14) lived. He was the engineer son of George Stephenson of *Rocket* locomotive fame. Robert built the first London to Birmingham railway and designed many large bridges.

Continue up Radnor Place, crossing Sussex Gardens into Norfolk Place to Praed Street. Ahead is St Mary's Hospital. A plaque here records that **Sir Alexander Fleming** (15) discovered penicillin in the second-storey room above. Turn to the left.

Before walking along Praed Street, pause to read the plaque on the Fountains Abbey public house. Walk on past Paddington Station to its continuation, Craven Road. Turn right into Westbourne Terrace and cross to the far side of the road. The politician and social reformer **Susan Lawrence** (16) lived at No.44 and further along at No.60 **Charles Manby** (17) lived 1870-6. He also was a civil engineer and is credited with the design of the first iron-clad steamship and the planning of the Suez Canal.

Return to the traffic lights and turn right into the continuation of Craven Road. No.34, which is past Gloucester Terrace, has a blue plaque on the home of the popular comedian **Tommy Handley** (18). His radio programme *ITMA* (*It's That Man Again*) did much to boost the morale of wartime Britain.

Walk ahead through Craven Hill and turn left at Leinster Terrace, which is at the top of the road. The building at the end of Lancaster Gate, called Leinster House, has a plaque recording that the American author and poet **Francis Brett Harte** (19) lived here from 1895 until his death. Before settling in London he served five years as US consul in Glasgow.

The house on the right at the bottom of Leinster Terrace, 100 Bayswater Road, was the home of the writer **J.M. Barrie** (20). He got his inspiration for *Peter Pan* while walking in Kensington Gardens, across the road.

At Bayswater Road turn to the right and then immediately right again into Porchester Terrace. Many famous people have lived in this road but the only plaque to be seen is at No.3, the home of horticulturists **John** and **Jane Loudon** (21). John designed the house, with its curved glass portico (below), in 1843. He edited several gardening magazines and wrote *The Gardening Encyclopaedia.*

Continue and turn left at Porchester Gardens, then turn left again at Queensborough Terrace. At No.14, Greek poet **Constantine Cavafy** (22) lived 1873–6. Further along, across the road, No.38, now a hotel, was the home of the pianist and composer **Sir William Sterndale Bennett** (23). He founded the Bach Society in 1849 and was a principal of the Royal Academy of Music. Proceed down to Bayswater Road and turn to the right.

If you are ready for lunch or refreshments, you may like to go into Queensway, where there are many restaurants and cafés, also the William Whiteley shopping mall. Queensway and Bayswater tube stations are both nearby.

Continuing the walk in Bayswater Road, go past the station and into Orme Square. This is a private square with iron gates, originally built by Edward Orme between 1815–24.

Several prominent people have lived in the square but the only one honoured with a plaque is **Sir Rowland Hill** (24). He lived from 1839–42 at No.1, which is at the end. The artist Lord Leighton lived at No.2 between 1859–66. Return to Bayswater Road and take the second turning right into Palace Court. The poet and essayist **Alice Meynell** (25) lived at No.47 near the end of the road. It is now approximately half a mile to the next plaque.

Turn left into Moscow Road and proceed along the length of Pembridge Square. Turning left into Pembridge Gardens will bring you down to Notting Hill Gate underground station. Turn right and right again into Pembridge Road. Cross over and fork left into Ladbroke Road. This is to the left of the Kensington Temple. The building at the rear of the Temple has two blue plaques (facing page, top). These commemorate **Dame Marie Rambert** (26) and her husband **Ashley Dukes** (27). The inscriptions are explanatory.

Now walk back to Pembridge Road, crossing over Kensington Park Road. Turn left into

Portobello Road. You may like to spend some time in Portobello Road as it is filled with antique arcades and interesting shops. Saturday is the market day when everything is open and antique stalls abound. The first plaque to be found is at No.22 and is a privately erected one on the house where **George Orwell** (28) lodged 1927–8.

Take the next turning to the left, Chepstow Villas. The corner house, No.39, was the home of **Louis Kossuth** (29) for a short time. He was a Hungarian nationalist who was appointed provisional governor of Hungary after the overthrow of the Hapsburg dynasty.

Cross over Kensington Park Road, past the centre traffic island, into Kensington Park Gardens. The physicist and chemist **Sir William Crookes** (30) lived at No.7 on the left side. Apart from his many discoveries and inventions he is credited with doing much to improve electric lighting.

Return to Portobello Road and turn left. A blue plaque was erected at No.167 in 1975, to honour **Susan Garth** (31) as the founder of the antiques market. This caused some disagreement with other traders at the time, as stalls have been there since the World War Two. The plaque has survived despite their protests.

Turn left at Elgin Crescent and cross over Kensington Park Road and Ladbroke Grove. On the right-hand side there is a plaque at No.60 Elgin Crescent. The first Indian Prime Minister **Jawaharlal Nehru** (32) lived here 1910–12 while reading for the bar.

Go back to Ladbroke Grove and turn to the left. Now walk up to the second set of traffic lights passing Ladbroke Grove underground station. Ahead you can see the elevated A40 (M) Westway. Turn right into Lancaster Road. A short way along on the right-hand side is the Serbian Community Centre. A plaque records that **Miodrag Purkovic** (33) lived here 1972–6. He was a historian and chairman of the Society of Serbian Writers and Artists abroad.

This is the last plaque of the regular walk and you can leave by Ladbroke Grove underground station. If you would like to extend the walk proceed as follows, the next plaque though is over 700 yards away. There are only six more plaques and two more miles.

Continue all the way up Lancaster Road, crossing Portobello Road again, to St Luke's Road at the end, where you turn left. There are two plaques on the corner house at No.40. The inscription on the tarnished bronze one is '**W.H. Hudson's** (34) friends' Society of Quilmes, near Buenos Aires, where the great writer was born on August 4th, 1841, and where he spent his youth, has placed this bronze plaque at 40 St Luke's Road, London. The house in which Hudson lived his last years, and died on August 18th, 1922 (LCC 1938)'. A second plaque was placed by the Anglo-Argentine Society to commemorate the 150th anniversary of his birth.

Cross over St Lukes Road and continue into Tavistock Road opposite. The second turning is Aldridge Road Villas, where a plaque can be seen at No.23. This commemorates **Sadar Patel** (35), an Indian politician who lived at this address. He was a follower of Gandhi and held several posts in Nehru's government. It will now be over 800 yards to walk to the next plaque.

Leaving Aldridge Road Villas, turn left then right, into Shrewsbury Road. Turn left at the end, into Talbot Road, then take the fourth turning right into Hereford Road. The radio pioneer **Guglielmo Marconi** (36) lived at No.71 in 1896–7. Again it is over 800 yards to the next plaque.

Walk back to Talbot Road and turn right. Continue past St Stephen's church into Westbourne Park Road. At the bottom turn left and then left again into Westbourne Park Villas. No.16 Westbourne Park Villas was home to the novelist and dramatist **Thomas Hardy** (37) from 1863 to 1874. His novels, which have been adapted for modern films and television, include *The Woodlanders, Tess of the D'Urbervilles* and *Far From the Madding Crowd.*

Turn back and right into Porchester Road. At Porchester Square, opposite the library, there is a green plaque commemorating **Szmul 'Artur' Zygielbojm** (38) who lived nearby 1942–3. He was a Polish councillor who was outspoken against Nazi tyranny during the 1930s. Having lobbied politicians and the press in his efforts to save the European Jewry, he finally took his own life because of the apparent indifference of the world to the plight of the Jews.

Continue past the library and take the next turning on the left, Porchester Square. Turn right at Porchester Terrace North and then turn left into Orsett Terrace. No.1 at the far end is where you will find the last plaque on this tour. The Russian Socialist writer **Alexander Herzen** (39) lived here 1860–3.

The nearest underground station is Royal Oak. To reach it, turn back along Orsett Terrace and right into Gloucester Terrace. Follow it round to Porchester Road, where you again turn right. This will bring you up to the station, which is about a third of a mile from the last plaque.

Walk 14
Maida Vale/
St John's Wood

Distance:	6 miles (9.65km)
Time taken:	2¾ hours
Number of plaques:	33
Nearest tube stations:	Edgware Road, Warwick Avenue, Maida Vale, St John's Wood
Bus routes:	6, 13, 16, 18, 46, 82, 98, 113, 139, 189, 274

THIS route starts in a market area, continues with an attractive canal-side walk and finishes with an interesting route through some of North London's most attractive residential streets. Many of the houses and mansion blocks were built during the mid to late 19th century. The walk commences in Edgware Road, starting from the underground station. If you have travelled on the Bakerloo Line the exit is in the right place. From the other lines it will be necessary to walk to the Edgware Road and turn right, going beneath the flyover. You then need to walk along Edgware Road, walking away from the flyover, and turn right into Church Street, which is by the second set of traffic lights. This street has contained a market since before World War One. It flourishes today with a variety of goods available, including antiques and furniture, as well as food and household goods. Its covered market has nearly 400 stalls. Past Penfold Street, at No.71, you will find a green plaque commemorating the **Theatre Royal** (1). This theatre was the home of Victorian music hall and stood on the site 1832–1959. Among those who performed here were Charlie Chaplin, George Robey, Harry Champion and Marie Lloyd.

Walk back to Edgware Road, cross at the traffic lights and turn right. Continue up to Maida Avenue, at the second set of traffic lights, and turn left. This road runs alongside the Regent's Canal. Near the beginning you will see a blue plaque on No.2. **Arthur Lowe** (2), who lived at this address, is best remembered as Captain Mainwaring in the *Dad's Army* television series.

Walking on alongside the canal you will find the blue plaque for the poet and writer **John Masefield** (3) at No.30.

Now retrace your steps a short way and turn right at Park Place Villas. A few yards further on turn right into Howley Place. The Indian patriot and newspaper owner **Lokamanya Tilak** (4) stayed at No.10, 1918–19, while taking part in a lawsuit. He was active in the quest for self-government for his country.

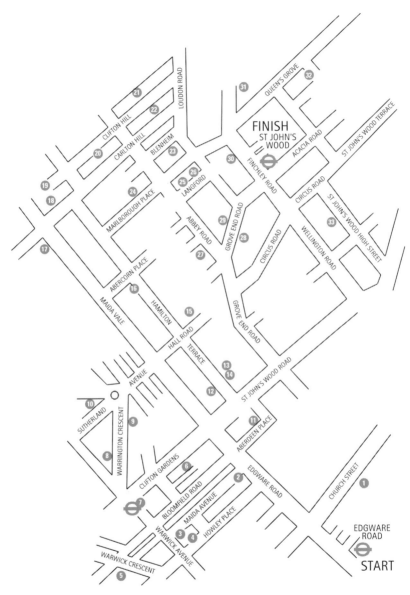

1 Theatre Royal
2 Arthur Lowe
3 John Masefield
4 Lokamanya Tilak
5 Robert Browning
6 Henry Hall
7 Sir John A. Fleming
8 Alan Turing
9 David Ben Gurion

10 Andreas Kalvos
11 Emily Davies
12 Sir Joseph Bazalgette
13 Sir G.A. MacFarren
14 William Strang
15 J.W. Waterhouse
16 Rabbi Joseph Hertz
17 Philip Lawrence
18 Dr A. Fleischmann

19 William Frith
20 W. Reid Dick
21 Melanie Klein
22 Charles Voysey
23 George Santley
24 Thomas H. Huxley
25 Laura & Harold Knight
26 John Adams-Acton
27 Sir Edward Elgar

28 Sir L. Alma-Tadema
29 Sir Thomas Beecham
30 Oskar Kokoshka
31 Thomas Hood
32 George Frampton
33 Britten/Pears

Continue forward, walk over the bridge and turn right into Warwick Crescent. Near the end of this short road, you will find a green plaque commemorating the poet **Robert Browning** (5). A memorial wall fashioned with two doves symbolising peace, love and learning is alongside. Browning lived in a house on this site 1862–87, after the death of his wife Elizabeth.

Take the bridge to the right, crossing over the canal. There is an excellent waterside café on this corner. Turn right into Blomfield Road, cross over Warwick Avenue and continue alongside the canal. Turn left into Randolph Road and then right into Randolph Mews. At No.8 a green plaque records that **Henry Hall** (6) lived here 1959–81. He was the dance band director who was regularly heard on the radio saying 'this *is* Henry Hall speaking'.

Return to Randolph Road and turn right and then left into Clifton Gardens. The physicist and engineer **Sir John Ambrose Fleming** (7) lived at No.9 on the left side. He was a pioneer in the widespread use of electricity. Warwick Avenue underground station is just ahead.

Turn right into Warrington Crescent, where there is a plaque to be found on the hotel at No.2, the birthplace of **Alan Turing** (8). He was a wartime code-breaker at Bletchley Park, and one of the pioneers of the modern computer. Formosa Street behind the hotel is the local area for restaurants and shops.

The first Israeli Prime Minister **David Ben Gurion** (9) lived for a time at No.75 Warrington Crescent. Nearby, you will find a good place for refreshment in the Warrington Hotel.

Crowds gathered for the unveiling of the plaque commemorating Alan Turing.

Take the next turning to the left of the roundabout, Sutherland Avenue. You will see a plaque across the road at No.182, where the Greek poet **Andreas Kalvos** (10) lived. Most of his life was spent in Italy but he established a school in Corfu and published many patriotic verses. From here it is over half a mile to the next plaque.

Now walk back past the roundabout and continue along Sutherland Avenue. Turn right at the main road, Maida Vale. Continue up to the third set of traffic lights and turn left into Aberdeen Place. This leads into Cunningham Place. You will find a plaque at No.17 on the left, for the founder of Girton College, Cambridge, **Emily Davies** (11) who lived here 1862–86.

Walk on, turn to the left and then turn right into Hamilton Terrace. This street was laid out in 1829 and named after James Hamilton, the Duke of Abercorn. No.17 was the home of the civil engineer **Sir Joseph Bazalgette** (12). He designed London's sewerage system and the Victoria Embankment. Opposite at No.20 there are two plaques. The composer and teacher **Sir George Alexander MacFarren** (13) lived and died here. A later occupant of the house was the painter and etcher, **William Strang** (14). He illustrated Kipling's short stories, *Don Quixote* and produced over 700 etching plates.

Continue along Hamilton Terrace and turn right into Hall Road. At No.10 on the left you will see the blue plaque commemorating the artist **John William Waterhouse** (15). He was a Pre-Raphaelite painter whose most well-known pictures were two versions of *The Lady of Shalott*.

Return to Hamilton Terrace, bearing right and continuing to No.103. **Joseph Herman Hertz** (16) lived here 1913–46, during which time he was Chief Rabbi of the British Empire.

Turn left at Abercorn Place and then right at Maida Vale. Across the road, past the high-rise apartment blocks, is St George's School. On the outer wall there is a large plaque

commemorating the headmaster **Philip Lawrence** (17), who was fatally stabbed while defending a pupil from an attacker (left).

At the traffic lights turn right into Carlton Hill. No.92 has a plaque commemorating **Dr Arthur Fleischmann** (18), who apart from being a medical practitioner, was a notable sculptor. He is credited with having made portrait busts of four popes.

Turn left into Greville Road, then left at Clifton Hill. At the end of the cul-de-sac there is a plaque on No.114 for the artist **William Frith** (19). He painted large canvases, notably *Ramsgate Sands* (1851) and *Derby Day* (1858). Walk back along Clifton Hill to No.95A, opposite the Clifton public house. A blue plaque on the gatepost records that the sculptor **Sir William Reid Dick** (20) worked here (facing page, top). Further along across the road at No.42, you can see the plaque for the psychoanalyst follower of Sigmund Freud, **Melanie Klein** (21).

Now turn right at the top of the road and then right again into Carlton Hill. No.6 was the home of architect and designer **Charles Voysey** (22). Many of his designs were influenced by the style of William Morris.

Return to Loudon Road and turn right and then right again into Blenheim Road. The baritone singer **Sir Charles Santley** (23) is commemorated with a plaque at No.13 (below). Continue on and turn left at Abbey Road. Go right past the synagogue. No.38 Marlborough Place was the home of the biologist **Thomas Henry Huxley** (24), from 1872 to 1890. He wrote many scientific works and was the originator of the word 'agnostic'. Return to Abbey Road and turn to the right.

The first turning on the left is Langford Place, where there are two plaques. The husband and wife artists **Laura** and **Harold Knight** (25) lived at No.16. No.14 was home to sculptor **John Adams-Acton** (26) from 1882 to 1906. He sculpted many statues for cathedrals and several of royal figures.

Walk back to Abbey Road and turn left. You will reach the Abbey

Studios on the other side of the road, where much graffiti is usually evident. There is a plaque commemorating **Sir Edward Elgar** (27), who opened the studios in 1931 and recorded here. Now cross the most famous pedestrian crossing in the world, immortalised by the Beatles. The memorial ahead is for Edward Onslow Ford RA and was erected by his friends and admirers. Turn left into Grove End Road.

Within a few yards there are two plaques almost opposite each other. No.44 was the home of the artist **Sir Lawrence Alma-Tadema** (28) from 1886 to 1912 and No.31 the home of the famous conductor, **Sir Thomas Beecham** (29). He founded the Royal Philharmonic Orchestra in 1947.

To continue, walk up to Finchley Road and St John's Wood station ahead. You have probably walked for about two hours and may like to leave at this point. However there are another four plaques within easy reach and to see these continue as follows.

Turn left at Finchley Road and walk along to the far end of Eyre Court. A blue plaque records that Austrian artist **Oskar Kokoshka** (30) lived here. He arrived in 1938 to escape the Nazis but finally retired to Switzerland after the war.

Continue and cross the road. Walk past Queen's Grove to No.28 Finchley Road. This is the house where the poet and writer **Thomas Hood** (31) lived and died. The English Heritage blue plaque was erected in 2001 as a replacement for the original inconspicuous LCC one.

Walk the short way back and turn left into Queen's Grove. At No.32 there is a plaque marking the home of the sculptor **George Frampton** (32), who created the statue of Peter Pan in Kensington Gardens. Frampton was a joint first principal of the Central School of Arts and Crafts with William Lethaby. Turn back and left into Ordnance Hill.

On Rossetti House you can see the busts of Christina and Dante Gabriel Rossetti. Walking along Ordnance Hill you will pass the barracks of the King's Troop Royal Horse Artillery. Cross Acacia Road and at the end of the road turn right and then left into St John's Wood High Street. This is a smart shopping street with excellent restaurants and cafés.

The last plaque of this tour is to be found opposite Allitsen Road, at No.45A. This was the home of the composer **Sir Benjamin Britten** (33) and also the singer **Peter Pears**. Both names are recorded on the plaque. They founded the Aldeburgh festival together in 1948.

St John's Wood tube station is about a quarter of a mile away. Walking back to Circus Road and turning left will bring you to Wellington Road. Turn to the right and you will find the station is just a short walk ahead.

Walk 15
Covent Garden/ Whitehall

Distance:	3¾ miles (5.63km)
Time taken:	1¾ hours
Number of plaques:	40
Nearest tube stations:	Leicester Square, Covent Garden, Charing Cross, Westminster
Bus routes:	6, 9, 11, 12, 13, 15, 23, 24, 29, 53, 77a, 88, 91, 109, 176

THERE has been a market on the Covent Garden site since 1656. The present market buildings date from the mid-19th century and were used mainly for the sale of fruit and vegetables. Today it is a tourist area with small shops, craft stalls and a variety of street entertainers. The walk continues to Whitehall, where the main government buildings are situated, and finishes at Westminster.

This tour begins at Leicester Square tube station, where you leave by exit No.2. Turning to the right on leaving the station leads into Leicester Square. Walk across the centre of the square towards the statue of William Shakespeare. Entering the gardens you will pass a bust of William Hogarth and a delightful bronze statue of Charlie Chaplin. Ahead you can see two plaques on No.48 that commemorate the painter **Sir Joshua Reynolds** (1). As the original LCC brown plaque is set rather high, a copy was made and placed at a lower level. Reynolds lived in a house on this site from 1761 until his death in 1792. You will see a bust of him as you walk out of the central gardens and you will shortly see another plaque commemorating him. As you walk back round the outer edge of the gardens you will notice bronze plaques set into the pavement. These have the handprints of many well-known film stars. Walk back past the Empire and Warner Bros cinemas into Cranbourn Street, crossing over Charing Cross Road.

The first building on the right past the traffic lights, No.38–44 Cranbourn Street, bears a green plaque on the site of the house where **Sidney Webb** (2) was born. He was a social reformer and founder of the London School of Economics.

A few doors away at Nos 77–78, another green plaque records the site of Old Slaughters Coffee House. This is where, on the 16 June 1824, a society was formed which later became the **Royal Society for the Prevention of Cruelty to Animals (RSPCA)** (3).

Walking forward you will see a large blue plaque on the left side, above the telephone

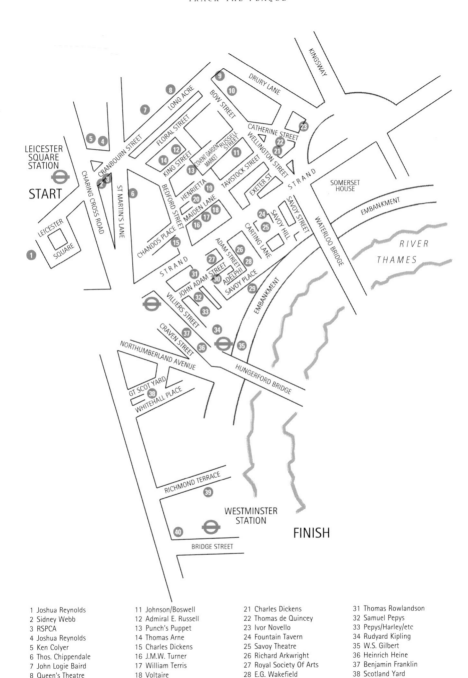

1 Joshua Reynolds	11 Johnson/Boswell
2 Sidney Webb	12 Admiral E. Russell
3 RSPCA	13 Punch's Puppet
4 Joshua Reynolds	14 Thomas Arne
5 Ken Colyer	15 Charles Dickens
6 Thos. Chippendale	16 J.M.W. Turner
7 John Logie Baird	17 William Terris
8 Queen's Theatre	18 Voltaire
9 Denis Johnson	19 David Garrick
10 Bow Street	20 Jane Austen

21 Charles Dickens	31 Thomas Rowlandson
22 Thomas de Quincey	32 Samuel Pepys
23 Ivor Novello	33 Pepys/Harley/etc
24 Fountain Tavern	34 Rudyard Kipling
25 Savoy Theatre	35 W.S. Gilbert
26 Richard Arkwright	36 Heinrich Heine
27 Royal Society Of Arts	37 Benjamin Franklin
28 E.G. Wakefield	38 Scotland Yard
29 Adelphi Terrace	39 Sir H.M. Stanley
30 Robert Adam	40 John Peake Knight

boxes. This is No.5 Great Newport Street, where **Sir Joshua Reynolds** (4) lived 1753–61. He obviously liked to live in the locality. Further along at 11–12 Great Newport Street, past the next set of telephone boxes, there is a plaque for the jazz musician **Ken Colyer** (5). This was formerly 'Studio 51' where he regularly played.

Walk back and take the second turning right, St Martin's Lane. Opposite the Albery Theatre a rectangular plaque can be seen on No.61. This is where the furniture designer **Thomas Chippendale** (6) established his workshop in 1753.

Turn and walk back a few yards to the street intersections. The second turning on the right is Long Acre. No.132 Long Acre, on the corner of Slingsby Place, is where **John Logie Baird** (7) first broadcast a television programme in 1929. This is a large rectangular stone plaque.

Continue down Long Acre, passing Covent Garden tube station. On the corner of Neal Streat there is a plaque commemorating the **Queen's Theatre** (8), which stood on this site from 1867 until 1878. Ahead you can see the impressive tower of Freemason's Hall. Continue past Bow Street to Acre House on the other side of the road. A decorative green plaque beside the entrance records that **Denis Johnson** (9) made and sold the first bicycle at premises on this site in 1819. Turn back and left into Bow Street.

A few yards into Bow Street you will find a square on the left called Broad Court. Here there is a delightful little bronze statue of a seated ballet dancer. On the wall behind is the **Bow Street** (10) plaque. This records the names of several notable former residents of the street.

Continue along Bow Street, walking past the Royal Opera House and its recent extension. The original building was opened in 1732. After a fire the replacement building was finished in 1809. However fire again took its toll and the present building designed by E.M. Barry dates from 1858. John Flaxman's coade stone frieze from the second building can be seen in the portico.

Turn right into Russell Street. At No.8 Russell Street there is a blue plaque recording that **Dr Samuel Johnson** (11) first met his biographer **James Boswell** in this building, which was occupied at the time by a bookseller named **Thomas Davies**.

Walk ahead through the centre of Covent Garden. If you have not been here before, there is much to see. The market came into existence in the mid-17th century and was the centre for flowers, fruit and vegetables for almost 300 years. The present structure is Victorian with later additions. Today it is a hive of shops and small traders. Street entertainers also abound.

Coming out of the main building there is a square ahead and the 17th-century church of St Paul. To the right is King Street, where at No.43 there is an elaborate bronze plaque at the house of **Admiral Edward Russell** (12). He commanded the British Fleet during the

war with France (1689–97) and was thrice First Lord of the Admiralty. Walk over to St Paul's Church and on the left rear pillar of the façade you will find an engraved inscription. It states that near this spot **Punch's Puppet Show** (13) was first performed in England and witnessed by Samuel Pepys in the year 1662.

Continuing along King Street you will find an unusually shaped blue plaque at No.31. This is where **Thomas Arne** (14), the composer of *Rule Brittania* lived.

Turn left into Bedford Street. Ahead, on the corner of Chandos Place, you can see a blue plaque. This records that as a boy **Charles Dickens** (15) worked here 1824–5. Turn left into Maiden Lane. The first plaque to be seen is in Exchange Court, at the site of the house where the artist **Joseph Mallord Turner** (16) was born. A few yards along, on the rear of the Adelphi Theatre, there is a plaque commemorating the actor **William Terriss** (17). It was here that he was stabbed and killed by a jealous rival. At No.10, on the rear of the Vaudeville Theatre, another green plaque records that the French author **Voltaire** (18) lodged in a house on this site 1727–8. Turn left at Southampton Street.

No.27 has a relief bronze plaque with a bust of the actor **David Garrick** (19). He lived at this address 1750–72. Turn left into Henrietta Street. **Jane Austen** (20) frequently visited her brother, who lived at No.10. Turn back and walk past the covered market towards the

The unveiling of the plaque for Jane Austen.

London Transport Museum. Now turn right and go back through Russell Street. Turn right into Wellington Street.

At No.26 Wellington Street, on the corner of Tavistock Street, there is another blue plaque with the name of **Charles Dickens** (21). He had apartments here 1859–70 and ran a magazine, *All The Year Round,* from these offices.

Continue into Tavistock Street. The writer **Thomas de Quincey** (22) lived at No.36. His best-known work was *Confessions of an Opium Eater.* Turn right into Catherine Street and left at Aldwych. Near the bus stop at No.11 there is a blue plaque on the home of **Ivor Novello** (23). This actor, dramatist and composer lived and died in a flat here.

Walk back past Catherine Street and turn right into Exeter Street, which leads off the same junction. Continue ahead, crossing over Wellington Street, where you can still see a gaslight on the exterior of No.15. Cross Burleigh Street and follow Exeter Street round to the Strand. You will see the Savoy Hotel across the road. Cross over the Strand and bear left. A short way along the road you reach Savoy Buildings, where there are large plaques set on either side of the entrance. This is the site of the **Fountain Tavern** (24) and the **Coal Hole** pub. The former was the meeting place of political opponents of Robert Walpole and the latter a bawdy house. In the mid-19th century the 'Judge & Jury Club' met at the Coal Hole and made a farce of current events ending with a tableau of girls dressed in skin-coloured costumes, nudity not being legal in those days.

Walk back a short way to the present day Coal Hole pub and turn left into Carting Lane. Continue down the steps, past the stage door, and you will find a green plaque on the wall of the theatre. It records that the **Savoy Theatre** (25) was the first public building in the world to be fully lit by electricity (1881). Go back up the steps and turn left in the Strand.

Now walk down to Adam Street, a short way along on the left. You will pass several well-known stamp dealers in this part of the Strand. Very few of the Adams brothers' original houses remain but No.7 Adam Street is a good example. The blue plaque at No.8 names **Richard Arkwright** (26) as a former resident. He was the inventor of a spinning frame in 1768 and was one of the main instigators of the industrial revolution.

Turn right into John Adam Street. The **Royal Society of Arts** (27) at No.8 has a brown plaque beside its entrance. Turn back and right into Adam Street. At the offices of Nos 1–5 **Edward Gibbon Wakefield** (28) conducted the plan for the colonisation of New Zealand, where a bronze plaque records the event.

Look across to the motor cycle parking bay at the rear of the Adelphi building. There is a colonnade here where an inscription can be found on the first column. This gives a list of notable former tenants of the original **Adelphi Terrace** (29), which had been built by the brothers Adam. Walk on and turn right into Robert Street.

A rectangular blue plaque records the names of **Robert Adam** (30) and other eminent people who have lived at Nos 1–3 in the street. Turn to the left. The building on the corner of Durham House Street has a blue plaque, which informs us that the cartoonist **Thomas Rowlandson** (31) lived in a house formerly on this site.

Continue on and turn left into Buckingham Street. There are two plaques in this cul-de-sac commemorating **Samuel Pepys** (32). No.12 has a brown circular plaque which states that he lived in this house 1679–88. No.14 has a large rectangular plaque, which also states that he lived there. Other names mentioned are **Robert Harley, William Etty** and **Clarkson Stanfield** (33).

Return to John Adam Street and turn left, then left again into Villiers Street. The end building on the left, No.43, has a plaque for **Rudyard Kipling** (34), the writer who lived here 1889–91. He was the renowned author of *The Jungle Books* and *Just So Stories* and received the Nobel Prize for Literature in 1907.

Go straight ahead and walk through the tube station entrance, emerging onto the Embankment on the other side. Cross over at the traffic lights to a bronze relief plaque with a bust of **Sir W.S. Gilbert** (35). He was the librettist in the partnership with Sir Arthur Sullivan. Come back through the traffic lights and walk under Hungerford Bridge. Across the Thames you can see the Royal Festival Hall and the London Eye.

Turn right into Northumberland Avenue. Branching off to the right is Craven Street, where many 18th-century terraced houses survive. There is a bronze plaque at No.32 where the German poet and writer **Heinrich Heine** (36) lived for six months in 1827. A few doors away at No.37, a similar bronze plaque names **Benjamin Franklin** (37). The American statesman and inventor lived at this address 1757–62. Other known persons to have lived in the street include wood carver Grinling Gibbons, author James Smith, architect Henry Flitcroft and the founder of Great Ormond Street Hospital, Dr Charles West.

Cross the road and enter Craven Passage. Walk ahead, cross Northumberland Avenue, and turn into Great Scotland Yard. Turn left at Scotland Place, going under the archway, then turn right into Whitehall Place. A blue plaque by the entrance of the building on your right records this as the former **Scotland Yard** (38) headquarters of the metropolitan police force.

Proceed to Whitehall, turning to the left. Walking along Whitehall you can see the mounted Queen's Life Guard sentries. The changing of the guard at 11.00am is well worth seeing. The government offices are all in this road. You will walk past the gates of Downing Street, the Cenotaph and have a good view of the London Eye. There are many statues. On the left side of the road is Richmond Terrace. Unfortunately, as this has been enclosed for a government car park, you can no longer enter to see the blue plaque at No.2, which was the home of **Sir Henry Morton Stanley** (39). You may get a glimpse of it though, near the end of the terrace, as you walk past. Stanley was the journalist who went to Africa in search of Dr Livingstone.

Turn left upon reaching Parliament Square. There is a green plaque on the corner building, No.12 Bridge Street. This commemorates **John Peake Knight** (40) who invented traffic lights and had the first ones erected at this junction. It is the last plaque of the tour and nearby is Westminster underground station.

Walk 16
Holborn/St Paul's

Distance:	5 miles (8 km)
Time taken:	2¾ hours
Number of plaques:	53
Nearest tube stations:	Holborn, Chancery Lane, City Thameslink, St Paul's, Bank, Cannon Street, Blackfriars, Temple
Bus routes:	8, 11, 15, 25, 26, 68, 76, 91, 168, 171, 188, 242

HOLBORN is now part of the borough of Camden, which extends as far as Hampstead. In former days it was the smallest of the metropolitan boroughs. This walk extends from the Inns of Court to the outer fringes of the City of London. It incorporates the areas of Fleet Street and St Paul's Cathedral and gives the visitor an opportunity to see the modern developments as well as the historic sights. Many of the commemorative plaques seen on this tour are rectangular blue ceramic and have been erected by the Corporation of the City of London.

Starting from Holborn tube station, turn left into Kingsway. Turning left again at Remnant Street will take you into Lincoln's Inn Fields. This is London's largest square. It was formed from two fields in the early 17th century, when permission to build was given. None of the original houses remain although there are some from the 18th century.

Turn right upon coming into the square. A blue plaque can be seen at No.65. This was the home of the surgeon **William Marsden** (1). He founded the Royal Free and Royal Marsden Hospitals. A few doors away at 59–60, a former Prime Minister, **Spencer Perceval** (2), lived from 1791–1808. He was the only British Prime Minister to have been assassinated while in office. The bronze plaque was placed by the LCC in 1914. This is one of the few remaining 18th-century houses in the square.

Cross the road and go into the fields via the path leading to the centre. This was a place of execution and the plaque recording this fact is no longer in the centre of the bandstand. If you would like to make a small diversion from the tour, take the path towards the left of the square and you will come out almost opposite the Sir John Soanes museum. This is one of the most interesting of London's smaller museums and well worth a visit if time permits.

To continue walking proceed past the bandstand to the opposite side of the square. The buildings ahead are Lincoln's Inn Library and Lincoln's Inn Hall. Turn to the right and cross over to the gateway, which is surmounted by two small domes. This takes you into New Square. Walk straight on past the war memorial and bear to the left into Old Square. There is a small plaque on the wall of the chapel recording that a nearby paving stone

START
HOLBORN STATION

FINISH
TEMPLE STATION

1 William Marsden
2 Spencer Perceval
3 Zeppelin Bomb
4 John Thurloe
5 Sun Yat Sen
6 Thomas Chatterton
7 Furnival's Inn
8 Charles Dickens
9 Giuseppe Mazzini
10 Labour Party
11 Edgar Wallace
12 The Daily Courant
13 Ludgate
14 Wynkyn de Worde
15 George Williams
16 John Newbery
17 St Paul's School
18 Cordwainers' Co.
19 St John Evangelist
20 London Salv. Corps.
21 St Thomas Apostle
22 St Mary Bothaw
23 Cutlers' Hall
24 Turners' Hall
25 Richard Whittington
26 Duke of Buckingham
27 Richard Whittington
28 Joiners & Ceilers Co.
29 Fred Cleary
30 Blacksmiths' Hall
31 Upholders' Hall
32 Doctors' Commons
33 Thomas Linacre
34 Bell Inn/Shakespeare
35 The King's Wardrobe
36 Blackfriars Priory
37 Bridewell Palace
38 Salisbury Court Playhouse
39 Robert Wakeman
40 Sunday Times
41 Samuel Pepys
42 P. O'Conner
43 Bright/Cobden
44 Tompion/Graham
45 William Hazlitt
46 Dr Samuel Johnson
47 Dr Samuel Johnson
48 The Mitre Tavern
49 Automobile Association
50 Old Sarjeants Inn
51 Devil's Tavern
52 Essex Street
53 Charles Lamb

marks the spot where a **bomb dropped by a Zeppelin** (3) fell. Continue on and go through the wrought iron gates, turning right. This is Chancery Lane. Walking down you will find on the wall on your right, opposite Cursitor Street, a plaque naming **John Thurloe** (4). He was a resident of Old Square and served Parliament as Secretary of State under Oliver Cromwell. After the Restoration, he continued to practice as a lawyer. Turn back down Chancery Lane and proceed past the London Silver Vaults to High Holborn.

Cross over High Holborn by the traffic lights and walk into Warwick Court, opposite. Before the archway, behind the railings, is a bronze plaque commemorating the Chinese leader **Sun Yat Sen** (5). He lived in a house, formerly on this site, while in exile. Return to High Holborn and turn left. There is an interesting statue of a robot man on Bracton House and a public house has stood on the site of the Cittie of Yorke since 1430. Continue past Gray's Inn Road. The greatly restored façade of Staple Inn, across the road, dates from the 16th century. Note the pedestal with a winged griffon, marking the boundary of the City of London.

Turn into Brooke Street on the left. The corner building has a City of London plaque set at first-floor level, below the fourth window. The young poet commemorated, **Thomas Chatterton** (6), took his own life in a house formerly on this site. He lived in great poverty and his poems, in a mediaeval style, were attacked by the critics.

Continue along High Holborn to the monolithic Prudential Assurance Co. building. By the main entrance is a blue plaque which records that it was built on the site of **Furnival's Inn** (7). Go through the entranceway into the courtyard where there is a plaque for **Charles Dickens** (8), immediately on the right. Ahead is a pointed canopy, above an alcove, below which is a bust of Dickens. A plaque below records that he lived here for a short time and wrote *The Pickwick Papers* while in residence. Return to High Holborn, turn left and proceed on to Hatton Garden.

Hatton Garden was originally built by Elizabeth I's chancellor, Sir Christopher Hatton, in the 1570s. None of these houses remain and today it is the centre of the diamond and jewellery trade. No.5 was the home of the Italian patriot **Giuseppe Mazzini** (9) 1841–2. The large bronze plaque is at first-floor level. Take the small alleyway, a few doors away, which leads to the Olde Mitre Tavern and Ely Place. A tavern was built here in 1546 and is an interesting place to stop for refreshment. Ely Place is Crown property and as such has a gated entrance. Turn left into Charterhouse Street. The green domes you can see ahead are set on Smithfield meat market. At the junction with Farringdon Street there is another pedestal surmounted by a griffon, marking the outer limit of the City of London. Turn right at the traffic lights into Farringdon Street.

Walk under the decorative bridge, which was built in 1868, and past Turnagain Lane. This street got its unusual name because people who wanted to go to the Fleet River had to turn round, as there was no bridge to cross over. It is interesting to see No.26 Farringdon Street, which was built in 1886 and is now sandwiched between two giant modern office blocks. Continue to Caroone House, No.14 Farringdon Street. This was the site of the Congressional Memorial Hall, where the **Labour Party** (10) was formed in 1900, which was built on the land where the ancient Fleet prison formerly stood. A bronze plaque is by the entrance. Ahead is Ludgate Circus, where on the corner with Fleet Street on the right, there is a large bronze plaque commemorating **Edgar Wallace** (11). Before receiving acclaim as a novelist and playwright, he worked as a Fleet Street journalist.

Cross back over Farringdon Street to the corner with Ludgate Hill. Here there is a blue plaque, which records that ***The Daily Courant*** (12) was printed in a house formerly near this spot. This was the first London newspaper, published over 300 years ago in 1702.

Continue along Ludgate Hill. On the wall of the church of St Martin within Ludgate there is a plaque commemorating **Ludgate** (13). This gate, originally built in Roman times, was demolished in 1760. Walking in the direction of St Paul's Cathedral you will find a turning on the left called Ave Maria Lane. At the end of the first building is the entrance to Stationer's Hall and in the courtyard you will find a plaque commemorating **Wynkyn de Worde** (14). A pupil of William Caxton, he set up a printing press on this site in 1500 from which he produced hundreds of books.

Now go to the left side of St Paul's Cathedral, where prior to redevelopment there was a large building called Juxon House. This is the site of a drapery house, where **George Williams** (15), with 11 other men, formed the YMCA in 1844. Walking on and bearing left will bring you into Paternoster Row. A plaque has been placed here by the Pennsylvania Library Association to honour **John Newbery** (16), a bookseller, author and publisher, who lived and worked in a house that was once on this site. He specialised in children's books. Now turn right into New Change.

Walk along New Change, past the rear of the cathedral, to St Augustine's House. Here there is a blue plaque marking the site of the first **St Paul's School** (17), which stood on this site from 1512–1884 (below). Continue on to the end of the road and the steps leading up to the churchyard. Round the corner, just past the steps, is a plaque on the boundary wall. This is easily missed because of the plants and shrubs surrounding. The plaque marks the site of six successive livery halls of the **Cordwainers' Company** (18). The last was destroyed in the Blitz of 1941. This plaque would have been better placed on the balustrade of the steps.

Turn back into New Change and then right into Watling Street. An interesting pedestal with a bust of Admiral Arthur Phillip (1738-1814), first governor of Australia, stands on the side. You will see a plaque ahead on the building marked 25 Cannon Street. This commemorates the church of **St John the Evangelist** (19). It was dedicated in the 13th century, and after improvements was finally destroyed in the 1666 Great Fire of London. At the other end of Watling Street, at No.61, there is a rectangular green plaque on the site of the headquarters of the **London Salvage Corps** (20). This corps was set up by insurance companies, its duties being taken over in 1984 by the London Fire Brigade.

Turn right into Queen Street and cross over Cannon Street. The black-painted brick building on the right, No.28, has a plaque on its boundary wall. This marks the site of the church of **St Thomas the Apostle** (21), which was also destroyed by the 1666 Great Fire of London.

Walk the short distance back to Cannon Street and turn right. The main entrance to Cannon Street station has another blue plaque which records the site of a church destroyed by the Great Fire. This was **St Mary Bothaw** (22). A 'haw' was a yard and the derivation of the church's name suggests that it was close to a boat yard. Opposite, at No.110 Cannon Street, you can see the ancient London Stone set into the wall. Its significance in pre-history is uncertain, but historians consider it to have been the measuring point for distances from London in Roman times. The leader of the 1450 rebellion, Jack Cade, is said to have struck the stone with his sword and proclaimed himself 'Lord of the City'. Turn back and left into Dowgate Hill. Then turn right into Cloak Lane.

Walk along Cloak Lane to the red-brick building, where you will find a plaque marking the site of **Cutlers Hall** (23). The first was built in 1285 in Poultry, and the earliest at this site was built in the 15th century. Successive halls continued here until 1883, when the company moved to its present site, at Warwick Lane. Turn left into College Hill.

There are four plaques in this short street. The first is at No.22 on the left. **Turners Hall** (24) stood here 1736–66. Turners made furniture and other items using a lathe. A few doors along a plaque records the site of the home of **Richard Whittington** (25). He was four times Lord Mayor of London, not thrice, as the nursery rhyme states. On the opposite side of the street another blue plaque informs us that the **Duke of Buckingham** (26) lived in a house on this site. He was a friend of Charles II and spent many years in Parliament. A further plaque for **Richard Whittington** (27) is ahead on the rear of the church of St Michael Paternoster Royal. This states that he was buried here. Turn left and right through the gardens, down to Upper Thames Street.

You can see a blue plaque across the road. This was the site of the hall of **The Worshipful Company of Joiners and Ceilers** (28). The hall was situated at this spot 1603–1796. It is not necessary to cross over Upper Thames Street unless you would like to see the plaque close-up.

Turn right and walk along Upper Thames Street, around the church of St James Garlickhythe and left at Doby court. Note the interesting clock. Continue on past the ascending staircase, under the bridge and turn right at Huggin Hill. Just past the barrier you will see an opening on the left leading to Cleary Garden. Walk in, going up the steps to a small delightful square (right). The blue plaque commemorates **Fred Cleary** (29). He was a councillor and property developer who seized every opportunity to add beauty to the city with the addition of gardens and open spaces.

Walk up and turn left into Queen Victoria Street. Continue on to the second turning, which is Lambeth Hill. A plaque here is on the site of the **Blacksmith's Hall** (30), which stood 1668–1785. The next turning to the left off Queen Victoria Street is Peter's Hill. On the international headquarters of the Salvation Army a similar style of plaque records the site of **Upholders' Hall** (31) (below), which was destroyed in the Great Fire of 1666. The upholders were upholsterers and the livery company is still in existence. Ahead you can see the Millenium Bridge and the Tate Modern gallery across the Thames.

Continuing along Queen Victoria Street you will see the Royal College of Arms across the road. Just past the next turning is Faraday House, almost opposite the church of St Benet and White Lion Street. This is on the site of the **Doctors' Commons** (32). The 'doctors' were advocates and doctors of law.

Turn in to Godliman Street, which you will have just passed. Knightrider Street runs across this turning. The left side is now contained in premises owned by British Telecom. To see the plaque of **Thomas Linacre** (33) it is necessary to gain permission from the gatekeeper. Linacre was the physician to kings Henry VII and VIII, and was the founder and first president of the Royal College of Physicians. He lived in a house on this site.

Continue the walk up Godliman Street and turn left into Carter Lane. A short way along you will see a sign denoting Bell Yard. Here there is a small stone plaque recording the site of the **Bell Inn** (34). It was from this spot that Richard Quiney wrote a letter to William Shakespeare in 1598. The original is still preserved at Stratford-upon-Avon. Continue past Addle Hill and turn left into Wardrobe Place. This entranceway is easily passed. It is before you get to St Andrew's Hill. No.5 Wardrobe Place is the site of **The King's Wardrobe** (35). Before the Great Fire of 1666, the king's ceremonial clothes and those of his ministers were stored here. Walk to the very end of Carter Lane. The last building on the corner is No.7 Ludgate Broadway. It is marked as the site of the 13th century **Blackfriars' Priory** (36).

Turn right and then left at Pilgrim Street, then turn left again at New Bridge Street. The plaque marking the site of **Bridewell Palace** (37) is across the road at No.14, past the traffic lights and Bridewell Place. This plaque gives full details of its history. Continue down, turning right at Tudor Street and again at Dorset Rise. On the left side, opposite Dorset Buildings, there is a plaque marking the site of the **Salisbury Court Playhouse** (38). This theatre opened in 1629 and had a chequered history. In 1649 its interior was devastated by soldiers. It reopened after the Restoration, to be finally destroyed in the Great Fire of 1666.

Continue to Salisbury Square, where there is a memorial in the middle to **Robert Wakeman** (39). He was a Lord Mayor of London and Member of Parliament. Walking on into Salisbury Court you will find a blue plaque on the left, commemorating the office of the first edition of the *Sunday Times* (40). Across the road there is a plaque marking the birthplace of **Samuel Pepys** (41).

Turn left into Fleet Street. At No.78 there is a bronze bust and plaque commemorating **T.P. O'Conner** (42). He was a journalist and Parliamentarian. It states 'His pen could lay bare the bones of a book or the soul of a statesman in a few vivid lines'. At No.68, which is on the corner of Whitefriars Street, there are two rectangular plaques (left). One states that the offices of the **Anti-Corn-Law League** (43) were situated here. This mentions **Richard Bright** and **Richard Cobden**. The other plaque mentions two famous clockmakers, **Thomas Tompion** and **George Graham** (44). Turn left into Bouverie Street. Beneath the overhanging windows of No.6 is a plaque on the site of a home of the essayist and critic **William Hazlitt** (45).

Return to Fleet Street and cross over to Johnson's Court, between Nos 166 and 167. Here a blue plaque records that **Dr Samuel Johnson** (46) lived in a house on this site 1765–76. Walk round to Gough Square and you will find an original house of **Dr Samuel Johnson** (47) with a brown RSA plaque. He lived here 1746–59. The house is now a museum devoted to him. Walking on you will see ahead the statue of Dr Johnson's cat Hodge. Also, through the archway, is a cannon in Gunpowder Square. Turn right into Wine Office Court. As you walk past Ye Olde Cheshire Cheese, read the interesting history. Returning to Fleet Street, turn right, cross over and continue to No.37. This was the site of the **Mitre Tavern** (48), which was a favourite haunt of Dr Johnson, his biographer, James Boswell and also Oliver Goldsmith. At No.18 Fleet Street a plaque marks the first offices of the **Automobile Association** (49). Cross over to Chancery Lane. A short way along at No.5 there is a plaque marking the site of the **Old Sarjeants Inn** (50), which stood here 1415–1910.

Return to Fleet Street, bearing right. The Wig & Pen, which was built in 1625, claims to be the only building in Fleet Street still standing that survived the Great Fire of London. A further plaque can be found at No.1 Fleet Street, where the **Devil's Tavern** (51) was formerly situated. You are now opposite the Royal Courts of Justice. In the centre of the road stands a plinth commemorating Temple Bar. Successive gateways to the City stood here from the 13th century until 1878. The memorial has a statue of Queen Victoria, surmounted by the City of London symbolic griffon. Walk on and turn left at Essex Street. Etched into the wall, next to the first door on the right-hand side, is a plaque headed **Essex Street** (52). This is followed by a list of notable persons who have lived in the street.

There is now just one plaque left on this walk before reaching the nearest underground station. Retrace your steps a short distance in Fleet Street and turn right into Middle Temple Lane. Halfway down you will find a turning on the left with an archway entrance, called Middle Temple Row. This is opposite No.1 Plowden Buildings. A short way along Middle Temple Row there is a white plaque on the red-brick building. This marks the birthplace of the essayist and critic **Charles Lamb** (53).

The tube station is less than a quarter of a mile from this point. Return to Middle Temple Lane, turn left and walk past the gardens to the Embankment. Turning right, you will find it is a short walk to Temple tube station. Looking across the River Thames en route, you have a good view of the London Eye, Big Ben and other landmarks.

Walk 17
Clerkenwell

Distance:	4½ miles, plus ¾ mile for variation (A) and ¾ mile for variation (B)
Time taken:	2 hours, plus 20 mins (A) and 20 mins (B).
Number of plaques:	37
Nearest tube stations:	Farringdon, King's Cross, Barbican
Bus routes:	8, 19, 25, 30, 38, 45, 55, 56, 63, 73, 171a, 214, 242

CLERKENWELL is an area that is seeing great change, and the recent building developments offer the walker an opportunity to see the old with the new. This walk touches a local historic trail, the London jewellery quarter, part of the City of London, Charterhouse and Bart's hospital. There are two additional sections that can be added to the walk.

The tour starts at Farringdon station, where you will emerge into Cowcross Street. Turn right and then left into Farringdon Road. At the traffic lights you can see the griffon in the centre of the road which signifies the boundary of the City of London. Cross over Charterhouse Street and turn left into Snow Hill. You will pass the commemorative plaque marking the opening of Smithfield Market in 1888. Just past Cock Lane, on the police station, there is a blue rectangular plaque marking the site where the **Saracen's Head Inn** (1) stood from olden

times until 1868. Stow described it in 1598 as 'a fair and large inn for the receipt of travellers'. Ahead you can see the gilt figure with the scales of justice surmounting the Old Bailey criminal court. Walk back and turn right into Cock Lane. It was on this very corner that John Bunyan collapsed and died in 1688.

On a corner building at the bottom of Cock Lane there is a statue of a gilt cherub. This is where the Great Fire of London is reputed to have ended. The accompanying plaque will give you the history of the cherub. Turn left on coming out of Cock Lane and cross the road. Just past the bus stop you will find a stone plaque next to the red telephone box. This was laid by Lady Ludlow to commemorate **Dame Joanna Astley** (2), the nurse of King Henry VI who lived in a house on this site.

Continue past the King Henry VIII gate, erected in 1702. If you wish to go into St Bartholemew's Hospital you will find that there are conducted tours at certain times, as well as a museum, which is unfortunately closed on Mondays. Proceeding on you will

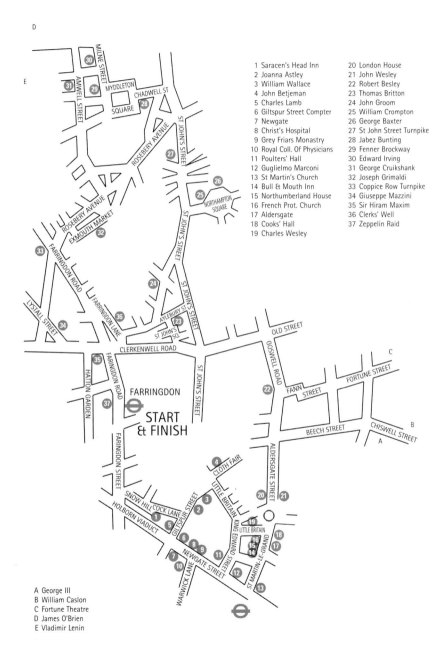

1 Saracen's Head Inn
2 Joanna Astley
3 William Wallace
4 John Betjeman
5 Charles Lamb
6 Giltspur Street Compter
7 Newgate
8 Christ's Hospital
9 Grey Friars Monastery
10 Royal Coll. Of Physicians
11 Poulters' Hall
12 Guglielmo Marconi
13 St Martin's Church
14 Bull & Mouth Inn
15 Northumberland House
16 French Prot. Church
17 Aldersgate
18 Cooks' Hall
19 Charles Wesley

20 London House
21 John Wesley
22 Robert Besley
23 Thomas Britton
24 John Groom
25 William Crompton
26 George Baxter
27 St John Street Turnpike
28 Jabez Bunting
29 Fenner Brockway
30 Edward Irving
31 George Cruikshank
32 Joseph Grimaldi
33 Coppice Row Turnpike
34 Giuseppe Mazzini
35 Sir Hiram Maxim
36 Clerks' Well
37 Zeppelin Raid

A George III
B William Caslon
C Fortune Theatre
D James O'Brien
E Vladimir Lenin

reach a large wall plaque recording that the Scottish patriot **William Wallace** (3) was executed near this spot. You will perhaps remember Hollywood's recreation of his story in the film *Braveheart*. Ahead is the priory church of St Bartholemew-the-Great, which was founded in 1123 by the prior Rahere. He was buried here in 1143 and the present tomb dates from the 16th century.

Next to the church is a small turning called Cloth Fair. This is named after the mediaeval Bartholemew's Fair which was held annually and where cloth merchants bartered. Walk through to the restaurant named Betjemans. A blue plaque in Cloth Court on the side of the building (above) records that the Poet Laureate **Sir John Betjeman** (4) lived here.

Return to Giltspur Street, passing Dame Joanna Astley's plaque again. At No.10, next to the Church of the Holy Sepulchre, you will see a bust of **Charles Lamb** (5) (left). He was a 'bluecoat boy' for seven years at the nearby school. The bust and plaque were moved to this position in 1962. In mediaeval times knights would ride through Giltspur Street on their way to tournaments at nearby Smithfield. Their shiny spurs were later made in this street. A debtors' prison, known as the **Giltspur Street Compter** (6) stood here from around 1790 until 1854. A Corporation of London plaque marks the spot on the last building across the road, next to the public house. Turn left into Newgate Street.

Across the road is the Old Bailey central criminal court. On the outer wall, which is in Newgate Street, there is a plaque commemorating **Newgate** (7). Traces of a Roman gate have been found and successive city gates stood here until 1777. A short way along Newgate Street, there are two more plaques on No.106. These are for the site of **Christ's Hospital** (8) (1552–1902) and the site of **Grey Friars Monastery** (9) (1225–1538). The former was founded by Edward VI as a hospital for orphans, the latter by four Franciscan friars.

Cross over the road to Warwick Lane. The 19th-century Cutlers Hall has an interesting terracotta frieze. Next door is a plaque commemorating the **Royal College of Physicians** (10). The college was located here after the Great Fire of London and remained until 1825, when it transferred to Pall Mall.

Return to Newgate Street and continue to King Edward Street on the other side. Here you will see the ruin of Christ Church, Greyfriars. This was one of Sir Christopher Wren's churches, destroyed by incendiary bombs in World War Two. Its history dates from 1228 and is detailed on the site. Just past the garden, in King Edward Street, there is a plaque recording the site of a **Poulters' Hall** (11), which did not survive the Great Fire of London. Ahead is the National Postal Museum, with a statue of Sir Rowland Hill standing by the curbside.

Return to the traffic lights and cross the road, to continue along Newgate Street. Ahead you can see the British Telecom building with a brown plaque recording that **Guglielmo Marconi** (12) made the first public transmission of wireless signals from this site on 27 July 1896. Continue along Newgate Street and turn left into St Martin-le-Grand.

Across the road on Empire House there is a plaque marking the site of the collegiate church of **St Martin** (13). This was founded in the 11th century, rebuilt in 1368, and remained until it was demolished in 1548. It was a safe sanctuary where jewellery and lace making flourished.

Cross back over the road and just past Angel Street you will find Nomura House at No.1

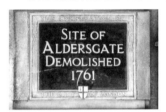

St Martin-le-Grand. There are three plaques here. The first commemorates the **Bull and Mouth Inn** (14). This was a large coaching inn, demolished in 1888. The inn sign is in the nearby Museum of London. The second plaque marks the site of **Northumberland House** (15). This dated from 1352 and belonged to the Dukes of Northumberland. The third plaque is on the site of a 16th-century **French Protestant Church** (16), which was also demolished in 1888. Immediately opposite this third plaque is another marking the site of **Aldersgate** (17), which was demolished in 1761.

A little further along on the same side a blue plaque on No.10 records the site of **Cooks' Hall** (18). This site was originally acquired for the Cooks' Company in 1500 and successive halls were built. The last was burnt down in 1771. Cross the road to Postman's Park.

Postman's Park is so named because of its proximity to the post office and the fact that postmen often relax here to eat their lunchtime sandwiches. In the centre, a long wall conceived from an idea of the artist G.F. Watts is emblazoned with plaques commemorating individual heroes. After you have read these interesting heroic stories, walk back a dozen paces from the right end of the wall. Turn and look across the road running alongside. This is Little Britain, where you can just see the blue plaque above the doorway of No.13, which reads 'Adjoining this site stood the house of John Bray, scene of **Charles Wesley's** (19) evangelical conversion, May 21st 1738'. Return to Aldersgate Street and turn left towards the Museum of London.

If you like, go down Little Britain for a close-up of the Wesley plaque. The Museum of London is well worth a visit if you have time and there is also an excellent restaurant for lunch or light refreshment.

To continue the walk, go left round the roundabout to the continuation of Aldersgate Street. At No.171 a new building named London House has been built on the site of the original **London House** (20), which is commemorated with two blue plaques. This was the home of the bishops of London after the Restoration, and was destroyed by fire in 1766. Across the road, near the telephone boxes, there is a small plaque set into the wall, which marks the probable place where **John Wesley** (21) encountered his divine inspiration.

It is at this point you must decide whether to continue the walk as outlined or add the extra twenty minutes of section (A) detailed on page 121.

To continue with the main tour walk to the very end of Aldersgate Street, to the point where it meets Goswell Road. This is past Barbican station and opposite Fann Street. A blue plaque at first-floor level commemorates **Robert Besley** (22). He was an alderman and Lord Mayor of London. A drinking fountain erected in his memory existed near here from 1878 to 1934. Across the road you can see a stone frieze mounted on a plinth. This was formerly on the premises of a local gold refinery and when the building was demolished in 1962 the frieze was rescued. From here it is over 700 yards to the next plaque.

Walk further along Goswell Road and turn left at the traffic lights into Clerkenwell Road. Cross over St John Street and turn right into St John's Square. Follow the pathway into Jerusalem Passage. At the very end, on the corner of Aylesbury Street, is a plaque on the site of the home of **Thomas Britton** (23). He was a remarkable man. A coal merchant by trade, he had many intellectual interests. He conducted a weekly musical evening, which several eminent composers of the day, including Handel, regularly attended. He was also one of the founders of the British Library.

Turn left at Aylesbury Street and take the first right into Sekforde Street. Don't be fooled by the stone plaque on the red-brick building. There is no inscription. The house at No.8 was the home of **John Groom** (24), who founded his first home for disabled people near here in 1866. This street is on the 'Clerkenwell Historic Trail'. It is over a quarter of a mile from here to the next plaque.

Walking on, cross the road at the traffic lights and continue in the same direction along St John Street. Take the second turning on the right, Wyclif Street, which will bring you into Northampton Square. Turning to the left you will see a bronze plaque commemorating **William Crompton, 1st Marquess of Northampton** (25), after whom the square is named. Further round, on the City University building, a plaque marks the site of the workshops of **George Baxter** (26). He was an engraver and printer who invented a process for colour printing. Return to St John Street and turn right.

The third turning on the left is Lloyd's Row, where there is a large block of flats named Tunbridge House at the junction. On the corner of the building there is a green plaque marking the site of the **St John Street Turnpike** (27). The turnpike stood here from around 1746 until 1830 and was thought worthy of a plaque by the local council.

Continue up St John Street, past Roseberry Avenue, where Sadlers Wells Opera House is situated, and turn left at Chadwell Street. Upon coming into Myddelton Square you will find a green plaque on the corner house on the left side. This is No.30, where **Dr Jabez Bunting** (28) lived 1833–58. He was the leader of the Methodist Church after the death of John Wesley. Myddelton Square, which was named after Sir High Myddleton, was built between 1824 and 1827.

Cross the top of Chadwell Street and walk around the right side of the square. Ahead you can see a brown plaque marking the home of **Lord Fenner Brockway** (29) from 1908 to 1910. You will notice it does not give the date of his death (1988), as it was erected during his lifetime. He was an eminent socialist politician and a founder of the Campaign for Nuclear Disarmament (CND).

Turn right into Mylne Street and upon entering Claremont Square turn to the left. Continue round the square to No.4, which is on the left before the main road. The plaque here commemorates **Edward Irving** (30), who was a clergyman who founded the Catholic Apostolic Church.

At this point you should decide whether to proceed with the regular walk or continue with the addition (B) on page 121. If not proceed as follows.

Turn around and walk ahead into Amwell Street. The engraver and illustrator **George Cruikshank** (31) lived at No.71 in 1824–49. Walk down Amwell Street past Great Percy Street, cross over Roseberry Avenue and continue through Rosomon Street. Turn right into Exmouth Market. A blue plaque at No.56 records that the great clown **Joseph Grimaldi** (32) lived here for 10 years. His name 'Joey' came to be used by later clowns.

Continue, turning left into Roseberry Avenue. Ahead is the GPO sorting office of Mount Pleasant. On the corner of that building there is a green plaque marking the site of the

Coppice Row Turnpike (33), which stood here at around the same time as the St John Street Turnpike.

Continue along Roseberry Avenue until you reach Laystall Street. Turning left, walk down to No.10. A large elaborate plaque here commemorates **Giuseppe Mazzini** (34), the Italian nationalist leader. Turn left again at Clerkenwell Road. You will see a blue plaque on the corner of Hatton Garden (left) as you pass. This is where **Sir Hiram Maxim** (35) invented his machine gun in 1883.

Walking along Clerkenwell Road, you will cross over Farringdon Road and Vine Street Bridge. Take the first turning left, which is Farringdon Lane. **Clerks' Well** (36) is at Nos 14–16. The well, which gave its name to the district, can be seen through the window of the present building. It was first recorded in 1174, when parish clerks performed miracle plays here, hence its name. There is a small rectangular blue plaque and details of the history can be read through the windows of the building.

Returning to Clerkenwell Road you pass the old courthouse, now a Masonic temple. Turn right and then left into Farringdon Road. Walk on to the last plaque of this tour at No.61. It informs you that the premises were totally destroyed by a **Zeppelin Raid** (37) in 1915 and were rebuilt two years later. Turn left at the traffic lights and you will have returned to Farringdon tube station.

Off route plaques, for the more energetic walker

(A) From **Wesley** continue along Aldersgate Street and turn right at Beech Street. This is a tunnel of the Barbican estate and leads on to Chiswell Street, where you will see the old Whitbread Brewery. Inset in the wall is a plaque stating that 'Their Majesties King **George III** (A) and **Queen Charlotte** were received in this brewery by **Samuel Whitbread** 24th May 1787'. Walk on to 21–3 Chiswell Street, which is the building just past Bunhill Row. A blue plaque marks the site of the foundry of the typesetter **William Caslon** (B). It stood here from 1737 until 1909. Retrace your steps along Chiswell Street and turn right at Whitecross Street. Turn left at Fortune Street, next to the Two Brewers public house. Opposite there is a plaque marking the site of the **Fortune Theatre** (C). This was built in 1600, burnt down in 1621 and rebuilt, finally being demolished in 1661. Walk along Fortune Street and cross to Fann Street. This will bring you to the next plaque of the main tour.

(B) From **Irving** continue to Pentonville Road. Turn to the left and cross over the road. Turn right at Cynthia Road, then left at the end into Donegal Street. On the wall of the school opposite is a green plaque commemorating **James 'Bronterre' O'Brien** (D). He was an Irish journalist and Chartist who lived near here 1863–4. There is now nearly one third of a mile to walk between this and the next plaque.

Turn left at the end of the road and cross over Pentonville Road at the traffic lights into Penton Rise. Turn left at Vernon Rise, which leads into Percy Circle. The corner building on your right sports a plaque with the name of **Vladimir Lenin** (E). The Russian revolutionary leader stayed at No.6 Percy Circus in 1905. Turn left, continuing along Great Percy Street and turning left at the end into Amwell Street. This will bring you directly to the next plaque of the tour (Cruikshank).

Walk 18
City

Distance:	4¾ miles (7.24 km)
Time taken:	2¼ hours
Number of plaques:	55
Nearest tube stations:	Bank, Liverpool Street, Monument
Bus routes:	8, 11, 15, 26, 35, 40, 47, 48, 56, 76, 78, 133, 149, 214, 242

THIS walk is centred on the business and financial heart of London. The area has suffered two great catastrophes in the last 350 years. Firstly, the Great Fire of London in 1666, and secondly the Blitz of the World War Two. There are very few old buildings surviving and the modern buildings are tall. The noise of traffic, together with the dust and noise of construction work, tends to deter the walker, but there are many interesting places to see and visit. Roman and Saxon remains are constantly being discovered, as excavations begin on new building sites. Remains of the old city wall have also been preserved.

In mediaeval times London contained more churches than any other city in Europe. Most of the plaques seen in this walk are of the rectangular blue glazed type erected by the Corporation of the City of London and commemorate many of these churches and the sites of livery halls.

Commencing the walk at Bank underground station, it is best to leave by exit No.5, emerging by the right-hand side staircase to Cornhill. The first plaque to be seen is a rectangular one commemorating the founder of Guy's Hospital **Thomas Guy** (1). He lived at No.1 Cornhill and had his bookshop on this site.

Now cross at the traffic lights, walking past the Royal Exchange and the Bank of England to Prince's Street, on the far side. Within a few yards on the left there is a plaque marking the site of the **General Letter Office** (2), which stood here 1653–66. The first ever postmarks were struck in 1661, 179 years before the first postage stamp was printed.

Walk back past the station entrances to the road junction. Across the road is the Mansion House, with its six magnificent Corinthian columns. On the front of the building you can see a blue plaque with the wording 'Adjoining this spot stood the **Stocks Market** (3) 1282–1737'.

A set of stocks originally stood on this site, after which the market was named. Successive buildings housed a fish and meat market and later a general market with fruit and vegetables. The area was cleared in 1737 to make way for the Mansion House and the market transferred to Smithfield.

Walk to the right and you will find, around the corner of the Mansion House in

Walbrook, a similar plaque recording the site of the church of **St Mary Woolchurch Haw** (4) (above). It got its name from the fact that wool was weighed in the churchyard. The word 'haw' means yard.

Cross the road at the traffic lights into Poultry. This street, as you probably will guess, was named after the many poulterers who once lived here. The left-hand side, at No.1, has been completely redeveloped, with new offices, shops and restaurants. Opposite are the iron gates of St Mildred's Court, where there are two plaques. **St Mildred's Church** (5), was first recorded in the 12th century. It was burnt down in the Great Fire of 1666 and rebuilt by Wren, before finally being demolished in 1872. To the right is the plaque of **Elizabeth Fry** (6), the great prison reformer who lived in a house on this site 1800–9. A few yards away, a plaque can be found on the Midland Bank, marking the site of the birthplace of **Thomas Hood** (7). This poet and humorist has four commemorative plaques in different parts of London.

Walk along Poultry to Old Jewry. On the corner building is the plaque of **St Mary Cole Church** (8). It was built by a man named Cole and was the church where St Thomas Becket was baptised. Continue to No.11 Old Jewry. The **Great Synagogue** (9) stood on this site from early times until 1272. The Jews were expelled from Great Britain in 1291 by Edward I and suffered many indignities. More than 500 of them were massacred in this area in 1262.

Across the road is Frederick's Place. No.3 has a plaque commemorating **Edwin Waterhouse** (10). He was an eminent accountant whose offices were in this building 1899–1905. Opposite, at No.6, a blue plaque informs us that the Prime Minister **Benjamin Disraeli** (11) worked in this building 1821–4. Retrace your steps and turn right into Cheapside, which is the continuation of Poultry.

No.90 Cheapside corners with Ironmonger Lane. **St Thomas Becket** (12) was born in a house near this spot in 1118. He became Archbishop of Canterbury and was murdered in the cathedral. Apart from the rectangular blue plaque there is a small bronze one below his effigy.

Cross over Cheapside and walk into Queen Street, almost opposite. Turn left at Pancras Lane, where halfway down in front of a small wooded enclosure is the plaque of **St Pancras Church** (13). This church, which was first recorded in 1257, was one of those destroyed in 1666 by the Great Fire. Continue to the blue plaque by the vehicle entranceway in the corner of the road. This marks the site of the church of **St Benet Sherehog** (14). On the adjacent wall similar wording is etched into the stonework. This church was in the centre of the wool district and a 'sherehog' was the name for a castrated ram.

Return to Queen Street, turn right and cross over Cheapside into King Street. As you cross Cheapside, glancing to the left you will see the church and steeple of St Mary-le-Bow, where the Bow Bells are housed. Anyone born within the sound of these bells is said to be a true cockney. Turn left at Trump Street and left again at Milk Street. There is a plaque at No.3, above a vehicle entrance, which commemorates the **City of London School** (15). This stood here from 1835 to 1882, before transferring to the Thames Embankment because of lack of space. Turn around and go under the archway, turning right and then immediately left into Gutter Lane. Almost opposite is a plaque marking the site of **Broderers Hall** (16), which was bombed in 1940. The Broderers Company was the livery company for embroidery and lace making.

Turn left and walk past Saddler's Hall to Cheapside. Continue right and then turn right again, passing St Paul's Cathedral, into Foster Lane. A blue plaque on the large red-brick building, Empire House, marks the site of the church of **St Leonard** (17). This church was another destroyed in the Great Fire of London. Proceed along Foster Lane and turn right at Gresham Street. Across the road, a further church destroyed in the Great Fire is commemorated. The plaque marking the site of **St John Zachary** (18) is set into the brick wall.

Walk on and turn left into Wood Street. The church tower ahead is all that remains of St Alban's after it was bombed in 1940. Cross London Wall and continue ahead to St Alphage Garden. On the side of Roman House, a plaque marks the site of **Cripplegate** (19). This was one of the city gates originally built by the Romans. It was rebuilt several times until it was finally demolished in 1760. Walk on to Fore Street on the other side of Roman House. Etched into the wall an inscription records that the **First Bomb** (20) to fall on the City of London during the World War Two landed here.

Return to Wood Street and walk back, again crossing London Wall, and turn left at Love Lane. At the end of this short street, cornering Aldermanbury, are the remains of the church of St Mary Aldermanbury. This church was first mentioned in 1181 and has been destroyed twice, in 1666 and 1940, when the second church, built by Wren, was bombed. Fabric from the church was used in a church in Fulton, Missouri, US, which was built as a memorial to Sir Winston Churchill. A bust of William Shakespeare stands in the grounds. It is worth stopping to read the narrative on the pedestal of this statue and the large stone plaque at the head of the church foundations.

Cross over Aldermanbury and take the steps down at the side of the Guildhall Library. Cross the square and continue past the offices of the Corporation of London, down the steps leading to Basinghall Street. On the wall at the centre of these steps is a blue plaque marking the site of **St Michael Bassishaw** (21). This was another of Sir Christopher Wren's churches. It was designed in 1676 and demolished in 1900.

Turn right and walk down Basinghall Street. An interesting diversion is to walk into Guildhall Buildings to see the newly restored exterior of the Guildhall and possibly the art gallery or library. Proceeding along Basinghall Street, turn left at the bottom and continue across the traffic lights into Lothbury. Just past the beginning of Moorgate there is a small alleyway called Founders Court, where a plaque at the entrance commemorates the first **Founders' Hall** (22). The original founders cast bronze and brass objects and their present day livery hall is at Cloth Fair, EC1.

Turn right into Moorgate and walk up to the second turning, Telegraph Street. A blue plaque on Kent House marks the site of the home of the poet **Robert Bloomfield** (23). Continue along Moorgate to London Wall. On the opposite corner of Moorgate and London Wall there is a plaque marking the site of **Moorgate** (24). This gate was built in 1415 and survived until 1761. Diagonally across London Wall you can see a large building called Moor House. Here there is a plaque on the site of the birthplace of **Sir Ebenezer Howard** (25). His town planning designs led to the first garden cities of Letchworth and Welwyn.

Continue along Moorgate a short way to the John Keats public house. This is No.85, where a plaque at the first-floor level marks the birthplace of the poet **John Keats** (26). Return to London Wall and turn left. On the corner of Circus Place there is a plaque recording the site of the **Second Bethlehem Hospital** (27), which stood here 1676–1815. John Evelyn compared this magnificent hospital to the Tuileries in Paris. It was afterwards transferred to Lambeth.

Proceed along London Wall and turn left at Blomfield Street. On the far corner of the Finsbury Circus entrance, a plaque marks the site of **St Mary Moorfields Church** (28). Turn

right into Liverpool Street and you will find the plaque commemorating the **First Bethlehem Hospital** (29), which is past the entrance of Liverpool Street Station, opposite White Hart Court.

Walk through 'The Arcade' and turn left at the end emerging into Old Broad Street. Cross London Wall and continue into Old Broad Street. At the foot of Tower 42 Financial Centre, formerly the NatWest Tower, there is a plaque marking the site of the home of **Sir Thomas Gresham** (30). He was a merchant and philanthropist who founded and built the Royal Exchange. Unfortunately a small kiosk type shop was built after the plaque was erected and it is now difficult to see.

Continue to the Stock Exchange building at the end of Old Broad Street. This was the site of the birthplace of **Cardinal Newman** (31) (1801–90). Turn right. The plaque on the site of **St Bartholemew by the Exchange** (32) is at 62–3 Threadneedle Street. This is almost opposite the statue of the philanthropist George Peabody.

Turn and walk the other way along Threadneedle Street. Just past Old Broad Street is a plaque marking the site of **St Anthony's Hospital and the French Protestant Church** (33). This is at No.53 Threadneedle Street, opposite Finch Lane. The very end building of Threadneedle Street, cornering with Bishopsgate, has a blue plaque marking the site of the church of **St Martin Outwich** (34). This was founded in 1403, burnt down in 1765 and rebuilt in 1796. It was demolished in 1874.

Turn right into Gracechurch Street and walk along to Bell Inn Yard. A blue plaque here records the site of the **Crosskeys Inn** (35), which once stood in the shadow of a church dedicated to St Peter.

Continue on to the junction with Fenchurch Street and cross over to the Royal & Sun Alliance building where you will see an inscription to the right of the main entrance. This records that a **Roman Basilica** (36) dating from around 120 AD stood on this site. Turn around and as you walk back across the traffic lights to Cornhill you will see a blue plaque on the corner building in Gracechurch Street. This marks the site of **The Standard in Cornhill** (37), which was a place where water was pumped from the Thames until around 1603 and also a measuring point for the City of London.

Further along Cornhill you will find that the poet **Thomas Gray** (38) was born at No.39 and is commemorated by a bronze plaque bearing his bust. He is remembered for his *Elegy Written in a Country Churchyard*.

Turn left into St Michael's Alley. Here you will see a plaque on the site of London's **First Coffee House** (39), which was opened in 1652 by a man of Turkish origin.

Continue through to George Yard and turn right upon reaching Lombard Street, then right again into Birchin Lane. About halfway along Birchin Lane you will reach the large plaque commemorating **Captain Ralph Binney** (40). His heroic story is detailed on the plaque. Now go into Change Alley on the other side of the road. In the centre you can see a large round blue plaque marking the site of the King's Arms tavern, where the **Marine Society** (41) was founded in 1756.

Turn left and then left again into Lombard Street, walking past the church of St Edmund the King. Cross over Gracechurch Street at the traffic lights to the corner of Fenchurch Street. There is a plaque on a pillar at the front of this building. It marks the site of the church of **St Benet Gracechurch** (42). This church was mentioned in 1181, destroyed in 1666 by the Great Fire and rebuilt. Being little used in the 19th century it was demolished in 1876.

Walk back from this plaque and continue along Fenchurch Street, turning left into Lime Street. Proceed up to the Lloyds building. This building was opened in 1986 and shows a marked contrast to the early business, founded by Edward Lloyd in a coffee house during the 1680s. At the front of the building, opposite Fenchurch Avenue, are steps leading down to a lower floor level. On the wall at the side of these steps you will see the plaque commemorating **William Dockwra** (43), who established the first penny post in 1680. This was 160 years before the first adhesive postage stamp.

Return to Fenchurch Street and turn right, crossing over Gracechurch Street into Lombard Street. On the left you will find Plough Court, where a blue plaque in the entranceway marks the birthplace of the poet **Alexander Pope** (44). Continue to No.15 Lombard Street, which was the site of **Lloyds coffee house** (45). This became a meeting place for businessmen and the founding place of Lloyds Insurance Company.

Across the road you will find another entrance into Change Alley, where a blue plaque can be seen commemorating **Jonathon's coffee house** (46), which stood here between 1680 and 1778. Further along, on Coutts Bank at No.72, another blue plaque marks the site of the home of **Gregory de Rokesley** (47). He was eight times Lord Mayor of London in the 13th century.

Walk back along Lombard Street a short way and turn right into Clements Lane, opposite the church of St Edmund the King, continuing to No.27, next to St Clement's Court. Here a stone plaque commemorates **Dositey Obradovich** (48). He was a Serbian statesman who lived in a house on this site in 1784 (below).

Walk on and proceed around the junction of King William Street into Cannon Street. Continue and turn left at Laurence Pountney Hill, which is past Laurence Poutney Lane. At the bottom there is a plaque on the brick wall, marking the site of **Laurence Pountney Church and Corpus Christi College** (49). Both were destroyed in 1666. Continue ahead and turn left at the second turning into Martin Lane. The plaque marking the site of **St Martin Orgar Church** (50) is on the wall below railings halfway along the street.

Walking on will bring you back to Cannon Street, where you turn right. Cross over the large road junction to the beginning of Gracechurch Street. There is a plaque on No.51, which is the site of the home of **William Curtis** (51). He was a noted botanist who had gardens in Bermondsey and Lambeth.

Cross Eastcheap at the traffic lights, where on the corner of Fish Street Hill you can see the blue plaque marking the site of **St Leonard's Eastcheap** (52). This church was first mentioned in 1214 and was also known as St Leonard's Milkchurch. Take the next turning right, Pudding Lane. This is famous as the starting point of the Great Fire of London in 1666. Just past the bollards you will find a commemorative plaque on the left, where the baker's shop of **Thomas Faryner** (53) was situated and the fire began.

Walk towards the Monument and at knee height on Lloyds Bank to the right there is a plaque commemorating **St Margaret Fish Street Hill** (54). On the other side of the Monument is Monument Street, where you will find the final plaque of this tour. It is on the end building and commemorates the **First City Terminus** (55).

Having seen 55 plaques, you are now conveniently by Monument underground station.

Walk 19
Around Regent's Park

Distance:	3 miles (4.80km), 6 miles (9.7km), or 7 miles (11.25km)
Time taken:	1 hour (short walk), 2¼ hours (regular walk) and 3 hours (full walk)
Number of plaques:	26, 43 or 46
Nearest tube stations:	Marylebone, Baker Street, Regent's Park, Chalk Farm, Swiss Cottage
Bus routes:	C2, 13, 18, 24, 27, 30, 31, 82, 113, 168, 274

REGENT'S Park is one of the most delightful recreation areas of London. The area enclosed within the Outer Circle contains 487 acres. This includes London Zoo, a boating lake, an open-air theatre, a bandstand and many sports facilities. The Prince Regent was an ardent supporter of John Nash, who designed the beautiful terraces surrounding a large part of the perimeter. These were built early in the 19th century and were effectively completed by 1828. After World War Two they were greatly restored and bomb damage scars removed. Most of the terraces are now used as offices. This walk takes in the plaques around the park and could be combined with a visit to the zoo, a visit to Queen Mary's Gardens, a row on the lake or just a leisurely stroll to feed the ducks.

The walk commences at Marylebone station, which is on the Bakerloo Line. You will seem to be going in the wrong direction to visit the first plaque, but as it commemorates two people, it is worth the extra walking. Walk towards the Jarvis Marylebone Hotel, cross Harewood Avenue and turn right into Lisson Grove. No.116 is on the corner of Rossmore Road. At the side of the building a blue plaque commemorates the former residents **Charles Rossi** and **Benjamin Haydon** (1). Sculptor Charles Rossi originally had the house built (1808) and worked in his studio here. The artist Benjamin Haydon rented rooms from him in 1817 and left three years later. Not being successful in his lifetime he lived in an impoverished state and committed suicide in 1846.

Now turn and walk back down Lisson Grove, then turn left at Harewood Row. Walk past Marylebone Station to Dorset Square. Turning to the left you will find a blue plaque at No.28 Dorset Square. This was the home of the comedy actor **George Grossmith Snr** (2). He frequently took leading parts in Gilbert and Sullivan operettas and was a co-author with his brother of *Diary of a Nobody* (1892). Dorset Square was the original site of Lord's cricket ground. If you cross the square to the green hut on the other side you will find two plaques there. One commemorates **Thomas Lord** (3) and the other the **MCC** (4), which had its first match here in 1787. Cross over the road to No.1 on the corner of Melcome Street.

1 Rossi/Haydon
2 George Grossmith Snr
3 Thomas Lord
4 MCC
5 Free French Forces
6 Bentley Motor Car
7 H.G. Wells
8 Arnold Bennett
9 Sherlock Holmes
10 Sherlock Holmes
11 José de San Martin
12 E.H. Shepard

13 Cochrane/ Beatty
14 H.G. Wells
15 Anthony Salvin
16 Ralph Vaughan Williams
17 Francis Turner Palgrave
18 Dr Ernest Jones
19 Sir Charles Wyndham
20 Frederick D. Maurice
21 Dame Marie Tempest
22 Sir Charles Wheatstone
23 Henry Brook Adams
24 Sir Joseph Lister

25 Kenneth Williams
26 Fabian Society
27 Henry Mayhew
28 Charles R. Cockerell
29 Sir J.M. Salmond
30 George Cruikshank
31 Walter Sickert
32 Peggy Duff
33 John Desmond Bernal
34 Dylan Thomas
35 W.W. Jacobs
36 Constant Lambert

37 Sir Henry Wellcome
38 Roger Fenton
39 W.B. Yeats
40 Sylvia Plath
41 Dr Jose Rizal
42 Friedrich Engels
43 B.R. Ambedkar
44 Sir Henry Wood
45 Dame Clara Butt
46 Robert Polhill Bevan

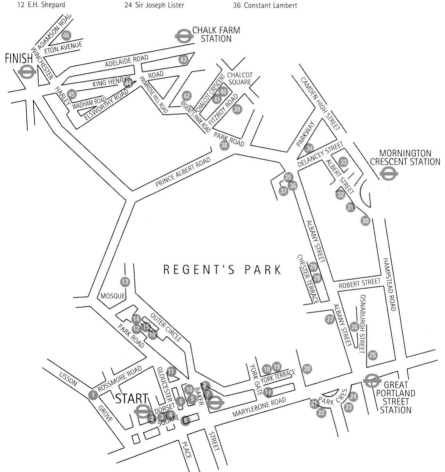

A bilingual plaque on this building states 'This plaque is erected to commemorate the deeds of the men and women of the **Free French Forces** (5) and their British comrades who left from this house on special missions to enemy occupied France and to honour those who did not return 1941–1944'. The stone plaque was unveiled by the Queen Mother in 1957.

Go into Melcome Street and turn left at Chagford Street. No.49 was the workshop where the first **Bentley Motor Car** (6) was produced in 1919. Return to Melcome Street and turn left to Baker Street. Looking across the road you can see two brown plaques set on either side of the entrance to Chiltern Court. These are for the novelists **Arnold Bennett** (7) and **H.G. Wells** (8). Both lived here in 1930.

Now re-cross Baker Street and walk up to the Abbey National Building Society, where there is a small oval plaque by the main entrance. This records the site of No.221B Baker Street, where the fictional detective **Sherlock Holmes** (9) lived. A few doors away can be found the **Sherlock Holmes** (10) museum. Although the museum is situated at No.237 Baker Street, there is a blue plaque marking it as 221B. If you have completed Walk 3 you will have already seen the last few plaques. Walk on and you will be in Park Road. At No.23 the South American leader and liberator **San Martin** (11) stayed a short time in 1824. Continue and cross the road, walking past the Royal College of Gynaecologists and Obstetricians, to Kent Terrace. A blue plaque at No.10 marks the home of **E.H. Shepard** (12). This popular cartoonist was the first to illustrate A.A. Milne's *Winnie the Pooh*.

Walk further along Park Road and turn right at Hanover Gate. Here you can see London's premier mosque, with its large golden dome. Turn left and the first house you will see is Hanover Lodge. It was built in 1827 to the design of the architect Decimus Burton and enlarged by Lutyens in 1909. The blue plaque on the house records two names, **Thomas Cochrane** (13) who lived here 1830–45, and another sailor **Admiral Beatty**, who lived here 1910–25. Walk back past the mosque and Hanover Gate and turn right into Hanover Terrace.

Hanover Terrace is a parade of houses designed by John Nash in 1822 and many notable people have lived here. The first of the three blue plaques to be found is at No.13. It is a second plaque on this walk for the novelist **H.G. Wells** (14) who lived and died at this address. The architect **Anthony Salvin** (15) lived at No.11. He was an authority in the restoration of ancient sites, notably the Tower of London and the castles of Windsor, Warwick and Caernarvon. No.10 was the home of composer **Ralph Vaughan Williams** (16) in 1953–8. There is now a walk of about one kilometre to reach the next plaque.

Continue through Hanover Terrace and walk along the Outer Circle, going in the same direction. You will pass more of the Nash terraces, which have in many cases been converted to offices since World War Two. Walk past Baker Street, staying on the Outer Circle, and you will have a good view of the Post Office Tower en route. When reaching York Gate you can see a blue plaque on the corner of York Terrace East. This was the home of the poet **Francis Turner Palgrave** (17) from 1862–75. He is best known as the editor of *The Golden Treasury of English Lyrics*.

Walk along York Terrace East and you will find plaques at Nos 19 and 20. The first is on the home of **Dr Ernest Jones** (18). He was a Welsh-born psychoanalyst and friend of Sigmund Freud. The actor-manager **Sir Charles Wyndham** (19) lived and died next

door (left). Turn right at the end of the road into Brunswick Place. No.2 was the home of **Frederick Denison Maurice** (20) 1862–6. He was an Anglican cleric and writer, who founded the Christian Socialist Movement with Charles Kingsley. Continue and turn left upon reaching Marylebone Road. Cross over to Park Crescent at the traffic lights. This was heavily bombed in World War Two and rebuilt for office use, Nash's original façade being retained.

There are four plaques in Park Crescent. The first is for the actress **Dame Marie Tempest** (21), who lived at No.24 from 1899 to 1902. The inventor and physicist **Sir Charles Wheatstone** (22) lived at No.19. Crossing over Portland Place you will pass the rear of the statue of Lord Lister.

At the next corner there is a plaque marking the former US embassy and the residence of **Henry Brook Adams** (23). He was a historian and descendant of two US presidents. Proceed on to No.12 Park Crescent, where there is a dark bronze plaque on the home of the surgeon and founder of antiseptic surgery **Lord Joseph Lister** (24). He lived here 1877–1912.

Continue round Park Crescent and turn to the right upon reaching Marylebone Road. Walk up to Great Portland Street station and cross over Marylebone Road to Osnaburgh Street. This is to the right of the Church of St Mary Magdalene. This church was built in the middle of the 19th century and is considered a perfect example of Victorian early Gothic styling. On the block of flats opposite, named Marlborough House, you can see a blue plaque commemorating the comedy actor **Kenneth Williams** (25). He is best remembered for his many parts in the *Carry On* films.

Ahead is the White House Hotel, where on the side of the building, in Osnaburgh Street, you will find a blue plaque commemorating the **Fabian Society** (26), which used to meet in a house formerly on this site. Its members included George Bernard Shaw, H.G. Wells and Sidney and Beatrice Webb.

At this point you will have walked about three miles and seen 26 plaques. You may like to finish and leave via Great Portland Street station. Alternatively it is a good point to stop for lunch or refreshment as several restaurants and cafés are in the vicinity.

To continue the walk, go past the front of the White House hotel and turn right into Albany Street. Cross over the street and walk along to No.55, opposite the Cape of Good Hope public house. A plaque at this address records the home of **Henry Mayhew** (27). He was an author and the joint first editor of *Punch* magazine.

Continue and turn left at Chester Gate. You will see the decorative archway leading into Chester Terrace (left). This terrace is one of Nash's most attractive designs and the properties are still used for domestic purposes. Walk through to No.13 to see the plaque of **Charles Robert Cockerell** (28). He was the architect who designed the Fitzwilliam Museum, Cambridge and the Taylorian Institute, Oxford. A little further along at No.27 you will see the blue plaque for **Sir John Maitland Salmond** (29), who was a Marshall of the Royal Air Force (below). It is now about two-thirds of a mile to the next plaque.

Return to Albany Street, via the same route, turn left past the Chester Arms and cross over to Robert Street. Walk through, turning to the left when you reach Hampstead Road at the end. Now walk up to Mornington Crescent, which is on the left-hand side. On the corner house, partly concealed by the large trees, you will see the plaque, erected in 1885, of the cartoonist **George Cruikshank** (30). He is best known for his illustrations of some of Charles Dickens's books and lived here from 1850–78. The large building ahead, formerly a cigarette factory, is a beautiful example of Art Deco styling and worth walking ahead to see if you are not already familiar with it.

A little further along Mornington Crescent you will reach the plaque of the artist **Walter Sickert** (31) at No.6. When living here his circle of friends became known as the Camden Town Group of artists.

Take the second turning on the left, Mornington Place, and then walk into Albert Street. No.11 was the home of CND campaigner **Peggy Duff** (32). Continue on to No.44 on the other side of the road. A blue plaque at this address marks the final home of the scientist **John Desmond Bernal** (33), who was one of the founders of molecular biology.

Walk up to Delancey Street at the end of the road and turn left. The Welsh poet **Dylan Thomas** (34) lived for a short time at No.54. Continue up to the traffic lights and turn left.

Go past Park Village East and turn left into Albany Street. The corner house shows the blue plaque of **W.W. Jacobs** (35). The most memorable of this author's short stories was *The Monkey's Paw*, which has been adapted for radio and television.

Now walk on to the end of the terrace. No.197 was the home of the musician and composer **Constant Lambert** (36). For several years he composed ballet pieces and worked for Sadler's Wells.

Return to the corner and turn left into Gloucester Gate. Follow right round the corner to the left and into the terrace still named Gloucester Gate. At No.6 there is a blue plaque for **Sir Henry Wellcome** (37). He was the philanthropic pharmacist who developed the Wellcome Trust and Foundation. Walk back past Gloucester Gate, staying on the Outer Circle of Regent's Park.

A short way along you will see the open-air car park for London Zoo on the right-hand side of the road. Just past this you will glimpse through the trees a red-painted Chinese restaurant at the canal side. At the traffic lights take the footpath signposted No.274 bus. This leads to the bridge crossing Regent's Canal after which you should turn left into Prince Albert Road.

Turn right into Albert Terrace. The photographer **Roger Fenton** (38) lived at No.2. He was the founder of the Royal Photographic Society in 1853. Turn left at the end and then right into Fitzroy Road. Primrose Hill Studios, opposite the old piano factory, is worth a visit. A weathered wooden plaque here lists the many notable former residents. Continue to No.23 Fitzroy Road. This was one of the homes of the Irish poet and dramatist **W.B. Yeats** (39).

Take the next turning left, Chalcot Road, which leads into Chalcot Square. The poet **Sylvia Plath** (40) lived at No.3 in 1960–61. She was married to the future Poet Laureate, Ted Hughes, and their troubled marriage ended when she took her own life.

Walk through and turn left into Chalcot Crescent. No.37 has a plaque for the Filipino patriot and writer **Dr Jose Rizal** (41), who lived at this address for a short time during 1888–9. Take the next turning right and then turn right again into Regent's Park Road. The political philosopher **Friedrich Engels** (42) lived at No.121 between 1870 and 1894. He was a friend of Karl Marx and assisted in the production of the *Communist Manifesto* (1848).

Proceed and turn left at Erskine Road. Turn right at the end of this road and you will see a plaque ahead. This is for **Dr Bhimrao Ramji Ambedkar** (43) who lived at 10 King Henry's Road during 1921–2. As a member of the Bombay Legislative Assembly and leader of 60 million 'untouchables', he was the principal author of the Indian Constitution.

Having walked six miles and seen 43 plaques you may now be feeling rather tired. You have the choice at this point of finishing the walk or seeing three more plaques before Swiss Cottage station. If you wish to leave the walk at this point, turn right at King Henry's Road and then left over the bridge to Chalk Farm tube station.

For the more energetic turn left at King Henry's Road then cross over Primrose Hill Road to Elsworthy Road, which is to the left of St Mary's Church. At No.4 you will find the plaque marking the home of the conductor **Sir Henry Wood** (44). He lived here from 1905 until 1937. It is interesting to see that the builder of the houses along this stretch of the road featured a small crouched figure at first-floor level.

Walk on and take the second turning right, Lower Merton Rise. Then walk immediately left into Wadham Gardens. Take the turning on the right named Harley Road. The popular contralto **Dame Clara Butt** (45) lived at No.7 from 1901 until 1929.

Continue straight on, crossing over Adelaide Road into Winchester Road. Cross over Eton Avenue and turn right into Adamson Road. The last plaque of this walk is to be found at No.14. This is for the artist **Robert Polhill Bevan** (46), who lived here 1900–25. He was a founder member of the Camden Town Group of artists, which included Sickert and Steer. Having studied in France, he brought Impressionist techniques to English painting.

If you now turn around, you will find it a short walk past the Embassy Theatre straight ahead to Swiss Cottage station.

Other nearby plaques not included in the walk:

Edward Goodrich Acheson, 31 Prince Albert Road, NW8.

Walk 20
Euston/Camden Town

Distance:	4½ miles (7.24km)
Time taken:	2 hours
Number of plaques:	18
Nearest tube stations:	Euston Square, Euston, Kings's Cross, Camden Town, Mornington Crescent
Bus routes:	10, 18, 24, 27, 29, 30, 46, 73, 91, 134, 135, 168, 214, 253

THIS area is a centre for national communications, having three main line railway stations and the Regent's Canal running through it. It has in this century become a centre for artists and, in recent times, tourists. The large markets and craft stalls attract visitors, particularly the young. Although there are not a great number plaques to be seen on this walk, it is thought worthy of inclusion because of its proximity to other walks and the aforementioned interest.

Starting from Euston Square station, exit at Euston Road North and turn right into North Gower Street. The first plaque to be seen on this walk is on the left side at No.187 North Gower Street. The Italian nationalist leader **Giuseppe Mazzini** (1) lived here 1837–40. This is one of the three plaques to be found commemorating him in London.

Walk on to No.200, on the other side of the road. Here you will find a green plaque on the home of the physician **Lord David Pitt of Hampstead** (2). He was a noted civil rights campaigner. Return to Euston Road and turn left, walking up to the third set of traffic lights. Cross the road to St Pancras parish church at Upper Woburn Place. This church, built 1819–22, is modelled on the Ionic temple of the Erectheum on the Acropolis at Athens.

Charles and Henry Rossi sculpted the caryatids (standing figures) in the early 19th century.

Having walked into Upper Woburn Place, turn left into Woburn Walk. This is a good place to stop for light refreshment, where you can sit, weather permitting, at one of the open-air tables. The attractive bow-fronted shops in this turning were designed by the architect Thomas Cubitt in 1822. At No.5 you will find a plaque recording that poet **W.B. Yeats** (3) lived here from 1895 to 1919.

Continue ahead through Flaxman Terrace and cross over into Bidborough Street. Crossing over Judd Street you reach Queen Alexandra Mansions, where you will see a blue plaque commemorating the artist **Paul Nash** (4). He was an official war artist in both world wars and is noted for his scenic landscape paintings.

FINISH

CAMDEN TOWN STATION

ROCHESTER TERRACE

KENTISH TOWN ROAD

CAMDEN STREET

CAMDEN SQUARE

AGAR GROVE

GREENLAND ROAD

CAMDEN HIGH STREET

BAYHAM STREET

PRATT STREET

CAMDEN STREET

COLLEGE STREET

ST PANCRAS WAY

DELANCEY STREET

ALBERT STREET

LIDLINGTON

OAKLEY SQUARE

HAMPSTEAD ROAD

NORTH GOWER STREET

EVERSHOLT STREET

WERRINGTON STREET

OSSULSTON STREET

PHOENIX

BRILL PLACE

BRITISH LIBRARY

ST PANCRAS STATION

PANCRAS ROAD

CHEYNEY ROAD

KING'S CROSS STATION

EUSTON ROAD

UPPER WOBURN PLACE

JUDD STREET

EUSTON SQUARE STATION

START

1 Giuseppe Mazzini
2 Lord David Pitt
3 W.B. Yeats
4 Paul Nash
5 Sir Nigel Gresley
6 Mary Wollstonecraft
7 Last Goon Show
8 George Cruikshank
9 Walter Sickert
10 Peggy Duff
11 John Desmond Bernal
12 Dylan Thomas
13 Charles Dickens
14 William Daniell
15 Krishna Menon
16 George James Symons
17 'Father' Henry Willis
18 Tom Sayers

Turning left through the passageway at the end will bring you to Euston Road. Ahead is St Pancras Station, to the left of which is the British Library. If you have not been there before and can spare the time, it is well worth a visit. If you are not going to the library, turn right upon emerging from the passageway and cross the road at the traffic lights, going forward into Pancras Road and right into Cheney Road, which is at the rear of King's Cross Station.

On the right hand side, by the station entrance, you will find the blue plaque of **Sir Nigel Gresley** (5). He was the foremost designer of classic trains between the wars. His *Mallard* held the speed record for steam trains in 1938, of 126mph.

Return to Pancras Road and turn right. Go under the three bridges on the left road and cross into Brill Place. Continue on into Phoenix Road and turn right at Werrington Street. On a wall of Oakshott Court is the plaque of feminist writer **Mary Wollstonecraft** (6), who lived in a house formerly on this site. She was the mother of Mary Shelley and author of *A Vindication of the Rights of Women* (1792).

Continue along Werrington Street, turning left at the end, then turn right into Eversholt Street. Proceed past the traffic lights and walk right up to the Camden Palace Theatre. Here you will find a blue plaque commemorating the production of the last radio performance of *The Last Goon Show* (7) in 1972. The traffic island in the middle of the road has a statue of Richard Cobden, who was instrumental in the repeal of the Corn Laws and is commemorated by plaques in two of these walks.

Now cross the road and walk past Mornington Crescent underground station. On the right you will see the beautifully restored Art Deco Carrera cigarette factory, with its black cat statues and motifs. If you have previously completed Walk 19, you will have already seen the next five plaques. At No.263 Hampstead Road on the corner of Mornington Crescent, almost hidden by the trees, is a brown plaque erected by the Royal Society of Arts in 1885. This commemorates the illustrator **George Cruikshank** (8), who lived here 1850–78. Walk into Mornington Crescent, where you will see a blue plaque ahead at No.6. The artist **Walter Sickert** (9) lived here in 1907.

Turn left at Mornington Place and right into Albert Street. No.11 on the left-hand side was the home of **Peggy Duff** (10). She was the first general secretary of the CND. Proceed along Albert Street to No.44 on the other side of the road. A blue plaque here marks the final home of **Professor John Desmond Bernal** (11), who was a founder of molecular biology and the social philosophy of science. Continue and turn left at Delancey Street. Cross Delancey Street to No.54, which was a home of the Welsh poet **Dylan Thomas** (12). Now turn and walk back down Delancey Street and cross over Camden High Street to Pratt Street. Take the first turning left, which is Bayham Street. At No.141, on the corner building of Greenland Road, there is a plaque commemorating **Charles Dickens** (13), who lived in a house on this site as a boy. This may be partly concealed by a mesh erected to prevent debris falling onto a lower level.

Cross the road and turn right into Greenland Road. Turn left at the end and then right into Camden Road. Continue under the bridge and then turn right at St Pancras Way, before the traffic lights. The artist **William Daniell** (14) lived and died at No.135. He travelled extensively in India with his artist uncle, Thomas Daniell, and they afterwards produced a six-volume work of aquatints.

Walk on and turn left at the traffic lights into Agar Grove. Turn left at Murray Street, which will bring you into Camden Square. On the left, at No.57, there is a plaque on the house where the Indian politician **Krishna Menon** (15) lived from 1924 to 1947. Another plaque can be found at No.62, where meteorologist **George James Symons** (16) lived for 32 years. Walk on to Camden Road and turn left. Cross over the road and proceed into Rochester Road. At the second turning by the children's playground turn left and then immediately right into Rochester Terrace. The plaque for **'Father' Henry Willis** (17) is at No.9. Among others, he built the huge organs for the Royal Albert Hall and St Paul's Cathedral.

Return to the playground and turn right then left at the next road junction to get back to Camden Road. Turning right at the traffic lights will bring you first to the main line rail station and, a little further on, to Camden Town tube station. The latter is about half a mile from the last plaque. The final plaque of this walk can be found at No.257 Camden High Street, which is just past the tube station. This commemorates the English heavyweight boxing champion of 1857, **Tom Sayers** (18). During his long career he lost only one fight and drew with the American John Heenan when competing for the championship of the world. Before departing, you may like to visit the nearby Camden Lock and market, or the many boutiques, shops and stalls in the area. There is a boat trip available for a short cruise along the Regent's Canal.

Walk 21
Islington

Distance:	5⅓ miles (8.58km) or 6⅓miles (10.20km)
Time taken:	3 hours or 3¾ hours
Number of plaques:	25 or 29
Nearest tube stations:	Old Street, Angel, Highbury & Islington, Arsenal
Bus routes:	3, 4, 19, 30, 38, 43, 55, 56, 73, 76, 141, 153, 153, 171a, 214, 271, 274

ISLINGTON has many historical associations. Its once famous music hall theatre has been replaced by small public house theatres. In recent years, due to its proximity to the City, Islington has become a fashionable residential area, but a high proportion of the housing remains council-owned. Many of the old buildings are gradually being replaced, but some of the historic landmarks remain. During this walk you will find street and antique markets, many public houses and several ethnic restaurants.

The walk commences at Old Street tube station. Leaving by exit No.8 you will immediately find a green plaque marking the site of the **City Road Turnpike** (1), which stood here from 1766 to 1864.

Go back down the steps into the station and now re-emerge at exit No.2. Walking along Old Street, you will see an interesting mural on the wall of Vince Court, depicting the history of this area. Continue past the Great Eastern Street fork and turn left at Pitfield Street. Now turn right into Boot Street and left into Hoxton Market. This quiet street was the centre of a fashionable market in the 17th century. Its main feature nowadays is the statue of a juggler in the centre. Ahead you can see the 1896 electric light station with a brown plaque proclaiming **'Shoreditch Electricity Generating Station & Refuse Destructor'** (2). Turning to the right you will find a plaque commemorating **John** and **Lewis 'Daddy' Burtt** (3). They were the founders of the Hoxton Market Christian Mission in 1886.

Walk through the turning at the end and follow it round into Hoxton Square. This square was built in the 1680s and it was here that Ben Jonson killed a fellow actor in a duel. The physician **James Parkinson** (4) lived at No.1 and you can see his blue plaque on the building on the left as you enter the square. He was the first to identify appendicitis and Parkinson's Disease, which he identified, bears his name. Continue round the square, turn right into Mundy Street and then left at Hoxton Street.

There are three plaques in Hoxton Street, all on the left-hand side. The first is on a brick column, supporting railings. **Pollock's Toy Theatre Shop** (5) was founded in 1851 and stood on this site until destroyed by bombing during World War Two. The present shop and museum is in Scala Street, W1.

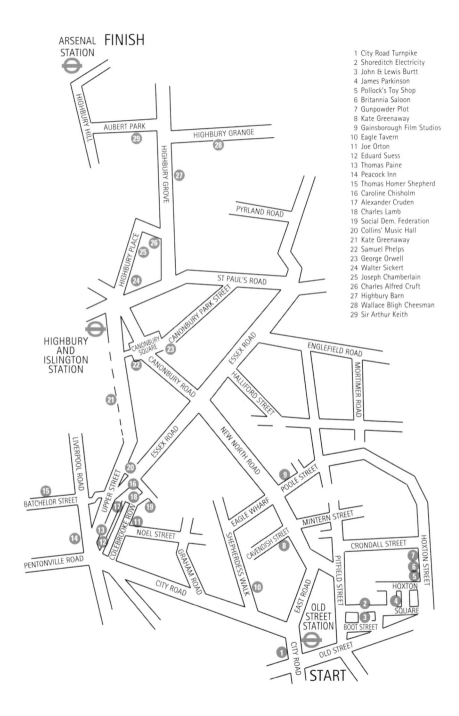

ARSENAL **FINISH**
STATION

1 City Road Turnpike
2 Shoreditch Electricity
3 John & Lewis Burtt
4 James Parkinson
5 Pollock's Toy Shop
6 Britannia Saloon
7 Gunpowder Plot
8 Kate Greenaway
9 Gainsborough Film Studios
10 Eagle Tavern
11 Joe Orton
12 Eduard Suess
13 Thomas Paine
14 Peacock Inn
15 Thomas Homer Shepherd
16 Caroline Chisholm
17 Alexander Cruden
18 Charles Lamb
19 Social Dem. Federation
20 Collins' Music Hall
21 Kate Greenaway
22 Samuel Phelps
23 George Orwell
24 Walter Sickert
25 Joseph Chamberlain
26 Charles Alfred Cruft
27 Highbury Barn
28 Wallace Bligh Cheesman
29 Sir Arthur Keith

HIGHBURY
AND
ISLINGTON
STATION

At No.107 a brown plaque marks the site of the **Britannia Saloon** (6). This opened in 1841, was rebuilt in 1848 and renamed the Britannia Theatre. It was demolished by German bombing in 1941. Further along, on the corner of Crondall Street, a brown plaque makes reference to the **Gunpowder Plot** (7). It is about a quarter of a mile from here to the next plaque.

Turn left into Crondall Street and right at Pitfield Street. Take the second left, which is Mintern Street. Walk through and cross over New North Road. Ahead is Cavendish Street, where you can see Sylvia Court. This was built on the site of No.1 Cavendish Street where the artist **Kate Greenaway** (8) was born. Return to New North Road and turn left. Cross over to the other side of the road and walk past Shoreditch Park to Poole Street. The corner building, which has recently been redeveloped, is the site of **Gainsborough Film Studios** (9). There is a brown plaque at the far end of the building recording their 25 years operating at this site.

Return to New North Road, cross over and walk into Eagle Wharf Road, turning left at the end into Shepherdess Walk. Continue all the way down to the **Eagle Tavern** (10) (left), which is just before City Road. The brown plaque relates the history of this site. It does not record though that the Eagle was the tavern mentioned in the nursery rhyme and song *Pop Goes The Weasel*.

Continue to City Road and turn right. Walk up to Graham Street, five turnings further. Proceed along Graham Street, turn right at Danbury Street and left into Noel Road. The playwright **Joe Orton** (11) is commemorated by a green plaque situated on the top floor of No.25. Orton, whose most memorable play was *Loot*, was killed by his lover Kenneth Halliwell at this address.

Walk on and turn left into Colbrooke Row. Take Duncan Street on the right and turn immediately left into Duncan Terrace, which runs parallel with Colbrooke Row. Near the end, at No.4, you will find a blue rectangular plaque on the birthplace of **Eduard Suess** (12). At the age of three he moved with his family to Prague. In adult life he became an Austrian statesman and noted geologist.

Walking forward, turn right at City Road and proceed round to Islington High Street.

You will pass the green clock tower, built in 1906, on the junction with Goswell Road. Angel Square can be entered from the High Street, to the right of the traffic lights. In the centre of the square there is an obelisk and sculpture above a plaque commemorating **Thomas Paine** (13), the British-born American citizen who wrote *The Rights of Man* at the Angel in 1791.

Returning to Islington High Street you can see a green plaque across the road at No.11. This is where the **Peacock Inn** (14) stood from 1564 until 1962. The inn was mentioned by Charles Dickens in *Boots at the Cherry Tree Inn* and by Thomas Hughes in *Tom Brown's Schooldays*.

Proceed along Islington High Street, cross at the traffic lights and take the left-hand fork into Liverpool Road. A few turnings along, on the left-hand side, you will find Batchelor Street. The engraver **Thomas Hosmer Shepherd** (15) lived at No.26 Batchelor Street between 1820 and 1842. Return to Liverpool Road, turning to the right. Cross over to Bromfield Street and walk through to Upper Street via Bromfield Street and Berners Road. Now cross over Upper Street to a narrow turning named Charlton Place.

No.32 Charlton Place was home to **Caroline Chisholm** (16) for a short time. She spent many years in Australia, where she did much to improve conditions for emigrants. Return to Camden Passage and bear right. Here you will find many interesting antique shops and stalls, especially on a Wednesday or Saturday. No.45 has an unusual plaque and relief bust of **Alexander Cruden** (17). He was a bookseller whose most notable literary achievement was a biblical concordance published in 1737.

Walk up to the Camden Head public house and turn right, going down the steps and through the car park. Turning to the left you will reach a white painted house (No.64), where the essayist **Charles Lamb** (18) lived 1823-7. Across the road in Colbrooke Row you can see a blue plaque for the headquarters (1926-37) of the **Social Democratic Federation** (19). Henry Hyndman, who founded this organisation in 1884, has his blue plaque on a house in Hampstead.

Continue on through St Peter's Street, crossing Essex Road and entering Islington Green opposite. A rectangular blue plaque on the first-floor level at Nos 10-11 Islington Green marks the site of **Collins' Music Hall** (20). Most of the famous music hall entertainers performed here, including Charlie Chaplin, Marie Lloyd, Harry Lauder and George Robey. The theatre closed after a fire in 1958, having been open since 1865.

Turn to the right at Upper Street and cross the road. At No.147 you will find a second plaque for **Kate Greenaway** (21). She lived here 1862-73. Walk on, cross the road at the pedestrian crossing and walk past the Town Hall. The Islington museum is closed on Mondays and Tuesdays.

Bear right into Canonbury Lane, which leads into Canonbury Square. Walking to the right you will see a bronze plaque at No.8. This is where the actor and manager **Samuel Phelps** (22) lived. Continue to the far end of the square, crossing over Canonbury Road. At No.27

Canonbury Square there is a plaque for the author **George Orwell** (23). This is one of five plaques in London situated on his many homes.

Continue round the square and turn right at the traffic lights into Canonbury Road. This will take you up to Highbury Corner, where there is an underground station, shops and restaurants. Before departing though, there are two more plaques to see in Highbury Place, which is immediately opposite, across the road junctions, facing the post office. The first plaque is at No.1, where **Walter Sickert** (24) established his school of painting and engraving. The second is at No.25 Highbury Place. The politician **Joseph Chamberlain** (25) lived here from 1845 until moving to Birmingham to look after the family business in 1854.

You can now either return to Highbury Corner for the tube station to finish the walk or continue.

If you would like to extend the walk a little further you can walk on to the end of Highbury Place and bear right at Baalbec Road. Then turn right at Highbury Grove. A short way along you will see a plaque on Ashurst Lodge. The dog show promoter **Charles Alfred Cruft** (26) lived near here between 1913 and 1938. From this spot it is nearly a quarter of a mile to the next plaque.

Turn back along Highbury Grove passing Baalbec Road again. Walking along Highbury Grove you will pass Christ's Church and on the other side the University of North London. Behind the church you will find the red-painted clock tower erected in 1897 to mark the 60th anniversary of Queen Victoria's reign.

Cross the road and walk up to the **Highbury Barn** (27) tavern (left). This pleasure area in the 19th century included a concert hall, music hall and a gas-lit 4000sq ft, open-air dance floor. Walk on and turn right at Highbury Grange. At No.8 you will see a green plaque which records that **Wallace Bligh Cheesman** (28) lived here 1926-7. He was a trade union leader who founded the Fawcett Association and the Civil Service Federation. Return to Highbury Park and turn right. The next turning on the left is Aubert Park.

The last plaque of this walk is to be found at No.17 Aubert Park. The Scottish physiologist and anthropologist **Sir Arthur Keith** (29) lived here 1908-33. He wrote several works on the study of embryology and the theory of evolution. It is now a walk of more than one third of a mile to Arsenal underground station. Continue and turn right at Highbury Hill. You will see the station ahead.

Walk 22
Hackney Borough

Distance:	6¼ miles (10.05km)
Time taken:	2¾ hours
Number of plaques:	25
Nearest stations:	London Fields, Hackney Central, Clapton, Highbury & Islington
Bus routes:	38, 43, 48, 73, 55, 106, 141, 236, 242, 253, 271, 276, 277, 341

HACKNEY at first appearances seems rather run down. It is however steeped in history and was a village in Saxon times. One of the few ancient buildings remaining is the tower of St Augustine's Church, which dates back to around 1300. From the 15th to the 18th century Hackney was home to much of the nobility. Sutton House, built in the early 16th century and now owned by the National Trust, is the best preserved of the old houses, but there are several buildings still inhabited dating from the 18th century. Today there are many immigrant families. Having suffered great damage during World War Two, many of the old houses have now been replaced with tower blocks. The borough was enlarged in 1965 with the inclusion of the districts of Stoke Newington and Shoreditch.

Although there are some plaques in South Hackney and Bethnal Green, they have not been included because of the distance involved. Most of the plaques on this walk are brown and have been erected by Hackney Borough Council.

The walk commences at London Fields station. London Fields itself is a green area of recreational ground of about 26 acres and is a refreshing site in a rather shabby area. Coming out of the station turn right and then left into Lamb Lane. This will bring you through to the main road junction. Cross the road to Well Street. The first brick building on the right-hand side has a brown plaque commemorating the diarist **Celia Fiennes** (1). She travelled extensively between 1685 and 1702, keeping a record of her journeys. In one year alone she covered 1,000 miles.

Return to Mare Street, crossing over to where you were previously and walk on to No.195. This is opposite Pemberton Place. On the gatepost there is a plaque recording this building as having been an **Elizabeth Fry** (2) refuge (left). A devout Quaker, she established many hostels and devoted her life to prison and asylum reform.

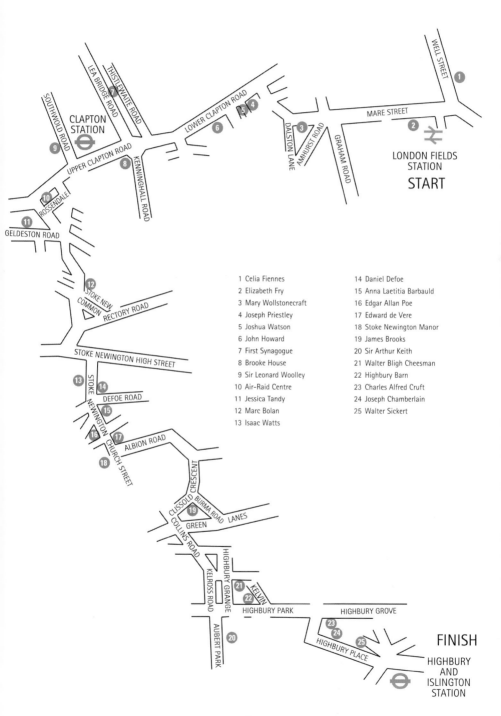

1 Celia Fiennes
2 Elizabeth Fry
3 Mary Wollstonecraft
4 Joseph Priestley
5 Joshua Watson
6 John Howard
7 First Synagogue
8 Brooke House
9 Sir Leonard Woolley
10 Air-Raid Centre
11 Jessica Tandy
12 Marc Bolan
13 Isaac Watts

14 Daniel Defoe
15 Anna Laetitia Barbauld
16 Edgar Allan Poe
17 Edward de Vere
18 Stoke Newington Manor
19 James Brooks
20 Sir Arthur Keith
21 Walter Bligh Cheesman
22 Highbury Barn
23 Charles Alfred Cruft
24 Joseph Chamberlain
25 Walter Sickert

Continue up Mare Street to the next plaque at No.373. This is past the 100-year-old Hackney Empire Theatre, Hackney Town Hall, Graham Road and Hackney Central station. The plaque for **Mary Wollstonecraft** (3) is on a pillar between shops on the left side. She was a feminist who wrote *A Vindication of the Rights of Woman* (1792) and was also the mother of Mary Shelley (author of *Frankenstein*).

Walking on you come into Lower Clapton Road, where you proceed past the church of St John-at-Hackney. This was built 1792–7 in the shape of a Greek cross and replaced a 16th-century church. The parish stocks and whipping post are still in the churchyard. Continue walking and bear left around the corner, after the Elephants Head. At No.113 a brown plaque records that **Joseph Priestley** (4) lived here 1792–4. He was a Presbyterian minister who studied chemistry. His pioneering work in gases identified oxygen, ammonia and sulphur dioxide. Unfortunately, as both this and the next plaque are set very high it is almost impossible to read the small wording.

Nearby, on the corner of Clapton Passage, there is a plaque for **Joshua Watson** (5). He was a philanthropist, active in many church associations and first treasurer of the National Society. The plaque states that he lived in a house on this site 1811–23 and 1841–55.

The next plaque is to be found at Nos 157–9 Lower Clapton Road, on the site of the house where the prison reformer **John Howard** (6) was born. Being appalled at the conditions in prisons in the 18th century, he undertook a programme of reforms, which resulted in two Acts of Parliament.

If you now cross the road you will find the next plaque about six turnings further up. This is at No.25 Thistlewaite Road. The **First Synagogue** (7) in the borough of Hackney was built 1779–80 on ground now at the rear of this house.

Return to Lower Clapton Road, cross over and walk towards the roundabout. Now cross Kenninghall Road to the community college called **Brooke House** (8). This building was erected on a house of that name which stood here from the late 15th century until 1955. The plaque, by the main entrance, gives its full history.

BROOKE HOUSE (King's Place)
Stood on this site
From late 15th century - 1955
Owned by Henry VIII, 1535-47

FULKE GREVILLE (Lord Brooke)
Poet and courtier
Lived here 1609-1628

LONDON BOROUGH OF HACKNEY

From the roundabout continue into Upper Clapton Road. Just past Clapton station is Southwold Road. You will see a plaque on the bridge that crosses over the railway lines. The archaeologist **Sir Leonard Woolley** (9) was born in a house formerly on this site. He published several accounts of his excavations in the Middle East.

Return to the main road, turn right, then turn left into Northwold Road. The first turning on the right is Rossendale Street. This seems an unlikely street to have anything of interest but at No.24 there is a plaque marking the site of the **Air-Raid Precaution Centre** (10), built in 1938. This was the Civil Defence Centre for Hackney during World War Two. Continue and turn left into Rossington Street.

Follow this road round to the continuation of Northwold Road and turn right, then right again into Geldeston Road. No.58 was the house where the actress **Jessica Tandy** (11) was born. Apart from the film mentioned on the plaque she appeared in many others, including

The plaque for Jessica Tandy was erected and unveiled simultaneously.

Forever Amber, *The Desert Fox*, and *The Birds*. Her first husband was the actor Jack Hawkins.

Walk back to Northwold Road and turn right. Just past the third turning on the left, Maury Road, there is a plaque on No.25 Stoke Newington Common (below). This is for the pop star **Marc Bolan** (12). He was the lead singer of the group T-Rex, and he died tragically

in a car accident. His real name was Mark Feld. Continue up Northwold Road.

Reaching the end of Northwold Road, turn left into Stoke Newington High Street, then right into Stoke Newington Church Street. The first plaque to be found in this road is on the gateway of Abney Cemetery and commemorates Abney House, which stood here from 1700 to 1843. **Isaac Watts** (13), hymn writer and poet, stayed here 1734–48. His most memorable hymn is probably *O God, Our Help in Ages Past.*

Close by, across the road, is Defoe Road. The corner house was built on the site of a house where the prolific writer **Daniel Defoe** (14) lived. His blue plaque can be seen on the side of the building. He wrote many books, published one of the first newspapers and is best remembered as the author of *Robinson Crusoe* and *Moll Flanders.*

The next commemorative plaque to be seen is a few doors along at No.113 Stoke Newington Church Street. This is for **Anna Laetitia Barbauld** (15), who lived here for 23 years. She was a poet and author, who published many volumes of work and also wrote a series with her brother called *Evenings at Home.* Note the faded advertising for the fountain pen shop that was once here.

Walking on you will find a brown plaque at No.172, opposite Woodlea Road. This was the site of the Manor House School, which the American short story-writer **Edgar Allan Poe** (16) attended for three years, while his family lived in England 1815–20.

Cross the road at the pedestrian crossing to the old red-brick building, which was built in around 1714. This is the site of a mediaeval mansion, the sometime home of **Edward de Vere, 17th Earl of Oxford** (17) (1550–1604). He was an Elizabethan courtier and poet who served against the Armada in 1588. He also sat as judge at the trial of Mary Queen of Scots in 1586.

A little further along you will see Stoke Newington Town Hall across the road. A brown plaque here informs us that this is the site of **Stoke Newington Manor House** (18) (1500–1695) and the terrace called **Church Row** (1695–1700), which was demolished in 1936.

Cross the road to Albion Road. A couple of turnings after Clissold Road you will reach Clissold Crescent. At No.42 you will see the house **James Brooks** (19) designed and built for himself in around 1862. An eminent church architect, he also designed rectories, schools and other private houses.

Continue to the end of Clissold Crescent, turn left and cross over Green Lane into Collins Road. At the far end take the passage through to Kelross Road and walk on to Aubert Park, which is past the main road, Highbury Park. At No.17 Aubert Park there is a green Islington plaque on the house where **Sir Arthur Keith** (20) lived 1908–33. He was a physiologist and anthropologist who wrote works on the theory of evolution and human embryology.

Return to the main road and turn right. Cross over to the first road, Highbury Grange. Another Islington plaque can be seen at No.8, where trade union leader **Walter Bligh Cheesman** (21) lived. He was a delegate to the founding conference of the Labour Party in 1900 and was a founder of the Civil Service Federation. As a former postal worker he founded the Fawcett Association, which aimed at achieving equality between postal sorters and telegraphists.

Come back to Highbury Park and turn left. Within a short distance you will reach the **Highbury Barn** (22) public house. A green plaque commemorates the lavish pleasure grounds that existed here from 1861 to 1871. The grounds included a theatre and restaurants but attracted many undesirable characters. For this reason the local inhabitants forced its closure. Continue walking along Highbury Grove. Take a look at the red-painted clock tower set behind the church before walking up to the next plaque.

Just past Baalbec Road there is a block of flats called Ashurst Lodge. On the front, a green plaque informs us that **Charles Alfred Cruft** (23) lived near here from 1913 until 1938. Many people do not realise that the huge annual dog show is named after this man. He was the general manager of dog-food manufacturers Spratts, and started the show in 1886.

The end of the walk is now in sight. Walk into Baalbec Road and turn left at the end into Highbury Place. There are two plaques in this road. The first is for the politician **Joseph Chamberlain** (24) at No.25. He was President of the Board of Trade in 1880, Colonial Secretary in 1895 and father of Prime Minister Neville Chamberlain. The second plaque is at No.1 and commemorates the artist **Walter Sickert** (25). He lived in several addresses in Islington and set up his school of painting here in 1927. The last four plaques are included in Walk 21.

Ahead is Highbury Corner where the main line and underground stations are situated.

Walk 23
East End (1)

Distance:	4 miles (6.43km)
Time taken:	2 hours
Number of plaques:	19
Nearest tube stations:	Aldgate East, Whitechapel
Bus routes:	8, 25, 26, 35, 47, 48, 55, 67, 78, 149, 242, 243, 253

1 Isaac Rosenberg
2 Viscount Milner
3 Dr James J. Mallon
4 Emmanuel Shinwell
5 Board of Guardians
6 Susanna Annesley
7 William Morris/Webb
8 Priory of St John
9 William Shakespeare
10 Holywell Priory
11 Mark Gertler
12 Bud Flanagan
13 Anna Maria Garthwaite
14 Miriam Moses
15 Mary Hughes
16 Edith Cavell
17 John Richard Green
18 Salvation Army
19 Elizabeth Garrett Anderson

THE area generally termed the 'East End' takes in a vast residential and industrial area that stretches from the City to Bow. It is centred mainly on the thoroughfares of Commercial Road and Mile End Road, which were built in the early part of the 19th century. It has long been an area where immigrant families have settled. These have comprised three distinctive groups who have left their mark on the area. First came the Huguenots, followed at the turn of the 19th century by the East European Jews and, since 1945, the Asian communities. It is a bustling area with many restaurants and street markets. It was severely bombed during World War Two and the shortage of accommodation resulted in the building of many high-rise apartment blocks.

Because of the widespread distribution of the commemorative plaques, the area has been divided into three separate walks.

Leaving Aldgate East tube station it is best to use the exit marked High Street (North). This is situated between the Whitechapel Art Gallery and the Whitechapel Public Library. If you do come out at another exit, proceed into the High Street. The art gallery has free entry and an excellent restaurant for a light lunch. Unfortunately it is closed on Mondays. Between the station and the library you will see a blue plaque on the wall commemorating the poet and artist, **Isaac Rosenberg** (1). He is best remembered for his poems written on the battlefields of World War One, where he lost his life in the Somme offensive. The entrance hall of the library contains some interesting wall plaques.

Walk back to the corner and turn right into Commercial Street. At No.28 you will find the narrow entrance corridor of Toynbee Hall. This is the Universities' Settlement in East London, founded in 1884 by Canon Samuel Barnett. Walking through you come into a small square courtyard. On the right-hand side is a clock with an embossed plaque in memory of **Viscount Milner** (2). On the adjacent wall there is a blue plaque, which commemorates **Dr James Joseph Mallon** (3), who was warden of Toynbee Hall 1919–54. He also served as a governor of the BBC for 15 years. The Youth Hostels Association had its first offices at Toynbee Hall and art exhibitions held there resulted in a subscription to build the Whitechapel Art Gallery. Many famous people have stayed here, including Prime Minister Clement Attlee.

Continue a short way along Commercial Street and cross at the traffic lights to Wentworth Street. Take the first turning on the right, Toynbee Street. A short way along you will reach Brune House on the left, where there is a red plaque. This states that '**Manny' Shinwell** (4) was born in a house formerly on this site. He first became a Member of Parliament in 1931 and after holding many Cabinet posts, became Father of the House. He was awarded a peerage in 1970 and lived to the ripe old age of 102.

Return to Wentworth Street and turn right. This takes you to Middlesex Street, known as 'Petticoat Lane'. The street was originally known as Hog's Lane, but an early 17th century map shows it as 'Peticote Lane', probably because of the abundance of traders selling clothes in the area. The name Middlesex Street was given about 1830. Turn right and enjoy looking for bargains on the many stalls.

You will pass Strype Street, which was named after a silk merchant name John Strype. His son, also called John, was a historian whose works included a biography of the Archbishop of Canterbury, Thomas Cranmer. An LCC plaque for Strype was erected in 1929 but due to refurbishment of the building, the plaque disappeared in 2000. Continuing along Middlesex Street you pass the unusually named Frying Pan Alley. Ahead on the left you can now see a blue plaque above the telephone boxes. This is on the Shooting Star public house, which once held the offices of the **Jewish Board of Guardians** (5). They did much to ease the resettlement of the immigrant families of the area in the 19th and early 20th century. Reaching the end of the road, turn right into Bishopsgate.

Walk down to the traffic lights and turn right into Spital Square. Leading off from this is a small cul-de-sac called Spital Yard. This was built in the 17th century and as you can see by the plaque on the end house **Susanna Annesley** (6) was born here. She was the mother of John and Charles Wesley as well as 15 other children.

Return to Bishopsgate, turn right, then take the pedestrian crossing before walking into Worship Street. You can see a City of London boundary griffon on this corner. At No.91 Worship Street there is a brown plaque of the Borough of Hackney erected in honour of **William Morris** and **Philip Webb** (7). Apart from their respective careers as designers and architects they were co-founders of the Society for the Protection of Ancient Buildings (1877).

Walk back a few yards and turn left into Curtain Road. Cross over Great Eastern Street and at Nos 86–8 you will see two plaques. This is the site of the **Priory of St John** (8) and the first London theatre. England's greatest playwright **William Shakespeare** (9) acted and performed his plays at this theatre as well as at the better known Globe and Rose theatres. A few doors away at No.98 there is a plaque marking the site of **Holywell Priory** (10). As the name suggests, there was a well and a priory, which was founded in 1152. It flourished until the dissolution of the monasteries in 1539. Now return to the road junctions.

Turn left into Great Eastern Street and then cross over Shoreditch High Street into Commercial Street. Walking on the right-hand side, proceed into the first turning, Elder Street. Many of the original 1730s houses have survived the passage of time. The artist **Mark Gertler** (11), who was born nearby, lived at No.32. He had associations with the Bloomsbury Group and is recorded also on two plaques in Hampstead.

Return to Commercial Street, bearing to the right. You can cut off the corner by taking the short street on the right. Cross over Commercial Street, walk past Lana House Studios and turn left into Hanbury Street. At No.12 you will see the blue plaque on the house where the comedian **Bud Flanagan** (12) was born. Flanagan, whose real name was Robert

Winthrop, was leader of 'The Crazy Gang' for 30 years. Many of his routines were with his partner Chesney Allen. Turn right into Wilkes Street.

Immediately you can see a blue plaque ahead on the corner of Princelet Street. This is for **Anna Maria Garthwaite** (13), who was a Huguenot silk weaver and designer. Across the street at No.17 there is a plaque on the birthplace of **Miriam Moses** (14), who was Britain's first female Jewish mayor (below). She was a founder member of the League of Jewish Women and the Board of Deputies. Next door is the 18th-century Princelet Street synagogue, now disused. Turn left into Brick Lane. Today this is the centre of the Asian community in the East End and has some of the finest Indian restaurants in London.

Turn right at Buxton Street, which is just past the tall chimney of Truman's Brewery. You may find it surprising to see the green open spaces contained in such a heavily built up area as this. Reaching the end of Buxton Street you will see a blue plaque on the left corner house, which is No.17 Vallance Road. This is for **Mary Hughes** (15), who lived and worked here, aiding the poor. She took in lodgers and held socialist meetings twice a week. Turn right in Vallance Road, walking past Underwood Road. This will lead you to Whitechapel Road.

Whitechapel was once the centre of Jewish life in the East End and many relics can still be seen above doorways and on the front of buildings. Like Petticoat Lane there are many stalls in Whitechapel Road. Cross over to the London Hospital on the other side. Walk into the main entrance and on the left you will see the bell cast in the nearby Whitechapel Bell Foundry in 1757. In the early days of the hospital this bell was rung when there was an emergency. Walk straight ahead and through the door to the courtyard on the other side. Ahead is a beautiful statue of Queen Alexandra and on the far wall to the left is a blue plaque, honouring nurse **Edith Cavell** (16), who trained and worked at the London Hospital. In World War One she helped British soldiers to escape and was captured by the enemy. Tried as a spy, she was found guilty and executed. Continue through the hospital and leave by the rear door.

Turn right and then left into Turner Street. The first turning on the left is Newark Street. Here you will find the London Hospital Museum, which is well worth a visit, time permitting. There is a fine collection of old surgical instruments, nurse's uniforms, records and other mementoes from the early days of the hospital. Immediately opposite, on John Garnett House, there is a blue plaque, recording it as having been the home of **John Richard Green** (17). He was a historian and author of many books on the history of England.

Return to Turner Street and continue to Walden Street, which will lead you into New Road. Turning to the left in New Road, walk down to No.23 on the other side. As the plaque records, the first indoor meeting of the **Salvation Army** (18) was held here in 1865. There is now just one more plaque to be seen before the end of the walk.

Continue and turn right upon reaching Commercial Road. On the London Guildhall University building you will see a plaque above the main entrance door. This marks the site of the birthplace of **Elizabeth Garrett Anderson** (19), who was the first woman doctor in Great Britain (1865). She founded the first hospital especially for women and was also the first woman to become a mayor (Aldeburgh, 1908).

These last four plaques are included in Walk 25. It is now just a short walk ahead to Aldgate East underground station and the end of the tour.

Walk 24
East End (2)

Distance:	5¼ miles (8.44km)
Time taken:	2 hours
Number of plaques:	22
Nearest tube stations:	Bromley-By-Bow, Bethnal Green
Bus routes:	8, 25, 106, 253, 277, 309

THIS walk commences on the eastern side of the tour, by the Blackwall Tunnel northern approach road. It is next to the River Lee, which in pre-motor days was an important means of transport to and from London. Bow is said to have taken its name from the 12th-century stone bridge that once spanned the river. The population of the area did not grow to any extent until the industrial expansion of the 19th century. Tradition has it that only a person born within the sound of Bow Bells can be considered to be a true cockney.

You may come across plaques during this tour that are not mentioned in the narrative. These are 'The Bow Heritage Trail' plaques, which have been placed by a local authority. Some have a strictly local interest and have therefore been left out of this account.

The walk commences at Bromley-by-Bow underground station. Coming from the station turn left and then left again at the first turning. Walk into St Leonard's Street at the side of the public house named the Imperial Crown. The first turning on the left past the right-hand side of the public house is Grace Street. Proceed to the end of this road, where you will find that the building on the right is Kingsley Hall (below). A blue plaque informs us that **Mahatma Gandhi** (1) stayed here in 1931. This great Indian leader visited

Britain on many occasions and also lived in South Africa. There is another plaque for him in Baron's Court Road, W14, where he stayed as a student.

Continue and turn left into Bruce Road. Near the end of this road you will see a school with high wire fencing around the playground. Look through and you will see the blue plaque commemorating the writer **H.G. Wells** (2), who officially opened the school in 1924. Turn back a few yards and go left into Stroudley Walk. Continuing ahead, passing Bromley High Street, you will reach the busy Bow Road. Ahead at the crossing is a raised statue of William Gladstone with outstretched arm. Cross the road and turn to the right. Walk past Bow Church, which dates from the 14th century, to Nos 215–7 Bow Road. These premises, currently owned by a company in the motor trade, are built on the site of a house once belonging to **Lord Edmond Sheffield** (3). He was a naval officer who fought against the Spanish Armada in 1588. Turn around and walk to the corner of Fairfield Road.

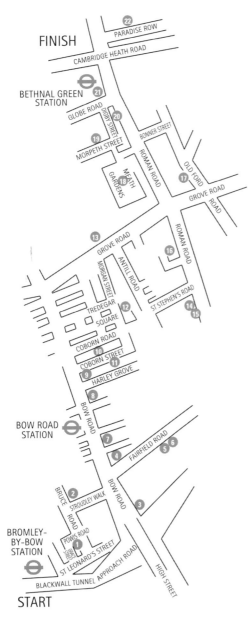

1 Mahatma Gandhi
2 H.G. Wells
3 Lord Edmond Sheffield
4 Bow Fair Field
5 Annie Besant
6 Match Girls
7 Match Tax
8 George Lansbury
9 Central Foundation
  Girls' School
10 Dr Barnado
11 Charles Coborn
12 Sir Charles Morgan
13 First Flying Bomb
14 Vernon Hall
15 John Passmore Edwards
16 Sylvia Pankhurst
17 Israel Zangwill
18 King Cole
19 Bradley Lynch
20 Sidney Godley VC
21 Wartime Disaster
22 Daniel Mendoza

The former Town Hall was built in 1937 and bears a plaque above a side door in Fairfield Road entitled **Bow Fair Field** (4). This was the site of an annual Whitsun fair stopped in 1823 due to the rowdyism and vice.

Go past the two bridges to the flats known as Bow Quarter. These buildings were the former Bryant & May match factory, built in 1874. On the outer gateway you will see two plaques. One is for the leader of the 1888 match girls' strike **Annie Besant** (5), who was a social reformer and advocate of birth control. The second is a Bow Heritage plaque remembering the **Match Girls** (6) who took part in the strike for better working conditions (top, next page). Return to Bow Road and turn right.

Just around the corner you will find another Bow Heritage plaque commemorating the building of the Town Hall in 1937. Next door is a school, where a plaque marks the site of a memorial fountain, which commemorated the abandonment of a proposed **Match Tax** (7) in 1872.

Walking on past the overhead bridge you will see the police station with a plaque

marking the starting point of the Bow Heritage Trail. Across the road is Bow Road railway station and on the right a little further along you will reach the corner of Harley Grove, where you will find Harley House. There are two plaques here for the statesman **George Lansbury** (8). One is in bronze, set on a stone plinth, and the other is from the Bow Heritage Trail. Lansbury was a Poplar borough councillor for 37 years, an MP, privy councillor, government minister and leader of the Labour Party. Walking on you come to an old school building with a plaque marking the former **Central Foundation Girls' School** (9).

Proceed to the next turning, Coborn Street, where there are two plaques. Opposite a school you will find a plaque for **Dr Barnado** (10) at No.30. He lodged here when he first arrived from Ireland in 1866. Although not medically qualified he was referred to as

'Doctor' by his associates and the name stuck. His homes for orphans were very successful and became a worldwide organisation. Across the road is an oval plaque commemorating the music hall entertainer **Charles Coborn** (11). He is remembered for his hit songs *The Man Who Broke the Bank at Monte Carlo* and *Two Lovely Black Eyes*.

Continue round the corner and cross over Coborn Road into Morgan Street. This leads into Tredegar Square. The only surviving part of the original construction of the 1840s is on the right-hand side. A plaque at Nos 25–26 mentions this as being part of the estate of **Sir Charles Morgan Bt of Tredegar Mon.** (12).

Continue to the very end and turn right. Cross the road at the pedestrian crossing and walk under the bridge. Turn around to see the plaque informing you that this is where the

First Flying Bomb (13) fell on London on 13 June 1944. The blue plaque is on the wall at the side of the bridge.

Turn right by the post box opposite into Antill Road. Now walk right to the far end and turn left into St Stephen's Road. This will bring you up to Roman Road, where you should turn right. Archaeologists consider this to have been part of the old Roman road from London to Colchester. Today it is a street market full of stalls. Walk up to the clock set on the library and you will find two plaques commemorating **Vernon Hall** (14) and **John Passmore Edwards** (15), who was a founder of free public libraries. Retrace your steps back along Roman Road and continue to Dane Place.

Walking into Dane Place and following it to the right you will see a Bow Heritage plaque on the house immediately ahead. This is No.45 Norman Grove, where the suffragette leader **Sylvia Pankhurst** (16) set up her toy factory and nursery in 1914. She was gaoled nine times during the struggle for emancipation.

Return to Roman Road and continue walking up to the traffic lights by St Barnabas Church, then turn right. Walk on to Old Ford Road at the roundabout. This is opposite Victoria Park and the lake. There is a refreshment café on the corner in the park where you can have a cup of tea and watch the ducks if you would like a rest. Continuing the walk, however, the next plaque is to be found nearby at No.288 Old Ford Road. This is for the writer **Israel Zangwill** (17), who lived here. His works include the novel *Children of the Ghetto* (1892) and the play *The Melting Pot* (1908).

Continue along Old Ford Road, going past the Regent's Canal, and turn left into Bonner Street. Turn to the left on reaching Roman Road and cross over to Usk Street. Carry on past

the allotments and go through the entrance gate into Meath Gardens. In the centre of the gardens you will see a tree, which is leaning at a crazy angle, situated between two park benches. Surprisingly there is a small metal plaque at the foot of this tree. This commemorates the Aborigine cricketer **King Cole** (18) who died from tuberculosis on the first unofficial Australian cricket tour of Britain (1868). He was buried in a pauper's grave at Victoria Park Cemetery, which is now Meath Gardens.

Leave Meath Gardens by the same exit but this time walk straight ahead. Facing you in Morpeth Street is a block of flats called Bradley Lynch Court. Next to the doorway marked 11–55 you will see a plaque for **Bradley Lynch** (19), who died from cancer at the age of 16. As the plaque states 'He worked selflessly and very hard to raise funds for the fight against the disease from which he was suffering'.

With your back to Bradley Lynch Court turn left, then left again at Knottisford Street. This leads into Digby Street, where you will find Sidney Godley House near the end of the road, just past the enclosed childrens' play area. The plaque for **Sidney Godley VC** (20) makes interesting reading.

Continue and turn right and then left at the traffic lights into Roman Road. Bethnal Green station is a short way ahead. Above the staircase leading down to the station you can see a plaque for the **Wartime Disaster** (21). This station suffered one of the worst

No.3 Paradise Row, home of the bare-knuckle boxer Daniel Mendoza.

civilian wartime disasters when in 1943 it was struck by a bomb and 173 men, women and children lost their lives.

Before you depart there is one more plaque to see. Cross over Roman Road towards the church of St John. Now cross Cambridge Heath Road to Paradise Row, where at No.3 there is a blue plaque on the home of the boxer **Daniel Mendoza** (22). He was one of the last bare-knuckle fighters and wrote *The Art of Boxing* (1789). Mendoza retired from the sport at the age of 56.

Nearby, on the other side of Cambridge Heath Road, is the Museum of Childhood, which is well worth a visit before departing from Bethnal Green station.

Walk 25
East End (3)

Distance:	3 miles (4.82 km) or 3½ miles (5.63 km)
Time taken:	1½ hours or 1¾ hours
Number of plaques:	10 or 13
Nearest tube stations:	Wapping, Whitechapel
Bus routes:	D3, 15, 100

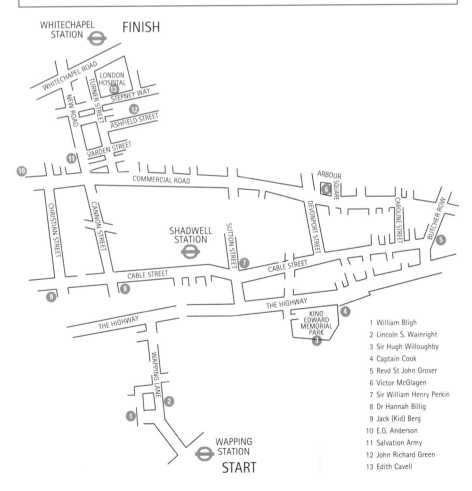

1 William Bligh
2 Lincoln S. Wainright
3 Sir Hugh Willoughby
4 Captain Cook
5 Revd St John Groser
6 Victor McGlagen
7 Sir William Henry Perkin
8 Dr Hannah Billig
9 Jack (Kid) Berg
10 E.G. Anderson
11 Salvation Army
12 John Richard Green
13 Edith Cavell

THIS walk is a little shorter than others and has fewer plaques. It has been included because it takes in an area close to the Thames and has many points of interest. Visitors who come with the intention of exploring the dock area find that many of the old warehouses have been converted into modern apartment blocks. Traffic on the main roads is heavy, as the coming of the Rotherhithe Tunnel brought an entry to south London. The area also suffered badly in World War Two. This walk could be lengthened with an exploration of the dock area at the start, before proceeding along the detailed route. Alternatively it could be combined with the Walk 23, which commences at Aldgate East Station.

Coming out of Wapping underground station, cross over Wapping High Street into Wapping Lane. Turn left at Watts Street and then take the second right into Reardon Street. Set high on a brick wall is a plaque marking the site of a home of William Bligh (1). He was captain of the famous *Bounty* and was cast adrift by mutineers before sailing 4,000 miles to safety. As the plaque states he served in the West Indies. After a colourful life he retired in 1811 with the rank of Admiral.

Turn right into Chandlers Street, almost opposite. Ahead, in Wapping Lane, is Clergy House (below), with the blue plaque of Lincoln Stanhope Wainright (2). This vicar of St Peter's served for 55 years and worked tirelessly for his parishioners. It is now about three-quarters of a mile to the next plaque.

Continue up Wapping Lane. You will pass Tobacco Dock, which is a 'white elephant' shopping centre existing with just a café and a wine bar. Turn right on reaching the Highway. Now walk on to the King Edward Memorial Park, which you can enter from Glamis Road. At the rear of the park is a large brick-built circular folly, in front of which is a glazed plaque (left). This records that **Sir Hugh Willoughby** (3) and other seamen set sail from nearby Ratcliff Cross to explore the northern seas. Having separated from other ships in the fleet, Willoughby's ship sank with the loss of all aboard. The journal of his ship, later discovered by Russian fishermen, was published in 1903. There is a wonderful view of the Thames and its apartment blocks from this site.

Walk past the bandstand to the far corner of the park, exiting again on the Highway. The brick building in front of the modern luxury apartment block bears a blue plaque for **Captain Cook** (4). This famous explorer lived in a house formerly on this site. He charted many unknown lands but was unfortunately attacked and killed by natives in Hawaii. There is another plaque for him in Mile End Road.

Continue further along the Highway and cross over to Butcher Row. On the Royal Foundation of St Katherine you will see an English Heritage plaque commemorating the **Revd St John Groser** (5), a priest and social reformer who lived here.

Now cross over the road to Cable Street. This street is famous for having been the scene of the 1936 battle, when local residents barricaded the road and prevented Fascist marchers from passing. Turn right at the second turning, Caroline Street, then left upon reaching Commercial Road. Cross over to the other side of the road. Just past Arbour Square and by the bus stop you will see the plaque of **Victor McLaglen** (6) on No.505. He was a boxer, but is best remembered for portraying a tough guy in many Hollywood films.

Cross back over Commercial Road and a few yards further on go down Devonport Street, turning right at the bottom into the continuation of Cable Street. Walk along to Gosling House, on the corner of Sutton Street. A plaque marks the site where **Sir William Henry Perkin** (7) worked when he discovered the first aniline dye in 1856. Proceeding along Cable Street, you pass Shadwell tube

The Distinguished
Physician

Dr Hannah Billig G.M, M.B.E
1901 - 1987

Known locally as
"The Angel of Cable Street."
Honoured for her Bravery in
World War II and
Famine Relief Work in India

Lived and worked here
1935 - 1964

station. At No.198 Cable Street you can see the plaque of **Dr Hannah Billig** (8). She was known as 'the angel of Cable Street', having tended the sick and injured throughout World War Two. She was awarded the George Medal and MBE, and spent her final years in Israel.

Further along you will reach Noble Court. At the far end cornering Hindmarsh Close you will find the plaque of the boxer **Jack 'Kid' Berg** (9), who lived near here. He was light-welterweight champion in 1930 and British lightweight champion in 1934. His nickname was 'Whitechapel Whirlwind', not 'Windmill' as stated on the plaque.

Now cross the road and walk up Christian Street to Commercial Road. Turn to the left and, a short way along, cross the road to the London Guildhall University building. Above the main entrance there is a plaque for the first woman doctor, **Elizabeth Garrett Anderson** (10). This and the next three plaques are included in Walk 23. If you have already seen them you could continue to Aldgate East station ahead. Otherwise walk back to New Road and turn left to No.23, which was the first meeting place in 1865 of the **Salvation Army** (11).

Cross the road and turn right into Varden Street. Turn left at Turner Street and then right at Newark Street. You will see a plaque for the historian **John Richard Green** (12) on John Garnett House. He was the author of *A Short History of the English People* (1874) and several other books in the same vein. The museum of the London Hospital is across the road. This contains many gruesome surgical tools, nurse's uniforms and items of interest from the archives of the hospital.

Return to Turner Street, turn right and then right again at Stepney Way. You are now going to enter London Hospital. Walk through the doors and you come to a courtyard. On the wall at the right-hand side there is a blue plaque honouring the bravery of the nurse **Edith Cavell** (13). She served during World War One and was executed by the enemy for aiding the escape of British servicemen.

Walk to the statue of Queen Alexandra, turn right and go through the main foyer of the hospital. On the way you will pass the giant warning bell, cast in 1757 at the Whitechapel Bell Foundry. Coming out of the hospital you can see Whitechapel underground station opposite.

Walk 26
Hampstead (1)

Distance:	4 miles (6.4km)
Time taken:	2 hours
Number of plaques:	32
Nearest tube stations:	Hampstead
Bus routes:	210, 268

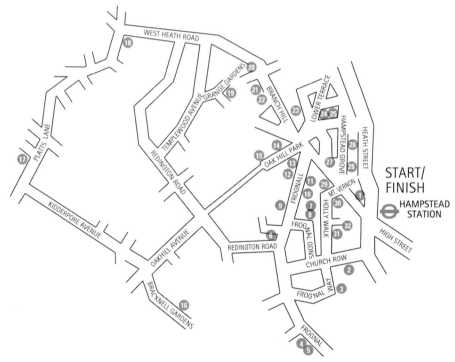

1 Clock Tower	9 Kathleen Ferrier	17 T.G. Masaryk	25 Sir G.G. Scott
2 T. & J.J. Park	10 T. Karsavina	18 F.O. Salisbury	26 George du Maurier
3 Gracie Fields	11 E.V. Knox	19 John Spedan Lewis	27 Joanna Baillie
4 Kate Greenaway	12 Charles de Gaulle	20 H. Beerbohm Tree	28 George Romney
5 Dennis Brain	13 Ramsey MacDonald/Ogden Stewart	21 Paul Robeson	29 Sir Henry Dale
6 Sir Harold Gillies	14 E. Rundle Charles	22 Alfred Reynolds	30 R.L. Stevenson
7 Sir Walter Besant	15 Gerard Manley Hopkins	23 John Constable	31 The Watch House
8 Hugh Gaitskell	16 Huxley Family	24 John Galsworthy	32 Sir William Walton

HAMPSTEAD is one of the most attractive of London suburbs and has for many years been the home of artists, authors and people of note. Due to its high ground, it was in mediaeval times considered a healthy area and was a place of refuge during the great plague of the 17th century. Today it contains some of London's most expensive and exclusive suburban residential properties. Although since 1965 part of the borough of Camden, the original boundaries extend from Golders Green in the north, to Swiss Cottage in the south and border Finchley and Hendon. The Heath, which consists of approximately 800 acres, was preserved as an open space in the late 19th century and is a popular skiing spot during the winter snow. Visitors come from far and wide for the regular bank holiday fairs. A warning to hikers is that Hampstead is very hilly and you can expect a walk in the vicinity to be more tiring than others detailed in this book.

We begin the walk from Hampstead underground station. Immediately opposite, on the corner of Holly Hill, is the **Clock Tower** (1). An oval cast plaque on the side of the building informs you that it started its life as the local fire station (below). A look-out used to be kept at the top of the tower. Cross over Holly Hill and continue along Heath Street a short distance to Church Row. At No.18 Church Row there is a large brown plaque that was unveiled in 1909. This commemorates the historians **Thomas** and **John James Park** (2).

The Clock Tower, Hampstead, a former fire station.

Continue towards the church of St John-at-Hampstead. If you are interested to see the cemetery opposite, you will find the graves of many notable people, including John Constable, Hugh Gaitskell, Anton Walbrook, Kay Kendall, Sir Herbert Beerbohm Tree and George du Maurier.

The walk continues from the plaque by taking the small turning with the bollards at its entrance, which leads into Frognal Way. The first house you will see is one that the popular singer **Gracie Fields** (3) had built for herself in 1934. Walking on through this unmade road you will reach Frognal. Turn to the left.

A short distance along Frognal is the University College School, built 1906-7. The statue over the main doorway is of Edward VII, who opened the school in 1907. Opposite at No.39 you will see a rectangular blue plaque marking a home of the author and artist **Kate Greenaway** (4). The noted architect R. Norman Shaw designed this house especially for her. Horn player **Dennis Brain** (5), who is commemorated by a regular round blue plaque, lived next door. He played with the Royal Philharmonic Orchestra. Now turn and walk back up Frognal.

The first plaque you will see is on the corner of Redington Road. This was the home of the noted surgeon **Sir Harold Gillies** (6). Take the next turning on the right, Frognal Gardens. At No.18 in the corner of the bend of the road is a driveway leading to a house with two plaques (left): both **Sir Walter Besant** (7) and later **Hugh Gaitskell** (8) lived here. The former was a novelist, antiquary and social reformer, and the latter was a leader of the Labour Party. Return to Frognal and continue. The blue plaque set high up on No.97, across the road, marks the home of the singer **Kathleen Ferrier** (9), who lived here 1942-53.

On the right at No.108 a blue plaque, surrounded by ivy, marks the home of the Russian-born ballerina **Tamara Karsavina** (10). She wrote several books on ballet and was a vice-president of the Royal Academy of Dancing. The next door corner house was the home of **E.V. Knox** (11), who was a humorous writer and former editor of *Punch* magazine. These two houses were joined together as a pub during the 18th century.

For a short time during World War Two the leader of the Free French forces and later president **Charles de Gaulle** (12) lived at No.99, opposite. Walk up the slope to the painted house, No.103, where there is an oval Hampstead plaque commemorating both Prime Minister **James Ramsey MacDonald** and American playwright **Donald Ogden Stewart** (13). The latter wrote scripts for many notable films and won an award in 1940 for *The Philadelphia Story.*

Turn left into the unpaved road Oak Hill Way. You will find a large isolated house called Coombe Edge, where the author **Elizabeth Rundle Charles** (14) lived 1874-96. Continue ahead through the pedestrian only barrier onto the footpath, which leads on to Oak Hill Park. At the end is a large white-painted house almost hidden by trees. This is Oak Hill House (No.9) and the oval plaque marks it as the home of **Gerard Manley Hopkins** (15). He was a poet and writer who became a Roman Catholic priest in 1877. None of his writings were published during his lifetime.

Continue through the footpath ahead and cross over the road into Oak Hill Avenue. Pass Greenaway Gardens and turn left at the end of the road into Bracknell Gardens. You will find a plaque at No.16 where the **Huxley Family** (16) lived. The father Leonard was editor of the *Cornhill Magazine* for 17 years, the older son Julian was a professor of zoology, and the younger son Aldous was a novelist, best remembered for his *Brave New World* (1932). The next plaque is nearly half a mile away and uphill.

Turn back and walk up Bracknell Gardens, continuing through Kidderpore Avenue. The neo-classical King's College was built in the early 1840s. Walk on to Platts Lane and bear right. At No.21 you will see a plaque that commemorates **Thomas Garrigue Masaryk** (17), who lived and worked here during World War One. He was one of the founders of the state of Czechoslovakia, becoming its first president from 1918–35. He was also the father of the better known Jan Masaryk. There is now an uphill walk of almost half a mile to the next plaque.

Continue up Platts Lane, passing Hollycroft and Rosecroft avenues, and turn to the right on reaching West Heath Road at the end. The huge house on the corner bears an oval Hampstead plaque (left), which states that **Francis Owen Salisbury** (18), known as 'Frank' lived here. He was a popular portrait and figure painter who also worked in stained glass.

Proceed along West Heath Road and take the second turning right, Templewood Avenue. A short way down you will see Grange Gardens, where there is an oval plaque for **John** and his son **John Spedan Lewis** (19). The father was a silk merchant and his son the founder of the John Lewis Partnership stores.

Return to West Heath Road and continue to Mansion Gardens, where you will find another oval plaque on the wall by a gateway. This commemorates the artist **John Constable** and also the theatrical impresario **Herbert Beerbohm Tree** (20). Details of their association with this spot are recorded on the plaque. Continue ahead to Branch Hill, where at the Chestnuts Hotel you will find the blue plaque recording that the black American bass singer **Paul Robeson** (21) lived here 1929–30. A few doors away there is a privately erected plaque for the Hungarian poet and philosopher **Alfred Reynolds** (22), who lived at Lower Lodge 1980–93.

Now turn left into Lower Terrace, where you will see another plaque for **John Constable**

(23) at No.2. He stayed in this house 1821–2. Turn around and walk through to Admiral's Walk. There are two plaques to be seen here on the large cream-painted houses (left). Firstly the novelist and playwright **John Galsworthy** (24), who is best remembered for *The Forsyte Saga*, and secondly the architect **Sir George Gilbert Scott** (25), whose designs include the Albert Memorial.

Coming out of Admiral's Walk turn right into Hampstead Grove. At No.28 on the left you will see the brown plaque of **George du Maurier** (26).

This French-born author and illustrator is remembered best for the novel *Trilby*. Opposite is the 17th-century Fenton House. This is the oldest house in Hampstead and is open to the public at restricted times. Apart from its many treasures it has one of the finest collections of harpsichords. Proceed onwards into Holly Bush Hill.

Bolton House, the large 18th-century house next door to Fenton House, bears another brown plaque, which commemorates **Joanna Baillie** (27). She was a poet and dramatist who lived in this house for nearly 50 years. The artist **George Romney** (28) had his studio in the painted half-timbered house on the side of the small green. Across the road is the huge old Consumption Hospital, now converted into luxury flats.

Cross over the road and go up the slope called Mount Vernon. The first plaque you will find is on Mount Vernon House and is for **Sir Henry Dale** (29). He was a physiologist who received the Nobel Prize in 1936 for work on the chemical transmission of nervous effects. On Abernathy House (No.7) you will see the plaque of the prolific novelist **Robert Louis Stevenson** (30). His works include *Treasure Island, Kidnapped, Dr Jekyll and Mr Hyde, The Black Arrow* and others. Walking round the corner you come upon a terrace of Queen Anne period cottages. No.9 Holly Place was **The Watch House** (31) of the 1830s police force

(below). The little turning next to it, Holly Place, has a plaque at No.10 marking it as a home of the composer **Sir William Walton** (32). Among his many compositions were the coronation marches of 1937 and 1953.

This is now almost the end of the walk. The most interesting way back to the underground station is by retracing your steps part of the way. Walk back through Holly Walk and Mount Vernon. Cross over to Holly Mount, walking towards the Holly Bush public house. At the end of Holly Mount there is a view across London. You can clearly see the Post Office Tower and the London Eye. Now walk down the steps opposite Holly Mount House, pausing to see Golden Yard and read its framed history conveniently placed on the wall. Continuing down the steps leads to Heath Street and, turning right, to the nearby underground station.

Walk 27
Hampstead (2)

Distance approx:	4 miles (6.4km), extra walk a further 1¾ miles (2.81km)
Time taken:	2 hours, extra walk a further hour
Number of plaques:	31, extra walk a further 10
Nearest tube stations:	Hampstead and Golders Green
Bus routes:	46, 214, 268

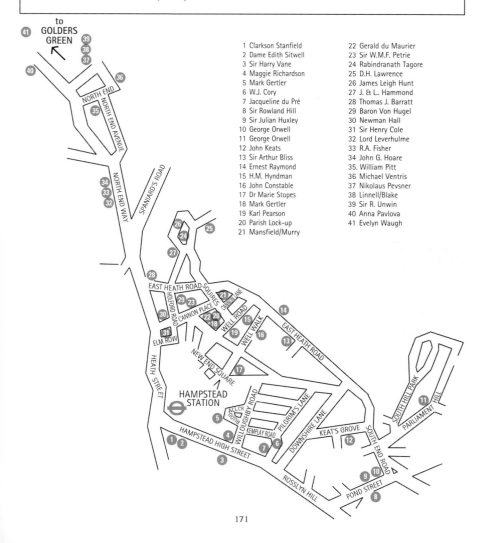

1 Clarkson Stanfield	22 Gerald du Maurier
2 Dame Edith Sitwell	23 Sir W.M.F. Petrie
3 Sir Harry Vane	24 Rabindranath Tagore
4 Maggie Richardson	25 D.H. Lawrence
5 Mark Gertler	26 James Leigh Hunt
6 W.J. Cory	27 J. & L. Hammond
7 Jacqueline du Pré	28 Thomas J. Barratt
8 Sir Rowland Hill	29 Baron Von Hugel
9 Sir Julian Huxley	30 Newman Hall
10 George Orwell	31 Sir Henry Cole
11 George Orwell	32 Lord Leverhulme
12 John Keats	33 R.A. Fisher
13 Sir Arthur Bliss	34 John G. Hoare
14 Ernest Raymond	35. William Pitt
15 H.M. Hyndman	36 Michael Ventris
16 John Constable	37 Nikolaus Pevsner
17 Dr Marie Stopes	38 Linnell/Blake
18 Mark Gertler	39 Sir R. Unwin
19 Karl Pearson	40 Anna Pavlova
20 Parish Lock-up	41 Evelyn Waugh
21 Mansfield/Murry	

THIS walk is based on the eastern side of central Hampstead. It starts and finishes at Hampstead tube station and could be taken in conjunction with the previous one. There is also an optional extra walk, should you decide to continue to Golders Green, where a further 10 plaques can be seen. This would add an extra 1¾ miles to the walk from Elm Row.

Coming out of Hampstead underground station turn left into Hampstead High Street. You cannot help noticing the lady looking down at No.28A. Cross over the pedestrian crossing next to the Victorian post box, towards the post office. Start walking up the slope and you will see that the corner house, named Stanfield House, has an oval plaque above the door. The gold coloured inscription reads 'Clarkson Stanfield (1) (1793-1867) Theatrical scenic artist, marine and landscape painter, Royal Academician, lived here 1847-65'. The large block of flats on the opposite corner is named Greenhill and there is a blue plaque set high on the front commemorating the poet Dame Edith Sitwell (2) who lived in flat 42. Continue over this raised part of the High Street. Across the road you can see, while walking, the entrance to the old brewery established in 1720.

Reaching the bottom you will find a wooden bench in front of an aged brick wall. The plaque to Sir Harry Vane (3) was placed here in 1897. He unfortunately lost his head after a distinguished career in Parliament. The house in which he lived is long gone, but the wall looks as though it has been here a considerable time. Cross over to Willoughby Road opposite. Behind the flower stall on the corner is a pretty floral plaque recording that Maggie Richardson (4) had her own flower stall here for 60 years.

Walk along Willoughby Road past the church, which has been neatly converted into housing, and turn left into Rudall Crescent. Penn Studio is in the corner at No.13. The building at the rear carries a plaque for the artist Mark Gertler (5) and is best viewed when standing outside No.17. Return to Willoughby Road and cross over to Kemplay Road. You will notice the interesting feature of this short road is the decorative stonework above the windows of the houses.

Reaching Pilgrims Lane and bearing right, the first noticeable thing to see is a ship's figurehead projecting from the wall of a house across the road. Next to this is a plaque marking it as the home of William Johnson Cory (6). He was an assistant master at Eton College and wrote the words of the *Eton Boating Song*. Carry on a little further to No.5A on the other side of the road. You will see a plaque on a home of the cellist Jacqueline du Pré (7), who lived here 1970-5 (left).

Continue and turn left at the main road. Walk on to the traffic lights and turn left into Pond Street. The huge Victorian Gothic St Stephen's Church stands on the corner. Past this is the Royal Free Hospital, which was built on the site of a house owned by Sir Rowland Hill (8), the creator of the adhesive postage stamp. His plaque is located on the outer wall of the hospital's covered car park at the right, found by going up the pathway on the side. It was originally erected in a different position by the Royal Society of Arts in 1892 and later moved to this site. Returning to Pond Street cross the road and go to the cream-painted house, No.31. An attractive plaque at this address records it as the home of **Sir Julian Sorell Huxley** (9). A noted biologist, he was secretary of the Zoological Society of London (1935–42) and first director-general of UNESCO (1946–8).

Proceed to the corner where there is an oblong stone plaque with a relief bust of the author **George Orwell** (10). This was at one time a bookshop where he lived and worked (1934–5). There is now an uphill walk of about 800 yards to the next plaque. It is worth it for the surprise waiting at the top.

Turn left and cross the road by Hampstead Heath station. The turning next to the station is South Hill Park, and bearing right leads to Parliament Hill. After the Art Deco flats at the beginning it appears a rather uninteresting street, but walk up to the top. A second plaque for **George Orwell** (11) can be seen at the last house, No.77. One can only imagine that he lived here for the seclusion and proximity to the Heath. Now take the footpath at the end of the road to the viewpoint 319ft above sea level. There are several benches around as this is a favourite local picnic spot. The views across London are superb. You can clearly see the City skyscrapers and St Paul's Cathedral, and on a clear day you will be able to discern many landmarks.

You now need to return to South End Road. If you do not fancy the walk back down Parliament Hill, you can make a small detour to get back to the same place. It is a little further but quite pleasant. Retrace your steps a short way and take the footpath ahead at the crossing. Follow this down to a footpath crossing between two lakes. Now take the footpath going around the left-hand lake, crossing back to a passageway between buildings ahead. This will bring you into South Hill Park. Turn to the right for the quickest way down to South End Road.

Reaching South End Road turn right and take the first turning left, which is Keat's Grove. **John Keats** (12) spent two years at No.10, the house that bears his plaque. It was here that he wrote 'Ode to a Nightingale'. The house is now a museum open to the public, but like many others, it is not open on Mondays.

Return to South End Road, turning left and continuing into East Heath Road. Walk past Downshire Hill and the large open car park, up to Heath Side. The large corner house was the pre-war home of the composer **Sir Arthur Bliss** (13) for 10 years. His blue plaque can be viewed from the other side of the road. Walking on you will see some large blocks of flats on the right named 'The Pryors'. You will find an oval Hampstead plaque here on the second block, which commemorates the novelist **Ernest Raymond** (14). He was the author of over 50 books including the winner of the 1936 Book Guild Gold Medal, *We The Accused*.

Cross the road to Well Walk. This was so named because of the spring water well. People flocked here in the 18th century to drink the chalybeate water. The red-brick house on the left, called 'Wellside', bears a stone plaque stating that it was built on the site of the old Hampstead pump room.

On the house behind the drinking fountain, No.13, you can see the blue plaque for **Henry Mayers Hyndman** (15). He was a socialist leader who lived here 1916–21. An earlier occupant of this house was the poet and novelist John Masefield. Turning round you can see a blue plaque opposite on the house where the painter **John Constable** (16) lived 1827–34. Ahead you will find an interesting board on the Wells Tavern, giving a history of the local spa water.

Further along at No.14 Well Walk there is an oval Hampstead plaque marking a home of the birth control pioneer **Dr Marie Stopes** (17). She lived here when married to her first husband R.R. Gates. Turn right at the traffic island into New End Square.

Ahead is Burgh House, which was built in 1703. This is open to the public Wednesday to Sunday. It also has a pleasant buttery restaurant and bookstall. Continuing past Burgh House turn right at Ye Old White Bear into Well Road. The creeper-covered Well Mount Studio has an oval plaque, which is the second on this walk commemorating the artist **Mark Gertler** (18). This talented painter had associations with the Bloomsbury Group and took his own life during a fit of depression. The next plaque is to be found at No.7 Well Road, the home of the mathematician and scientist **Karl Pearson** (19).

The turning a few yards further on the left is Cannon Lane, where you will find the old **Parish Lock-up** (20) at No.11. This dates from around 1730 and ceased to function in 1829. Take the turning to the right and then go left at East Heath Road. You will need to cross the road, as there is no footpath on the left-hand side. The white-painted house, No.17, is

surrounded by a high fence. A blue plaque here commemorates the novelist **Katherine Mansfield** (21) and her second husband **John Middleton Murry**, himself a writer and critic. They were friends of the author D.H. Lawrence and are said to have given him the inspiration for the two central characters of his novel *Women in Love*.

Turn left into Squires Mount, where you will see the date 1704 on the second terraced house. Continue right into Cannon Place. The corner house, Cannon Hall, was the home of **Sir Gerald du Maurier** (22). He was a theatrical impresario and actor, who lived here from 1916 until his death in 1934. Further along at No.5 Cannon Place the egyptologist **Sir William Matthew Flinders Petrie** (23) lived from 1919 to 1935. He excavated the pyramids at Giza as well as other important historical sites. Now retrace your steps back along Cannon Place and Squires Mount. Cross over East Heath Road and proceed into the Vale of Health.

The Vale of Health was so named because it was considered a healthy area to live during the time of the great plague of 1666. The first plaque to be found is on the painted house on the left. This is for the Indian poet and philosopher **Rabindranath Tagore** (24), who stayed here in 1912. He received the Nobel Prize for literature in 1913 and was knighted in 1915, but gave up the knighthood in protest against English policy in the Punjab. Walk further into the Vale of Health and turn to the right. You can see the blue plaque of the author **D.H. Lawrence** (25), who lived at 1 Byron Villas in 1915.

Continuing in the Vale of Health turn left at the end then left again into the narrow turning with the two bollards. There is a small terrace of cottages here where a blue plaque on South Villa marks the home in 1816–21 of the poet and essayist **James Leigh Hunt** (26). This may be partly obscured by plant growth. Continue on past the Tagore house.

Just after the red post box you will see a footpath which branches off to the right. The red-brick house on this corner is named 'Hollycot'. This was the home of the social historians **John** and **Lucy Hammond** (27) between 1906 and 1913. They jointly published many works detailing the harshness of English social conditions. Continue up this footpath towards the buildings visible at the top.

These buildings are flats named 'Bellmoor' and were built on the site of a large house of the same name. The brown plaque at the far end informs us that the Hampstead historian **Thomas J. Barratt** (28) lived in the original house 1877–1914. He was chairman of the soap manufacturers A. & F. Pears. A second large rectangular plaque points out that 'The surface of the soil is 435ft 7ins above sea level or 16ft 7inches higher than the top of St Paul's Cross'.

Cross over to Holford Road opposite, where you will find a GLC plaque at No.4 for **Baron Friedrich Von Hugel** (29). This Austrian-born theologian was the founder of the London Society for the Study of Religion. He was the author of several books and lived here 1882–1903.

Continue on to Hampstead Square. On the right, on the end wall of No.8, there is a brown plaque which records that these cottages were given to the aged by the widow of the clergyman **Newman Hall** (30), in memory of her husband. They lived at nearby Vine House at the time of his death. Take the footpath alongside down to the square and turn right at the end into Elm Row. This short road was built in the 1720s. On a brick wall, bordering No.3, there is an oval plaque informing us that **Sir Henry Cole** (31) lived here. He was a founder and director of the Victoria and Albert Museum and was also responsible for the first Christmas cards and the production of the first adhesive postage stamps, proposed by Sir Rowland Hill. He lived at this address 1879–80. A blue plaque also commemorates him opposite the main entrance of the Victoria and Albert Museum.

Turning left you can now walk down a short way to Hampstead underground station to complete the walk. If you wish to continue for another mile and three-quarters to Golders Green, you can see a further 10 plaques.

Additional walk

Walk back up Heath Street, passing East Heath Road, then cross over and walk past the Whitestone Pond. Continue along North End Way. On the left is Inverforth House, which was once a private house, then a hospital, and is now luxury flats. On the outer wall there are two blue plaques which commemorate former occupants **Lord Leverhulme** (32) and **R.A. Fisher** (33). The latter was a foremost statistician and geneticist who lived here in childhood. Lord Leverhulme, the soap millionaire, who greatly extended the house and grounds, lived and died here. An oval Hampstead plaque can be seen a little further along on the building for the banker **John Gurney Hoare** (34). He was a prime mover in the 19th-century battle to save Hampstead Heath as an open site. An interesting diversion here is to see the pergola at the back of the house. To do this turn left into Iverforth Close and go through the Hill Garden.

To continue the walk, go up the elevated path at the side of the main road and upon reaching the bottom, take the turning across the road, North End. This is next to the Old Bull and Bush, which was immortalised by the old music hall song. Bearing right again you come into North End Avenue, where you will see Pitt House. Here you will find a neglected wooden plaque on the gatepost. It informs you that **William Pitt the Elder, Earl of Chatham** (35) lived in a house formerly on this site.

Return to North End and walk on to the next plaque at No.19. This is for **Michael Ventris** (36)

who was an architect and linguist whose claim to fame was his translation of the ancient Minoan script known as Linear B. He tragically died in a road accident before his work was published.

Continue on to Wildwood Terrace. At No.2 there is a plaque marking it as the home of **Sir Nikolaus Pevsner** (37), who was an architectural historian who fled to Britain in 1933 to escape the Nazis. He became an authority on English architecture and wrote several books on the subject.

Walk on through the unmade road to the large house on the left called Old Wyldes. There are two plaques here. The first, an oval plaque, bears the names of **John Linnell** and **William Blake** (38), who lived here in earlier years. Linnell was an artist, engraver, sculptor and a patron of Blake. There is a copy of this plaque on a house in SE23, where there is no foundation for it to exist. The second is a round plaque, which commemorates **Sir Raymond Unwin** (39), who was an architect and planner of new towns. He was prominent in the development of Letchworth, Hampstead Garden Suburb and Wythenshawe and lived here 1906–40. Return to North End Road, take the pedestrian crossing over the road and continue walking down.

A short way along is the entrance to Golders Hill Park, where there is an excellent refreshment café and other amenities.

The next blue plaque is past this entranceway on the main road. It was the home of the Russian ballerina **Anna Pavlova** (40). She purchased Ivy Cottage in 1912 and lived here until her death in 1931.

The final plaque of the walk is at No.145 North End Road, which was the home of the novelist **Evelyn Waugh** (41). He is best remembered for *Brideshead Revisited, Men at Arms* and *Officers and Gentlemen*. It is now about half a mile downhill to Golders Green underground station.

Walk 28
South and West Hampstead

Distance:	6 miles (10.45km), extra walk a further ¾ mile
Time taken:	2¼ hours or 2¾ hours
Number of plaques:	25 or 28
Nearest tube stations:	Chalk Farm, Belsize Park, West Hampstead, Finchley Road
Bus routes:	13, 31, 82, 113, 139, 168, 328

THIS is primarily a residential area first developed in late Victorian times. It is a mixture of Victorian, Edwardian and modern houses, flats and mansion blocks. Like the two previous walks it has seen many authors, artists and people of note living within its boundaries. Many of the houses are architecturally interesting and even the many terraces have features worth noticing. A cosmopolitan area, the many European immigrants have made their impression on this neighbourhood. There are now many schools in West Hampstead.

The walk commences at Chalk Farm underground station, where you need to turn left upon exiting. The main road is Haverstock Hill and you can see the Salvation Army Hall, next door to Marine Ices. This old established Italian ice-cream manufacturer serves some of the most delicious ice cream to be found anywhere. Cross the road by the traffic lights and bear to the left. The first commemorative plaque you will see is a few doors along, past the school, at No.60. This is for **Noel Bertram Farman** (1), who was a physician and surgeon serving the local community for 40 years.

Cross over Haverstock Hill and take the first turning on the left, Eton Road. A short way along turn left into Eton Villas. Opposite St Saviour's church at No.9 there is an LCC blue plaque on the home of **Alfred Stevens** (2) (below). He was an artist and sculptor whose most

notable works were the Wellington monument at St Paul's Cathedral and the lions at the British Museum.

Returning to Eton Road turn left, then turn right into Fellows Road. Follow it around the bend and then turn right at the Hampstead Britannia Hotel into Primrose Hill Road. Turn right again at the Washington public house into England's Lane. There

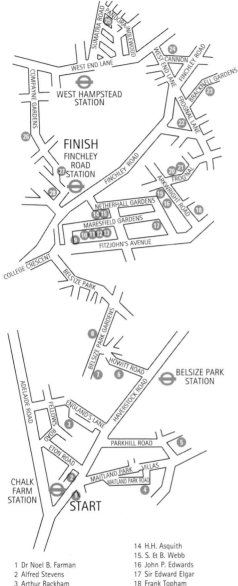

1 Dr Noel B. Farman
2 Alfred Stevens
3 Arthur Rackham
4 Karl Marx
5 Piet Mondrian
6 Ramsay MacDonald
7 Frederick Delius
8 Henry N. Brailsford
9 Philip de Laszlo
10 Cecil Sharp
11 Westfield College
12 Sigmund Freud
13 Anna Freud

14 H.H. Asquith
15. S. & B. Webb
16 John P. Edwards
17 Sir Edward Elgar
18 Frank Topham
19 Tobias Matthay
20 Dennis Brain
21 Kate Greenaway
22 Cecil Beaton
23 Huxley family
24 Sir Adrian Boult
25 Alfred Harmsworth
26 Dr N. Sokolow
27 Lindsay Anderson
28 M.B. Osterberg

are several cafés in this area. A short way along you will find Chalcott Gardens set back from the road on the right. The first house, No.16, was built in 1881 and was the home from 1903 to 1920 of the Art Nouveau-style illustrator **Arthur Rackham** (3) (below). Among other books, his drawings appeared in first editions of *Peter Pan* and Hans Andersen's *Fairy Tales*.

Continue along England's Lane and turn right upon reaching the main road. While walking down Haverstock Hill you will notice the Sir Richard Steele public house and the next turning, Steeles Road. Sir Richard Steele lived 1672–1729. He was a dramatist and politician who had a very varied career. His literary works included periodical magazines and his parliamentary career resulted in a knighthood from George I.

When you reach the church turn sharp left into Maitland Park Road, keeping to the right fork. This is to the right of the statue of the family group. On the large block of flats near the end of the road, numbered 101–108, you will surprisingly see a brown plaque with the name **Karl Marx** (4) on it.

The house formerly on this site was his home for eight years and he died here. As you are probably aware he is buried at Highgate Cemetery.

Walk through the entranceway of Nos 109–134 to the road at the back, turn to the left and then turn right on reaching Southampton Road ahead. Between St Dominic's Priory and School there is a footpath called Alan Cheales Way, which leads into Tasker Road. Turn right into Parkhill Road. A couple of doors along at No.60 there is a blue plaque which commemorates the Dutch abstract artist **Piet Mondrian** (5). He lived here for two years prior to World War Two, before emigrating to New York. There is now a walk of about one kilometre to the next plaque.

Turn and walk back down Parkhill Road to Haverstock Hill. Parkhill Road was built on the site of St John's Park, hence its name. The most architecturally interesting building is near the end of the road. It is called Tower Cottage, and was built in 1884.

Upon reaching Haverstock Hill again, bear right and walk up to Howitt Road, which is opposite Belsize Park tube station. At No.9 Howitt Road you will see a blue plaque for the first Labour Prime Minister **James Ramsay MacDonald** (6). He lived here 1916–25 before moving to a larger house in nearby Frognal. The plaque is easily missed because of plant growth.

Continue along Howitt Road. It is interesting to see the decorative embossed frieze above the windows of these terraced houses. Turn left at the end of the road. This is Belsize Park Gardens. There is a blue plaque at No.44 on the left, where the English composer **Frederick Delius** (7) lived 1918–19. Walking back along Belsize Park Gardens you will find another plaque at No.37 on the other side of the road. This commemorates the political journalist **Henry Noel Brailsford** (8). He joined the Labour Party in 1907 and regularly wrote leader columns for the *Manchester Guardian* and *Daily Herald*. From here it is over half a mile to the next plaque.

Continue along Belsize Park Gardens and turn left at the end into Belsize Park. Where the road forks off, keep to the right and this will continue to College Crescent and the start of Fitzjohn's Avenue. On the corner of Belsize Lane you will see a statue of Sigmund Freud, whose house you will shortly see. Across the road, on the corner of Maresfield Gardens, there is a blue plaque on the home of **Philip de Laszlo** (9). He was a Hungarian-born portrait painter of royalty and many other famous persons. From 1930 he was the president of the Royal Society of British Artists. Walk into Maresfield Gardens.

There are five plaques to be seen in this road. Follow the road round the bend to the first plaque at No.4. This is for **Cecil Sharp** (10) who was the founder of the English Folk Dance and Song Society (1911), the headquarters of which are named after him. Next door at No.6 there is a black oval plaque marking it as the first premises of **Westfield College** (11). The original college opened here in 1882 and it is now a part of London University with over 1,000 students.

No.20 Maresfield Gardens (facing page, top) was the home of the psychoanalysts **Sigmund Freud** (12) and his daughter **Anna Freud** (13). He managed to bring many of his possessions with him when escaping the Nazis, and these are now available for the public to view in this house. Opening times are from Sunday to Wednesday. Immediately opposite

at No.27 you will see another black oval Hampstead plaque on the house where **Herbert Henry Asquith** (14) lived. He was Prime Minister in 1908 and also led a coalition government in 1915–16. Continue and turn left into Nutley Terrace.

Emerging from Nutley Terrace, turn left and walk down Netherhall Gardens to No.10. This was the home of **Sidney** and **Beatrice Webb** (15) when first married in 1892. They were social scientists and political reformers who apart from being instrumental in founding the London School of Economics, founded *The New Statesman* and were active members of the Fabian Society. Sidney was created Baron Passfield in 1929.

Now turn and walk back up Netherhall Gardens. This is an uphill walk, but it is interesting to see the large Victorian houses en route. Continue around the bend in the road to No.51. The blue plaque here records this four-storey house as being a home of the journalist **John Passmore Edwards** (16). He is best remembered for his construction of free public libraries. Almost opposite, on the corner of Maresfield Gardens, there is a house bearing two plaques. This was built on the site of a house formerly occupied by the composer **Sir Edward Elgar** (17). The round private convex plaque is on the front of the house in Maresfield Gardens. Round the corner in Netherhall Gardens there is a bronze oval one erected by the Hampstead Plaque Fund.

Continue up Netherhall Gardens, turn left and then left again at the traffic lights into Arkwright Road. The large house, No.4, was the home of the artist **Frank Topham RA** (18) (1838–1924), who lived and worked here in the 1870s. The plaque is completely obscured by a vine in the summer, and can only be seen when this is not in leaf. Further down, at No.21 across the road, you will find a blue plaque commemorating **Tobias Matthay** (19). He was a pianist and teacher who numbered Myra Hess and Harriet Cohen among his pupils.

Now turn right into Frognal. This is a fine street with many Victorian and Edwardian houses. No.37 was built in 1888 and was the home of the horn player **Dennis Brain** (20) for the last five years of his life. He was the chief horn player of the Royal Philharmonic and Philharmonia orchestras. The house next door, No.39, was one of three remaining houses in Hampstead designed by R. Norman Shaw. He built this for the popular illustrator of children's books **Kate Greenaway** (21) and her blue plaque is a rectangular one. Opposite is University College School with its impressive entranceway. It is built in the Edwardian baroque style and has a statue of King Edward VII on its frontage. You will have already seen these two plaques if you have completed Walk 26.

Walk on past Frognal Close and turn left into Frognal Lane. The next turning on the left is Langland Gardens, where at No.21 you will see an oval plaque on the house where **Cecil Beaton** (22) was born and lived in childhood. He is best remembered for his photographs of royalty but was also a designer of scenery and costumes for stage and film productions.

Return to Frognal Lane, bear left and then take the second right into Bracknell Gardens. At No.16 you will see a blue plaque on the home of the **Huxley family** (23). The father Leonard was a teacher at Charterhouse school before joining *Cornhill Magazine*, of which he was editor 1916–33. The elder son Julian was a biologist and zoologist as well as the first director-general of UNESCO. Aldous was a novelist and many of his books had a science fiction content, such as *Brave New World* (1932). This plaque also will have been seen on Walk 26.

Retrace your steps to Frognal Lane and turn right. Cross over Finchley Road and proceed into West End Lane. The first turning on the right is Cannon Hill. You will see Marlborough Mansions and the blue plaque for **Sir Adrian Boult** (24). He was the conductor of the BBC Symphony Orchestra 1930–50 and the London Philharmonic 1950–70.

Continue down West End Lane and turn left. In this area you will find many restaurants, cafés and public houses. Cross over to Inglewood Road. This leads on to Pandora Road, where you will find the last plaque of the regular walk at No.31, opposite Solent Road. The newspaper magnate **Alfred Harmsworth** (25) once lived here. He founded the *Daily Mail* (1896) and the *Daily Mirror* (1903) and took control of *The Times* in 1908. In 1917 he was created 1st Viscount Northcliffe.

Walk on and turn left into Sumatra Road, which will bring you back to West End Lane. Turning right, you will find it a short walk to West Hampstead Thameslink and underground stations.

If you would like to walk for about another 20 minutes, continue past Broadhurst Gardens and turn left at Compayne Gardens. The writer and statesman **Dr Nahum Sokolow** (26) lived and worked at No.43 from 1921 until 1936. He was president of the World Zionist Organisation. Reaching the top of the road you can see Sterling Mansions on the corner of Canfield Gardens. A plaque commemorates the film and theatre director **Lindsay Anderson** (27) who lived here 1977–94. He directed *This Sporting Life* and appeared as an actor in *Chariots of Fire*.

Bear left around Sterling Mansions and turn to the right into Broadhurst Gardens. The cream-painted house at the end of the road bears a blue plaque for **Martina Bergman Osterberg** (28), who was born in Sweden and was a qualified physical training instructor. She opened a school of gymnastics here in 1882, which was later transferred to Dartmouth. This was the prime centre for the instruction of physical training for women in England and merged with the Thames Polytechnic in 1976.

Having completed the tour you can now turn left to Finchley Road, where there are many restaurants, shops, bus stops and the underground station.

Walk 29
Southwark/Lambeth

Distance:	5 miles (8km)
Time taken:	2½ hours
Number of plaques:	25
Nearest tube stations:	London Bridge, Borough, Elephant & Castle, Oval
Bus routes:	C10, 1, 3, 21, 35, 36, 40, 45, 59, 63, 68, 76, 100, 133, 159, 168, 171, 172, 176, 185, 188, 341, 343, 344, 381

SOUTHWARK traces its history back to Saxon times and traces of a Roman wooden bridge spanning the Thames have been found during excavations. Today it has much to offer and several of the places of interest are included in this walk. In fact it could be recommended to make a day of it and visit some of the interesting sights mentioned in the narrative.

Arriving at London Bridge tube station, exit by the Tooley Street entrance. Opposite the London Dungeon you will find a stone inscription on No.33 Tooley Street. This inscription, which is encircled by a stone wreath and firemen's tools, is set high on the corner of Cottons Lane. It commemorates **James Braidwood** (1), a fireman who lost his life in the execution of his duty on 27 June 1861, and is possibly the oldest of London's commemorative plaques. The first official plaque was erected in 1867 and the oldest surviving date from that year.

Turn back past the station, going under the bridge. Ahead you can see the four pinnacles on the tower of Southwark Cathedral. On your right are the Southwark tourist information centre and the Southwark Needle. This is made from Portland stone, is 16 metres long and set at an angle of 19.5 degrees. It marks the site of the mediaeval gateway to Southwark. Cross Borough High Street at the traffic lights and walk past the Barrow Boy & Banker. Take the narrow turning down the steps leading to the cathedral. It is well worth visiting this ancient building, which is the earliest Gothic church in London.

Continuing along Cathedral Street you will reach Sir Francis Drake's ship *The Golden Hind*. For a small charge, you can go aboard. Walking on to Clink Street you come to the remains of the palace of the bishops of Winchester, which dates from about 1150. On a wall just past this is a blue plaque, which records that it formed part of the original **Clink Prison** (2). There is a museum here now which you may like to visit.

Walk along Bankside, next to the river, and go under Southwark Bridge. There is a wonderful view of St Paul's and the London panorama. Within a short distance you will come to the reconstructed Shakespeare's Globe Theatre, where conducted tours are on offer. Close by, on the painted house at No.49 Cardinal's Wharf, there is a small plaque informing

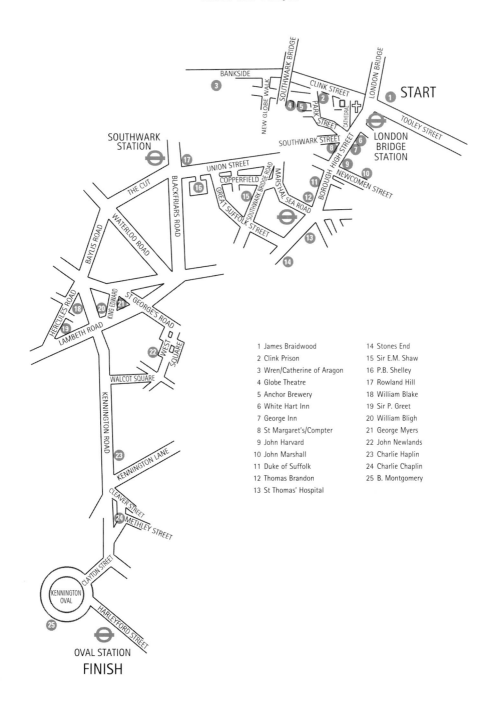

1 James Braidwood
2 Clink Prison
3 Wren/Catherine of Aragon
4 Globe Theatre
5 Anchor Brewery
6 White Hart Inn
7 George Inn
8 St Margaret's/Compter
9 John Harvard
10 John Marshall
11 Duke of Suffolk
12 Thomas Brandon
13 St Thomas' Hospital

14 Stones End
15 Sir E.M. Shaw
16 P.B. Shelley
17 Rowland Hill
18 William Blake
19 Sir P. Greet
20 William Bligh
21 George Myers
22 John Newlands
23 Charlie Haplin
24 Charlie Chaplin
25 B. Montgomery

you that **Sir Christopher Wren** (3) lived here at the time of the construction of his masterpiece across the river. **Queen Catherine of Aragon** also stayed here upon her arrival in England.

Walking a little further you will pass the Millenium Bridge and reach the Tate Modern art gallery.

Now return to the street called New Globe Walk, next to the Globe Theatre. Take the first turning left, Park Street, and continue past the bridge. There is a large bronze relief plaque at the site of the original **Globe Theatre** (4). Behind the plaque are boards displaying details of the theatre and information about the modern excavations. A little further, past Porter Street, you will see a terrace built on the site of the **Anchor Brewery** (5). This plaque records the names and dates of the brewers established here from 1616 to 1986. Turn right at the end of the road and follow it round, going through Park Street and turning right, past the fruit and vegetable market in Stoney Street. You have now arrived at the junction of Southwark Street and Borough High Street. Cross the road at the traffic lights and cross Borough High Street to White Hart Yard.

There are several plaques in Borough High Street, which have been erected by Southwark Council. These are rectangular in shape and are becoming faded with the

passage of time. The first of these is to be found at the entranceway of White Hart Yard. This is for the **White Hart Inn** (6), which was burnt down in 1676, rebuilt, then finally demolished in 1889. A few doors away on Lloyds Bank you will find the plaque of the **George Inn** (7), which is London's only surviving galleried inn (left). The present building dates from 1677 and is owned by the National Trust.

Cross the road to the war memorial on the centre traffic island. The building next to it has a listing of World War One dead. Beneath is a plaque stating that it is the site of **St Margaret's Church and Borough Compter** (8). The 13th-century church was partly used as a courthouse and prison. A pillory used to stand in the middle of the street and Southwark Fair was also held here for many years.

Re-cross the road and continue to nearby Queen's Head Yard. The Queen's Head Inn, which was owned by the family of **John Harvard** (9), once stood on this site. He sold it and used the proceeds to found Harvard University in America.

Continue and turn left at Newcomen Street. The red-brick building, No.9, was the offices of the **John Marshall** (10) charity until 1967. He lived in a mansion nearby and set up the charity in the early 17th century, mainly for the preservation of old churches. The present-day offices are next to the King's Arms public house, across the street.

The building on the site of St Margaret's Church and Borough Compter, Borough High Street.

Return to Borough High Street, turning to the left. Passing Chapel Court you can glimpse Lopex House, which is an original timbered building that survived the Southwark fire of 1676. Cross the road at the traffic lights. At Lyon House a Southwark plaque states that this was the site of the **Duke of Suffolk's Palace** (11) in the 16th century. A second plaque for this site can be found on Brandon House, on the corner of Marshalsea Road.

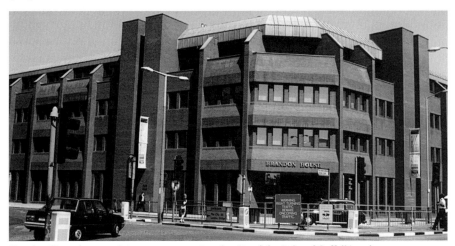

Brandon House bears a plaque commemorating the site of the Duke of Suffolk's palace.

Thomas Brandon (12) was the brother-in-law of Henry VIII and the first Duke of Suffolk. His uncle, also called Thomas Brandon, (died c.1509) is probably the one referred to.

Continue along Borough High Street past the traffic lights and cross over to the post office. A plaque here informs us that this is the site of the original **St Thomas' Hospital** (13), which was founded in 1225. After rebuilding in 1552 the hospital survived until 1865. The present building is in Lambeth Palace Road. Walking on you will reach the police station, where there is a similar plaque with the title **Stones End** (14). This was a fort designed to protect London.

Cross the road and walk back a few yards to Great Suffolk Street. This leads on to Southwark Bridge Road, where you turn right. Cross the road and walk past Sawyer Street to Winchester House, next to the fire station. The first chief officer of the metropolitan fire brigade, **Sir Eyre Massey Shaw** (15), lived here 1878–91.

Walk on a short way and turn in to Copperfield Street, which is at the junction with Guildford and Doyce Streets. Turn right at the end into the continuation of Great Suffolk Street and then left into Union Street. Go under the bridge and then turn left into Nelson Square. Ahead is Applegarth House, where a faded plaque informs us that the poet and dramatist **Percy Bysshe Shelley** (16) lived in a house formerly on this site. Return to Union Street and turn to the left, walking past Rowland Hill House to the crossroads. On the corner, across the road, is Orbit House, where you will see a plaque for **Rowland Hill** (17). This was not the founder of the penny post, but a preacher who founded the national Sunday school movement in 1803. His chapel on this site was later used for boxing tournaments. The next plaque on this walk is nearly two-thirds of a mile further along.

Now cross over towards Southwark Station and continue down The Cut. Walking along this road you will pass the Young Vic theatre and reach the Old Vic. Cross over Waterloo Road at the second set of traffic lights and continue along Baylis Road. At the end cross over Westminster Bridge Road into Kennington Road then fork right into Hercules Road. The plaque we seek is on Blake House, opposite Centaur Street. This is for the artist and poet **William Blake** (18), who lived in a house on this site in 1793.

Continue down Hercules Road and turn left at the end. Just past Briant House you will find the blue plaque of **Sir Philip Greet** (19) who lived at 160 Lambeth Road between 1920 and 1936. He was an actor-manager and worked with Lilian Baylis at the Old Vic theatre. Walk on and cross Kennington Road. At No.100 Lambeth Road the captain of the famous *Bounty*, **William Bligh** (20), lived from 1794–1813 when not at sea.

Opposite is the Imperial War Museum. This is also a place well worth a visit, time permitting. Continuing, turn left at the next turning, King Edward Walk. At the end turn right and you will see a blue plaque at No.131 St George's Road for **George Myers** (21). He was a master builder who worked in the Gothic style and also did much restoration work. His work included the House of Commons and over 90 churches. Opposite is St George's Roman Catholic Cathedral.

Walk on and cross over Lambeth Road to the continuation of St George's Road. The Imperial War Museum is now on your right. The first turning is Geraldine Street, which leads into West Square. In a corner of the Square at No.19 you will see the blue plaque for the chemist **John Newlands** (22). His discoveries led to the numbering of atomic elements and he was awarded the Davy Medal by the Royal Society in 1887. There is now a walk of about three-quarters of a mile to the next plaque.

Come out of the square via Austral Street and turn right. Cross the road and then go left into Sullivan Road, turning right again into Walcot Square. Upon reaching Kennington Road at the end turn left. It is now a straight walk along to No.287 Kennington Road, where the next plaque is to be found. This is for **Charlie Chaplin** (23) and is one of three addresses in the area where he is recorded to have lived. The second one is close by.

Continue and cross over Kennington Lane, noticing the flamboyant library as you pass. Turn left into Cleaver Street and right into Bowden Street. You can see **Charlie Chaplin's** (24) second plaque ahead of you at 39 Methley Street. His third plaque is at his birthplace in Walworth Road and just too far to be included in this walk.

There is one more plaque left to see. This is again quite a distance away, but it is located by the tube station. Take the turning on the right, Milverton Street. Cross over Kennington Road at the traffic lights and turn left. Turn right again at Clayton Street, which will lead you up to Kennington Oval and the cricket ground. Walk to the left on reaching the Oval and follow it round. Just past the Surrey Tavern you can see a white-painted house across the road. This was once a vicarage and the birthplace of the famous World War Two Field Marshall, **Viscount Bernard Montgomery of Alamein** (25).

You have now reached the end of the tour. Walk back towards the pedestrian crossing, which is the start of Harleyford Street. You will see the sign of Oval underground station ahead.

Other nearby plaques not included in the walk:

David Cox, 34 Foxley Road, SW9.
Charlie Chaplin, 277 Walworth Road, SE17.

Walk 30
Greenwich/Blackheath

Distance:	6¾ miles (10.86km)
Time taken:	3 hours
Number of plaques:	19
Nearest stations:	Cutty Sark, Greenwich, Blackheath, Lewisham
Bus routes:	53, 54, 177, 180, 188, 189, 199, 202, 380, 386

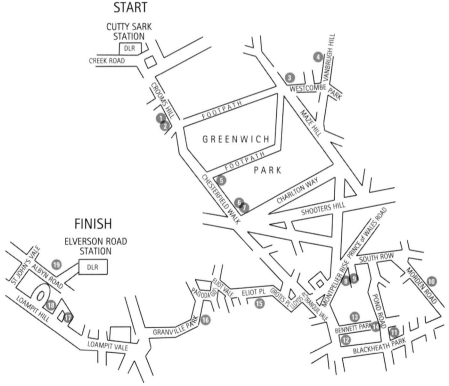

1 Cecil Day-Lewis	6 4th Earl of Chesterfield	11 Nathaniel Hawthorne	16 Samuel Smiles
2 Revd Benjamin Waugh	7 Viscount Wolseley	12 Sir Arthur Eddington	17 Edith Nesbitt
3 Sir John Vanbrugh	8 Blackheath FC	13 Donald McGill	18 Cecil Hepworth
4 Sir Frank Dyson	9 1st Int. Rugby Union Game	14 GPO Film Unit	19 Thankfull Sturdee
5 General James Wolfe	10 Charles Gounod	15 Sir James C. Ross	

BOTH Roman and Saxon remains have been found in this area. It did not come into prominence though until the time of the Tudor kings, when a royal palace was built. This was a favourite home of Henry VIII, and both he and Elizabeth I were born here. The 17th century saw the building of the Queen's House, the Royal Naval College and the Royal Observatory. Blackheath was only a village until the speculative building began in the early 19th century and the railway link to London opened in 1849, bringing new life to the region.

As you will notice, with only 19 plaques in a distance of six miles, they are in most cases well spaced out. However, the ground is fairly flat and there are some wide-open spaces. The walk begins from the Docklands Light Railway station at Cutty Sark. As the name implies it is next to the sailing ship resting in dry dock. Sir Francis Chichester's yacht *Gypsy Moth IV* is also to be seen here.

From the station turn right into Greenwich Church Street and walk towards the traffic lights. This continues past Greenwich market, Nelson Road and the front of St Alfege's church. The church was rebuilt by Nicholas Hawksmoor in 1712–18, on the site of an earlier building. It is believed that the first church was erected on the site where Alphage, then Archbishop of Canterbury, was murdered by Danes, in the year 1012.

Turn left into Stockwell Street, leading on to Croom's Hill. At No.6 you will see a blue plaque on the home of the Poet Laureate **Cecil Day-Lewis** (1). Apart from his poetic works, he wrote a series of detective novels under the pseudonym Nicholas Blake. A few doors away is the Fan Museum. Like many others it is not open on Mondays.

Another blue plaque is to be found at No.26 for the **Reverend Benjamin Waugh** (2), who founded the NSPCC in 1884. Other plaques for him can be found at Christ's Church, Friern Barnet and The Green, Southgate.

Now take the park entrance almost opposite and follow the signs for the Royal Observatory and General Wolfe statue. This path crosses a road and you will see the weather vane of the observatory ahead, above the trees. There are a few steps and then a very steep path to the top. The foundation stone of Sir Christopher Wren's observatory building was laid in 1675, and among the many early visitors was Sir Samuel Pepys. There are many historical items available to see, as well as the planetarium, and you can stand astride the actual Greenwich meridian line, set in concrete. The view across London from this hill is magnificent.

Walk past the rear of the statue of General Wolfe and take the footpath to the left of the refreshment cabin. Continue straight ahead, going past Queen Elizabeth's Oak and proceeding forward following the sign pointing to the playground and boating lake. Across the park you will be able to see a blue plaque on the wall of Vanbrugh Castle. This is for **Sir John Vanbrugh** (3), the distinguished architect, who designed and lived in this house. He was the architect of Blenheim Palace and Castle Howard, Yorkshire. He also wrote several dramas and was imprisoned for two years in the Bastille, during the war with France.

Walk into Westcombe Park Road and take the second turning left. At No.6 Vanbrugh Hill you will see the English Heritage plaque for **Sir Frank Dyson** (4) the Astronomer Royal of 1910–33 who lived here for 12 years.

Return to the park by the same entrance and take the pathway leading towards the Roman ruins. These have actually been removed to the local museum but the site is located on a mound by iron railings. Continue towards the park restaurant via the roadway. Then take the pathway with the wooden barriers, which leads towards McCartney House. The tennis courts will be to your left. McCartney House was the home of **General James Wolfe** (5), although he spent little time here, due to military commitments. The bushes in front of the house now partly obscure the blue plaque. It is set behind the left of the two highest shrubs. Continue through the wrought iron gate at the right of the house to the road on the other side.

Now keep to the left and walk past the other side of the house, through the avenue of lime trees, laid out in 1977 to commemorate the Queen's Silver Jubilee. This is Chesterfield Walk and the large house at the end is called Ranger's House (built 1699–1700). It is owned by English Heritage and is open to the public. The inscriptions set in concrete on either side of the main entrance commemorate former residents **Phillip, 4th Earl of Chesterfield** (6) and **Garnet, 1st Viscount Wolseley** (7).

Ranger's House, owned by English Heritage, the former home of Phillip, 4th Earl of Chesterfield, and Garnet, 1st Viscount Wolseley.

Leaving Chesterfield Walk, cross over the busy A2 road and bearing left, take the diagonal footpath across the heath. Turn right at Prince Charles Road and walk down to the junction with Montpelier Row. Across the road you can see the Princess of Wales public house. There are two green plaques here. The first records **Blackheath Football Club** (8),

which was founded here in 1858. The second commemorates the **First International Rugby Union Game** (9), which was organised here in 1871. Four Blackheath players took part. If you are thinking of lunch here, it is worth mentioning that the author waited 35 minutes for a simple snack.

Continue past Paragon Place and continue into South Row. This leads into Morden Road. At No.17 you will find the blue plaque of the French composer **Charles Gounod** (10) who stayed here in 1870. He is best remembered for the operas *Faust* and *Romeo et Juliette*.

Walk on and turn right at Blackheath Park. Then turn right again into Pond Road, where you will see the next plaque at No.4. This is for the American novelist **Nathaniel Hawthorne** (11), who stayed here in 1856. Return to Blackheath Park and continue past the church on the corner. Turn right again at the main road, then right into Bennett Park, where there are three plaques.

The first plaque you will find in this short road is at No.4, where **Sir Arthur Eddington** (12) lived. He was a physicist who was a leading exponent of Einstein's theory of relativity. The second is at No.5, across the road. This was the home of cartoonist **Donald McGill** (13). His saucy seaside postcards are now collectors' items. Looking to the end of the road, you can see a blue plaque on the building facing. This was the headquarters of the **GPO Film Unit** (14), later called the Crown Film Unit. They had their studios here from 1933 to 1943.

Return to the main road, turn right and continue into Tranquil Vale. Turn left at Lloyds Place, then continue bearing left into Grote's Place and Eliot Place. At No.2 you will see the plaque of the polar explorer **Sir James Clark Ross** (15). He discovered the magnetic North Pole in 1831 and later led an expedition to the South Pole. Polar lands are named after him.

Walk to the end and bear right into Eliot Vale, then left into Pagoda Gardens, taking the right fork. This leads into Granville Park, where you turn left. A short way along, at No.11, there is a blue plaque on the home of **Samuel Smiles** (16). Although trained to be a physician he became an editor of the *Leeds Times* and secretary of two Yorkshire railways. He also wrote the book mentioned on the plaque and biographies of rail pioneers. There is now a long walk to the next plaque: over three-quarters of a mile.

Continue all the way down Granville Park to Lewisham High Street, where you turn left. You now need to cross over the busy crossroads to the railway bridge past the bus station. Lewisham's Riverdale shopping centre is nearby, should you wish a diversion. Go under the bridge into Loampit Vale. Continue under the second bridge and turn right into Elswick Road. This terrace was built in 1879. The children's writer **Edith Nesbit** (17) lived at No.28 from 1882–5. Among her many publications she was the author of *The Railway Children* (1906) and *The Enchanted Castle* (1907).

Return to the main road and turn right. Three turnings further along you will reach Somerset Gardens, a cul-de-sac with a centre island. Keep to the right of the island and go to No.17. There is no obvious plaque to be seen, but look at the far side of the house. A plaque erected to commemorate the centenary of the British film industry marks this as the birthplace of film pioneer **Cecil Hepworth** (18). From 1898–1927 he made many films and during World War Two he made films for the Ministry of Agriculture.

To reach the final plaque of this route return to the main road and turn to the right. Take the next turning right, St John's Vale, and then turn right again after the railway bridge into Albyn Road. Turn left into Bolden Street, where you will see a plaque at No.16. Historian and photographer **Thankfull Sturdee** (19) lived here. He was known as 'the father of Fleet Street photographers'.

Continue and turn right at the main road. The first turning on the left is Elverson Road, where you will reach the DLR station of the same name.

Other nearby plaques:

Margaret & Rachel McMillan, McMillan College, Creek Road, SE8

Peter the Great, 146 Deptford High Street, SE8

James Glaisher, 20 Dartmouth Hill, SE10

Ernest Christopher Dowson, Dowson Court, Belmont Grove, SE13

Edward Owen Greening, Dowson Court, Belmont Grove, SE13

Leyland Lewis Duncan, 8 Lingards Road, SE13

James Elroy Flecker, 9 Gilmore Road, SE13

Sir Francis Baring, Manor House Library, Old Road, Lee, SE13

Ladywell Mineral Spring, Ladywell Road, SE13

Margaret and Rachel McMillan, 127 George Lane, SE13

Walk 31
Around Clapham Common

Distance:	5½ miles (8.85km)
Time taken:	2½ hours
Number of plaques:	16
Nearest tube stations:	Clapham Common, Clapham South
Bus routes:	35, 37, 77, 137, 255, 319, 417, G1

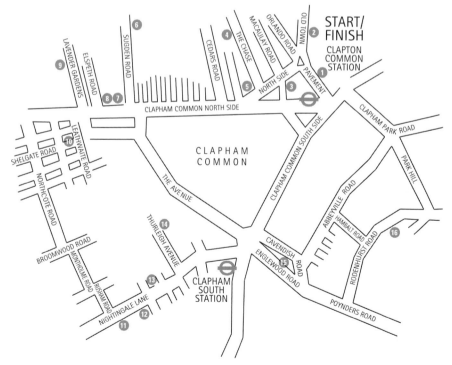

1 Z. & T.B. Macaulay	5 Sir Charles Barry	9 G.A. Henty	13 H.M. Bateman
2 John F. Bentley	6 Frederick Knee	10 Edward Thomas	14 Gus Elen
3 Wilberforce/Clapham Sect	7 John Burns	11 Baron Wandsworth	15 Jack Hobbs
4 Natsume Soseki	8 John Walter	12 Charles H. Spurgeon	16 Arthur Henderson

CLAPHAM Common was drained and planted in 1722 by Christopher Baldwin and comprises approximately 220 acres. In the 18th and 19th century the surrounding area was a fashionable place to live and many elegant and impressive houses were constructed in the streets around the common. Several of these magnificent buildings are still to be seen and add interest to the walk.

Commencing at Clapham Common station, leave by the exit marked 'The Pavement', turning to the left, where you will find public conveniences. Look across the road at No.5 to see a plaque commemorating the philanthropist and anti-slavery campaigner **Zachary Macaulay** (1) and his son **Thomas Babington Macaulay**. The younger Macaulay was a historian and author of *History of England*.

Cross the road at the traffic lights, turning left and walking past the Prince of Wales public house. Continue to No.43 Old Town to see the plaque of the architect of Westminster Cathedral, **John Francis Bentley** (2).

Cross the road again bearing left and continue past Orlando Road. Now cross to Holy Trinity church with the pillared portico on its front. Here you will see a blue plaque commemorating the **Clapham Sect** (3) and **William Wilberforce** who was a prominent member. This sect was an Anglican movement for evangelical reform, active in the 1780s and 1790s.

Cross back over the road, taking extra care as traffic is coming from the left on both lanes. Continue along Clapham Common North Side, passing Macaulay Road. Turn right into The Chase, where a long way down at No.81 a blue plaque can be seen commemorating the novelist **Natsume Soseki** (4), one of Japan's greatest writers. Return to Clapham Common North Side and you will see that the large house on the right corner is called The Elms. This was the home of the architect **Sir Charles Barry** (5) who designed the Houses of Parliament.

Walk on past Victoria Rise and the Parkside Hotel, with the common on your left. Just past the traffic lights turn right into Sugden Road. This is a street of rather uninteresting terraced houses. Again you will find the plaque in this road to be a long way down. It is at No.24 and commemorates **Frederick Knee** (6), who was a pioneer of the Labour Party and housing reformer.

Return again to Clapham Common North Side and continue. Just past the bus stop at No.110 you can see the rectangular blue plaque of the socialist politician **John Burns** (7). Continue past Marjorie Grove to the attractive mansion Gilmore House at No.113. This was home to **John Walter** (8), who was a wealthy printer and founder of *The Times* newspaper.

Continue on to St Barnabas church and turn right into

Gilmore House, home of John Walter, founder of The Times newspaper.

Lavender Gardens. Notice the different styling of these terraced houses to those in Sugden Road. The novelist and war correspondent **G.A. Henty** (9) lived at No.33. He wrote a large number of historical stories for children.

Walk back along Lavender Gardens and turn right. Past the traffic lights you will see Leathwaite Road on the other side of the street. Having probably walked for about one hour, you will find this is a good place to stop for a coffee or other refreshment. There are several cafés and restaurants in this area. If you would like to continue a little further before stopping, however, the same can be said for Northcote Road, which you will shortly reach.

Walk into Leathwaite Road and take the second right into Shelgate Road, where you will see a plaque at No.61 commemorating **Edward Thomas** (10). He was a World War One poet and writer, who lost his life at the front.

There is now a long walk down to the three plaques in Nightingale Lane. Continue and take the second turning left, which is Northcote Road. This is a road full of shops, restaurants and many antique and art shops. Walk on past the library, crossing Broomwood Road, going left and right into Montholme Road. At the end, again go left and right into Rusham Road. This will bring you to Nightingale Lane. Across the road you will see Nightingale House, a former home of **Baron Wandsworth** (11), a banker and philanthropist who generously left the building to be used as a home for Jewish aged. The blue plaque is next to the main entrance of the old house. You can see that modern additions have been added on either side of the building.

Leaving with your back to Nightingale House, bear right. There is an impressive looking school across the road, where you will notice the ruined remnants of the wall of an earlier building on the left side. On your right, opposite the school, is Queen Elizabeth House, No.99, where a metal plaque marks the home of the Baptist preacher **Charles Haddon Spurgeon** (12). He preached to huge congregations and published many of his sermons and other works.

No.40 Nightingale Lane was a home of the cartoonist **H.M. Bateman** (13), who worked for many periodicals including *Punch* magazine.

Turn left at Thurleigh Avenue and walk along almost to the end of this road. The cockney music-hall comedian **Gus Elen** (14) lived at No.3 for the last six years of his life.

Return to Nightingale Lane and continue to the end, where it meets Clapham Common South. Turn left at the traffic lights by the underground station. Pass the vandalised toilets and cross the road at the traffic lights to the next turning right, Englewood Road. No.17 was the home of the famous cricketer **Jack Hobbs** (15). During his career he played in 61 test matches and made 197 centuries. He was also the first English cricketer to be knighted.

Walk on to the end of the road and bear left into Cavendish Road. Cross over to Abbeville Road on the other side. Now take the fourth turning on the right, which is called Hambalt Road. This leads to Rodenhurst Road, where you bear left to the last plaque of this walk. This is at No.13, on the house of Labour politician **Arthur Henderson** (16). He was chairman of his party three times and served as Home Secretary and Foreign Secretary.

You can now continue back to Clapham Common station by turning left at the end of the road. This will take you through Park Hill, which has an interesting mixture of both old and modern houses and flats. The route continues on through Clapham Park Road up to the station.

Nightingale House, the former home of Baron Wandsworth, with its modern additions.

Walk 32
Wimbledon

Distance:	6¾ miles (10.86km)
Time taken:	3 hours
Number of plaques:	14
Nearest tube stations:	South Wimbledon, Wimbledon
Bus routes:	57, 93, 131, 152, 156, 163, 164, 200, 219

WIMBLEDON is known worldwide as the home of the lawn tennis championships. It has, however, many other attractions. The common, which comprises some 1,100 acres is loved by golfers, horse-riders and hikers. The town developed mainly in the 19th century after the coming of the railway, but a tavern is known to have existed since Tudor times. Wimbledon village is believed to have Saxon origins. The route of the walk proceeds through the town and across an attractive part of the common. It is one of the longest in the book and has the smallest number of plaques.

Emerging from South Wimbledon station, turn right into Merton High Street and walk along to Doel Close, which is just past Pincott Road. Above the sign you will find a rectangular plaque recording that the famous admiral, **Horatio Nelson** (1), lived in a house formerly on this site in 1801.

Return to the station and cross over to Kingston Road, continuing for about three-

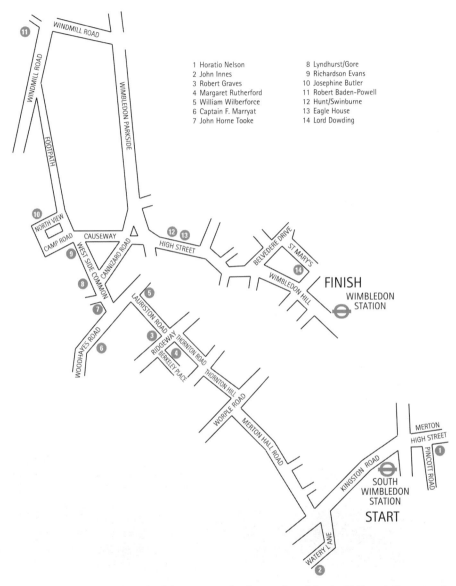

1 Horatio Nelson
2 John Innes
3 Robert Graves
4 Margaret Rutherford
5 William Wilberforce
6 Captain F. Marryat
7 John Horne Tooke

8 Lyndhurst/Gore
9 Richardson Evans
10 Josephine Butler
11 Robert Baden-Powell
12 Hunt/Swinburne
13 Eagle House
14 Lord Dowding

quarters of a mile. This will take you past the fire station, Merton Hall and the council offices. Turn left before the Nelson Hospital into Watery Lane, opposite the Leather Bottle public house. Continue down Watery Lane to the Rutlish School (facing page). Here you will see the blue plaque for **John Innes** (2), after whom the well-known potting compost is named. There is now more than a mile to go before reaching the next plaque.

Retrace your steps along Watery Lane and cross Kingston Road into Merton Hall Road.

The main point of interest in this road seems to be the tiling on the front of many of the houses, where owners have attempted to individualise their homes. Continue all the way along and take the footbridge over the railway into Elm Grove. Turn right upon reaching Worple Road and then first left into Thornton Hill. This is a long uphill road culminating in a zig-zag that leads into Thornton Road. Reaching the end of this road you will have reached the Swan public house. The large plaque prominently displayed on the front of the building gives its interesting history. Looking across to Lauriston Road you can see a blue plaque on the first house. This was the birthplace of the poet and novelist **Robert Graves** (3). He is best remembered for the stories *I Claudius* and *Claudius the God*.

Continue left in The Ridgeway and then take the second left into Berkeley Place. No.4 was the home for 25 years of the famous stage and screen actress **Margaret Rutherford** (4).

Return to the main road and turn right, then take the first left back to Lauriston Road, this time walking through and up to the common. On the end wall of the corner house of Lauriston Road and West Side Common, you will find a plaque commemorating **William Wilberforce** (5). This is one of six plaques in London recording his name.

Now walk left, having the common on your right side. This will take you past King's College School into Woodhayes Road. Southside House is open to the public for an interesting tour on Wednesday, Saturday and Sunday afternoons in the early part of the year. Gothic Lodge at No.6 was the home of **Captain Frederick Marryat** (6). You will recall that he was the author of *Children of the New Forest* and *Mr Midshipman Easy,* among other novels. Because of the high hedging you may find it easier to cross the road to see the location of this plaque.

Walk back a short way and cross the road to West Side Common. The large house called Chester House bears a plaque stating that **John Horne Tooke** (7) lived here. He was a radical politician who supported the American colonists. Tried for high treason, he was acquitted and later entered Parliament. Walk a little further to No.6, Westside House, just past Chester Road. This was the home of **Lord Lyndhurst** (8) who was twice Lord Chancellor of England. It was also the home of the first Wimbledon tennis champion (1877) **Spencer Gore.**

Continue along West Side Common and just past the red letterbox you will reach a large house surrounded by a high wall, named The Keir. Above the main entrance of the house, which was built in 1789, a blue plaque states that **Richardson Evans** (9) 'Protector of natural beauties' lived here. In 1903 he founded the John Evelyn Club, now called the Wimbledon Society.

Walking on you will come into West Place, which has some interesting old houses and cottages. One wonders if in earlier times, the servants of the owners of the magnificent houses in West Side Common might have lived in these cottages. Follow the road round into North View, where the next plaque can be seen at No.8. This was the home of **Josephine Butler** (10), who was a leading campaigner for womens' rights.

You are now going to walk across the common and the distance to the next plaque is nearly three-quarters of a mile. There are several footpaths but the quickest route is to return to the previous corner, where you will see an entranceway opposite with a map of the common displayed alongside. Take the right-hand footpath, which leads on to Windmill Road. The next plaque is actually on the windmill. As the plaque states it was

here that **Robert Baden–Powell** (11) wrote part of his *Scouting for Boys*. The windmill is also a museum open 2–5pm on Saturdays and 11am–5pm on Sundays and public holidays, April to October. The adjoining teashop is a welcoming oasis for refreshments or lunch. It will now be a walk exceeding one mile to the next plaque.

Taking the right fork of Windmill Road will bring you to Parkside, where you again turn to the right. This main road has the common on one side and a string of magnificent houses all the way along to Wimbledon village. Follow this down to the High Street where you will see the Rose and Crown public house, which was built in the early 17th century. A plaque on its wall states that the poet **Leigh Hunt** (12) met **Charles Swinburne** here. This is a fact that has been much disputed, although they are both known to have visited.

Next door to the Rose and Crown is **Eagle House** (13). This is a fine Jacobean house (left), built in 1613, by Robert Bell, who was a founder of the East India Company. William Pitt was a frequent visitor when his foreign minister William Greville lived here. It is now an Islamic study centre.

Continue through the village past the mini-roundabout and the drinking fountain and then turn left into Belvedere Drive, which is after Belvedere Grove. This leads into St Mary's Road, where you turn right. The last plaque of this walk is to be found at No.3, the home of **Air Chief Marshal Dowding** (14). He was the World War Two Chief of Fighter Command and leader of the Battle of Britain.

Turn right at the end of the road and then left on reaching the main road. It is now just a short way along to Wimbledon station.

Index to Plaques